Siegfried Sassoon

Siegfried Sassoon

A Study of the War Poetry

by
Patrick Campbell

McFarland & Company, Inc., Publishers
Jefferson, North Carolina, and London

Frontispiece: Siegfried Sassoon: The Soldier-Poet (ca. 1917). *Photography collection, Harry Ransom Humanities Research Center, the University of Texas at Austin.*

British Library Cataloguing-in-Publication data are available

Library of Congress Cataloguing-in-Publication Data

Campbell, Patrick, 1935–
    Siegfried Sassoon : a study of the war poetry / by Patrick Campbell.
    p.   cm.
    Includes bibliographical references and index.
    ISBN 0-7864-0525-2 (library binding : 50# alkaline paper) ∞
    1. Sassoon, Siegfried, 1886–1967 — Criticism and interpretation.
2. World War, 1914–1918 — Great Britain — Literature and the war.
3. Soldiers' writings, English — History and criticism. 4. War poetry, English — History and criticism. I. Title.
PR6037.A86Z64   1999
821'.912 — dc21   98-46275
                                                                                                 CIP

©1999 Patrick Campbell. All rights reserved

No part of this book may be reproduced or transmitted in any form or by any means, electronic or mechanical, including photocopying or recording, or by any information storage and retrieval system, without permission in writing from the publisher.

Manufactured in the United States of America

McFarland & Company, Inc., Publishers
   Box 611, Jefferson, North Carolina 28640

To the memory of
Corporal Herbert Campbell, 34403,
13th Yorkshire Regiment, who was awarded
the Military Medal in World War One
for "Bravery in the Field"

Acknowledgments

Grateful acknowledgment is made to the publishers and copyright holders listed below for permission to quote from the following material in copyright:

George Sassoon, Sir Rupert Hart-Davis, Faber and Faber and Penguin, U.S.A., for permission to quote from the following poetry and prose of Siegfried Sassoon: *The War Poems*, edited by Sir Rupert Hart-Davis (1983); *Letters to a Critic*, edited by Michael Thorpe (1976); *Letters to Max Beerbohm*, edited by Sir Rupert Hart-Davis (1983); *The Old Century* (1938), *On Poetry* (1939), *The Weald of Youth* (1942), *Siegfried's Journey* (1946), *The Memoirs of George Sherston* (1936), *Diaries: 1915–1918*, edited by Sir Rupert Hart-Davis (1983).

The Harry Ransom Humanities Research Center, University of Texas at Austin, for permission to quote from unpublished letters from Siegfried Sassoon to Lady Ottoline Morrell and Roderick Meiklejohn.

The photography collection of the Harry Ransom Humanities Research Center, University of Texas at Austin, for permission to reproduce a photograph of Siegfried Sassoon (circa 1917).

The trustees of the Imperial War Museum, London, for granting access to the Siegfried Sassoon papers, lodged in the Department of Documents, and for allowing me to quote from unpublished letters to Lieutenant Siegfried Sassoon from Lieutenant Julian Dadd and Quarter-Master Joe Cottrill, and to Lieutenant "Birdie" Stansfield from Joe Cottrill.

Carcanet Press for permission to quote from Robert Graves, *Goodbye to All That* (1929); from *Robert Graves: Broken Images: Selected Correspondence*, edited by Paul O'Prey (1988); and from *Robert Graves: Complete Poems*, volume one (1995), edited by Beryl Graves and Dunstan Ward.

The literary trustees of Lady Ottoline Morrell for permission to quote from *Ottoline: The Early Memoirs* (1963) and *Ottoline at Garsington: The Memoirs of Lady Ottoline Morrell: 1915–1918* (1974), both edited by Robert Gathorne-Hardy.

Oxford University Press for permission to quote from Paul Fussell, *The Great War and Modern Memory* (1975).

Michael Thorpe for permission to quote from Michael Thorpe, *Siegfried Sassoon: A Critical Study* (1966).

Manchester University Press for permission to quote from Adrian Caesar, *Taking It Like a Man: Suffering, Sexuality and the War Poets* (1993).

Associated University Press for permission to quote from Patrick Quinn, *The Great War and the Missing Muse* (1994).

Peters Fraser and Dunlop Group for permission to quote from Bernard Bergonzi, *Heroes' Twilight: A Study of Literature of the Great War* (1968).

Princeton University Press for permission to quote from John H. Johnston, *English Poetry of the First World War* (1964).

Oxford University Press for permission to quote from Wilfred Owen, *The Collected Letters*, edited by H. Owen and J. Bell (1967).

Macmillan Press for permission to quote from Jon Silkin, *Out of Battle: The Poetry of the Great War* (1972, 1987, new edition 1998).

Routledge for permission to quote from Vivian de Sola Pinto, *Crisis in English Poetry* (1951).

Thanks are also due to Bolt and Watson and Stanbrook Abbey for quotations from Dame Felicitas Corrigan, *Poet's Pilgrimage* (1973).

Contents

Acknowledgments   vii
Preface   1
Abbreviations   7

Part One

    Chapter 1:   Introduction   11
    Chapter 2:   The Progress of the Poet   23
    Chapter 3:   Frail Women and Glorious Boys   31
    Chapter 4:   "O World God Made!"
        Pacifism, Pantheism, Self-Sacrifice   42
    Chapter 5:   Working Methods and Formal Concerns   49
    Chapter 6:   Literary Influences   61
    Chapter 7:   The Poetic Achievement   76

Part Two

    Chapter 8:   1915–1916: "War Is Our Scourge;
        Yet War Has Made Us Wise"   87
    Chapter 9:   "Goodbye to Galahad":
        The Somme and Its Aftermath   109
    Chapter 10:   "Unmasking the Ugly Face of Mars":
        August 1916 to April 1917   122
    Chapter 11:   "When Will It Stop?"
        May 1917 to January 1918   148
    Chapter 12:   "Waiting for the End, Boys":
        January 1918 to March 1919   176

Appendix: Diary Poems 207
Select Bibliography 219
Index 223

Preface

A number of impulsions lie behind the writing of this book. It is dedicated to the memory of my uncle, Herbert Campbell, who was awarded the Military Medal for "bravery in the field" in the Great War. The Military Cross, awarded to Siegfried Sassoon, was, of course, reserved for officers. Such classist ironies were not lost on the poet. In "Arms and the Man," Captain Croesus observes that while "disabled heroes" from the ranks must pay for new "arms and legs," as an officer he qualifies for them "free of cost." Happily Uncle Bert never became a "disabled hero" but, like the troopers in Sassoon's verse, he is the unseen and unsung presence behind this book.

But my interest in Siegfried Sassoon himself was fostered by a link of another kind. For most of my working life, I have occupied an office in the Trent Park mansion that the poet's cousin, Sir Philip Sassoon, bought and effectively rebuilt in 1921 with eighteenth-century bricks purloined from a grand townhouse in Piccadilly. It is tempting to imagine Siegfried riding to hounds across the estate, but in fact the cousins never hit it off; the reclusive Siegfried disliked Philip's lavish socializing and his much-publicized attempts to climb the greasy pole of political preferment. Nonetheless, I am daily reminded of the family connection as I look out on a Trent Park that still bears the imprint of the Sassoon ownership.

Of course, neither of these coincidences explains an enthusiasm for Sassoon's poetry. Like most students, I read and warmed to Wilfred Owen's verse before encountering that of his Craiglockhart friend and confidant. But Sassoon's own realization that, in the estimation of critics, he "came a poor second" to Owen as a trench poet is a judgment that now seems an unduly harsh one. What this book attempts, in its own small way, is to nudge Sassoon's reputation up another notch, to argue that certainly in terms of satiric intensity and veracious reportage, perhaps even in terms of compassionate involvement, his poetry deserves to rank alongside his friend's. Indeed Sassoon's sheer output and variety — there are 150 poems discussed in this study — makes him arguably a more representative poet of the First World War.

This last point is an important one, the final nudge I needed to write this book. For a number of Sassoon's war poems have not previously been featured in a critical study of this kind. Not a consequence of any critical negligence, this omission relates to the fact that only in the 1980s did Sir Rupert Hart-Davis's splendid editions of the Sassoon diaries — and I am thinking particularly of the 1915–1918 notebooks — become available to the reading public. Such exposure had two effects: One, it meant that the personal revelations and reflections in the diaries could be used to cast new light on familiar poems; two, it allowed the emergence, into the light of day, of a significant number of poems incarcerated in the notebooks for more than 60 years. Of course, Sassoon had his reasons for not publishing the diary poems in his own lifetime: sometimes too personal, they are often rough-hewn versions he would not have wanted his admirers to read. But they are important documents, important enough to be discussed in the text of this book and to be included in an appendix. They help to complete both the picture of the imaginative life of a front-line officer and the oeuvre of the war poet.

One of the consequences of this inflection is that the much-loved *Memoirs of George Sherston*, a retrospective view of experiences at the Front twenty years on, are allotted only a cameo role in this study. In part this is because these memoirs inevitably present a distanced and sanitized view of events. The distaff side of trench warfare and its necessarily horrendous impact on the poet are largely erased from a prose account which, while it wants for nothing in terms of readability — as its devoted readership testifies — throws relatively little light on the trench poetry. Indeed, it is noteworthy that in order to highlight certain details when writing his memoirs, Sassoon returned to the "evidence" of those early poems.

In any case, by then the poet's attitude to the war verse was undergoing a sea-change. As though in illustration of the truism that artists are notoriously bad judges of their own work, Sassoon later recorded his regret that he was still lionized as a trench poet when he wanted to be remembered as a devotional poet first and foremost, and as a prose memoirist second. In a letter to the critic Michael Thorpe in 1966, the now reclusive poet emphasized this personal hierarchy of value, declaring, "I am a firm believer in the Memoirs; and am inclined to think that the war poems (the significant and successful ones) will end up as mere appendices to the matured humanity of the Memoirs" (*Letters to a Critic*, 1966, p. 14).

In the same letter Sassoon consigned his war poems, if not to oblivion, then at least to the bottom of his filing cabinet. Not only were they, in his estimation, inferior to his mature work, they frequently got in the way of readers' proper appreciation of it. "My renown as a War Poet," he declared, "has now become a positive burden to me, which makes your kind recognition of the later poems specially valuable to me." Moreover, Sassoon was at pains to remind his correspondent that the verses of *Counter-Attack* (1918), and to a lesser extent those of *The Old Huntsman* (1917) and *Picture-Show* (1919), had been dashed off by a headstrong young officer too caught up by events to view them dispassionately. His artistic success, now almost half a century back, was still cause for astonishment: "I was immature, impulsive, irrational and bewildered by the whole affair, hastily improvising my responses and only saved by being true to the experiences which I drew upon" (p. 14). But that last observation was of course the nub of the matter. It was precisely Sassoon's insistence on the truth, his desire to tell it how it was or at least how it felt at the time, that endeared him both to increasing numbers of his fellow soldiers and to a discerning public at home.

Sassoon's considered judgment on his early progress as a poet was equally sweeping, not to say disingenuous. Characterizing his development in terms of schoolboyish clichés, he maintained:

> I was never a professional writer and in some ways a complete amateur. In 1919 I was still in "the Lower Fifth" and the next six years were spent in trying to get into "the Upper Sixth." *Satirical Poems* (published in 1926) was an exercise in learning to use words with accuracy (the content was only playing a mental game without deep seriousness) and those years were a process of getting the war out of my system.... I did not find my real voice until 1924... [*Letters to a Critic*, 1966, p. 14].

Allowing for the fact that the whole notion of professionalism was abhorrent to Sassoon — witness his patrician perspective on fox-hunting, race-riding, golfing and cricketing — and for his recurrent wish to leap back to a pre-war Edwardian idyll, it is nonetheless extraordinary that he should disparage the trench poetry as "Lower Fifth" versifying. It is a critical commonplace that *Satirical Poems* (1926) are, to use Sassoon's own words, "exercises," occasional verses often composed without any compelling sense of occasion, misnomers in that they precisely lack that intensity which typified the "Blighty" satires or, for that matter, the bulletins from the battlefield. His contention that he did not discover his "real" poetic voice until 1924 is not shared by admirers of the war poetry.

Posterity has, furthermore, failed to uphold Sassoon's wish to be remembered as a significant devotional poet. At the end of his life no one knew that reluctant truth better than the poet. In *Letters to a Critic*, he bemoaned the fact that "most reviewers have shied away (the equine metaphor is instructive) from my spiritual pilgrimage." Where critics had responded, they offered not only "heart-breaking" reviews of *Sequences* (sixteen years in gestation), but a crippling denial of the poet's spirituality. Only Blunden, he recollected, "asserted that I am essentially a religious poet" (p. 15).

No one today, encountering Sassoon's *Collected Poems*, would deny this assertion: his spiritual pilgrimage, begun in the twenties and haltingly presaged in such war verses as "A Mystic as Soldier," slowly gathered momentum and culminated in his being received into the Roman Catholic Church in 1957. In terms of sheer quantity, the religious poetry bulks large. But it pales in comparison with the blood and thunder of verses imbued with fierce anger at Home Front hypocrisies, or with strenuous compassion for the suffering soldier. No spiritual experience, no matter how intensely felt, is likely to reach a significant readership unless it is couched in vividly realized imagery; on the battlefield the all too tangible events and experiences were a quarry of memorable images waiting to be encapsulated in verse.

In one sense the mature poetry owed its lukewarm critical reception to factors beyond the poet's control. For Sassoon the post-war writer was projected into an essentially irreligious age, an age for whom the "Great War for Civilization" had proved barbaric, its supposedly Christian impetus a hollow sham. In the estimation of the rising generation, now increasingly alienated from its elders and so-called betters, the war had not only exacerbated divisions of generation and class, but had contributed to the "Death of God." Ironically, it was a process to which Sassoon had unwittingly subscribed. The Anglican Church, variously represented in his verse by "fierce-browed prelates" and "Bishop Byegumbs," had revealed itself as a repository of hypocrisy and spurious xenophobia. To many post-war readers the great spiritual poetry of Sassoon's later mentors, Vaughan and Herbert, seemed an anachronistic monument to a religious age that could never return. The early Eliot and Pound, the socially committed poets of the thirties — all writers derided by Sassoon — seemed to reflect more accurately the values of an irreverent age.

Sassoon did find a final solution in a Wordsworthian "central peace, subsisting at the heart of endless agitation." It was in part a way of coping with the horrendous events of the past, of assuaging a sense of guilt that had dogged his footsteps ever since the bloodbath of the Somme. Unfortunately the assumption of this contemplative persona led Sassoon to underestimate the very poetry he should have cherished. How paradoxical that this personal revaluation should contribute to the generally held view that his war verse is inferior to that of Wilfred Owen.

My work on this book has been eased by the cooperation and consideration of a number of institutions and people. I am indebted to Middlesex University for a semester-long period of leave which enabled me to complete the bulk of my research. The staff of the British Library, where I did most of that research, were unfailingly helpful; the Reading Room was an oasis of scholarly calm in which to work. I am grateful to the Imperial War Museum, and in particular Nigel Steel of the Department of Documents, for answering queries and allowing me access to letters written to Sassoon by his fellow soldiers. The granting of access to correspondence between the poet and Lady Ottoline Morrell and Roderick Meiklejohn has given the book a dimension it would otherwise lack. For this material I owe a substantial debt to the Harry Ransom Humanities Research Center at the University of Texas, and in particular to Clifford Farringdon in the Office of the Research Librarian, who courteously fielded my requests. Though I have not quoted from Sassoon's letters to Robert Graves and Paul Lemperly, my thanks are due to Robert Bertholf and Michael Basinski, respectively curator and assistant curator of the Poetry/Rare Books Collection at the State University of New York at Buffalo, for providing photocopies of the material. Professor John Stallworthy of Oxford University has offered encouragement during the project's gestation, as has Professor Patrick Quinn. His knowledge and above all his infectious enthusiasm have been a real stimulus. To Jean Moorcroft Wilson I tender my thanks for her willingness to share her perceptions about Sassoon the man. Although I have on occasion dissented from their opinions, I am grateful for the insights in a number of critical studies: namely Michael Thorpe's pioneering *Siegfried Sassoon*, Bernard Bergonzi's *Heroes' Twilight*, John H. Johnston's *English Poetry of the First World War*, Jon Silkin's *Out of Battle* and Paul Fussell's compendious *The Great War and Modern Memory*. Among more recent books, Adrian Caesar's *Taking It Like a Man* has proved provocative and lively. While the material has been modified herein, I am grateful to Heldref Publications for allowing me to include analyses of "They," "Blighters" and "To Any Dead Officer," short articles that were originally published in *The Explicator*. Finally, I would like to thank Ann Lea, who patiently and expertly brought some semblance of order to my manuscript.

Almost all critical studies — and this one is no exception — are indebted to all those students who have, over the years, questioned their teachers' preconceptions about literature. It is with them very much in mind that I have divided the book into two sections. Part One, the contextual section, offers a general discussion of the war poetry — themes, poetic progress, working methods, stylistic features, literary influences and an evaluation of Sassoon's achievement. Part Two, which concentrates on textual analysis, consists of a chronologically arranged discussion of every existing poem that Sassoon wrote during The Great War. My modest hope is that future generations of students of Sassoon will discover, in these critiques, an instructive guide to the poems themselves.

Abbreviations

The following abbreviations are used in the text. Works are by Siegfried Sassoon unless otherwise indicated.

Diaries	*Siegfried Sassoon: Diaries 1915–1918*, edited by Rupert Hart-Davis
GTAT	Robert Graves: *Goodbye to All That*
IBI	*In Broken Images: Selected Letters of Robert Graves 1914–1946*, edited by Paul O'Prey
IWMP	Imperial War Museum Papers (letters to Siegfried Sassoon)
Memoirs	*The Complete Memoirs of George Sherston*
OC	*The Old Century and Seven More Years*
SJ	*Siegfried's Journey*
ULUT	Unpublished letters from Siegfried Sassoon, The Harry Ransom Humanities Research Center, University of Texas at Austin, Texas
WP	*Siegfried Sassoon: The War Poems*, arranged and introduced by Rupert Hart-Davis
WY	*The Weald of Youth*

Part One

Chapter 1

Introduction

In *The Complete Memoirs of George Sherston,* Sassoon recalled his gentle introduction to soldiering: "I had slipped into the Downfield troop by enlisting two days before the declaration of war. For me, so far, the war had been a mounted infantry picnic in perfect weather" (Memoirs, p. 219).

Four years and three months later, the conflict finally ground to a halt. Sassoon was strolling by the water-meadows in Oxford when he heard the news. He dashed off to London to be confronted by the sight of people "all waving flags and making fools of themselves — an outburst of mob patriotism. It was a wretched night and very mild. It is a loathsome ending to the loathsome tragedy of the last four years" (*Diaries*, 11 November, p. 282).

The change in the weather was symbolic. The war, which began as a "picnic," had degenerated into a "loathsome tragedy." Despite the fact that it had been, in essence, a localized conflict conducted mainly on the Western Front — Sassoon, Owen, Sorley, Graves, Blunden and Rosenberg all served there — the casualties suffered by the participants dwarfed those of previous wars. The figures make melancholy reading. Some 8,500,000 soldiers died as a consequence of wounds or disease; British casualties alone ran to 3,190,000, of whom more than a third were recorded as killed or missing, presumed dead. The German figures were even more catastrophic: combined with the Austria-Hungary losses there were total casualties of 14,000,000, an appalling 77 percent of their mobilized troops.

Almost two years into a war already bloody and attritional, and convinced that an immense breakthrough was required, Haig set in motion a master-stroke that had been six months in the planning. At 7:15 a.m. on 1 July, 1916, a huge mine exploded under the German lines. It signaled the start of the British offensive on the Somme. The soldier-volunteers had waited for a week while the enemy had been subjected to the biggest artillery barrage ever mounted, a million and a half shells from 1,537 guns. The war was, to all intents and purposes, over. Men were told they would barely need rifles, that not even a rat had survived the shelling. That morning, a line of foot soldiers, shoulder to shoulder and a dozen miles wide walked, uncomprehending, into a deadly hail of bullets. The immediate cost in human misery was 57,000 British casualties. It was said that battalions, two years in the making, were ten minutes in the destroying on that July morning. What was promoted as a breakthrough assault — the "Great Advance" — became the most notorious of endless battles of attrition. Only in November — more than four months on — did Haig call off an offensive which had crawled forward six miles, four miles short of the opening *day*'s expectation.

The Somme, which came to be known by the infantry as the "Great Fuck-Up," was the single most absurdly mismanaged campaign of an absurdly bungled war. British casualties alone amounted to 620,000; the sheer scale of the carnage meant that soldiers became rapidly inured to experiences beyond their worst nightmares. Joe Cottrill (Sassoon's quarter-master) wrote, almost matter-of-factly, to "Birdie" Stansfield: "the old Battalion is having a rough time at present — losing 200 men in three days. 10 men and the doctor all killed in a dug-out" (letter from Cottrill to Stansfield, 3 September, 1916, IWMP). Things were no better in 1917: the April head-on assault near Arras gained 5000 yards at a cost of 160,000 casualties; after the wettest early Autumn on record, thousands of troopers literally disappeared in the viscid mud and yellow slime pits of Passchendaele.

In this carnage the main instruments of destruction were machines — the crack of the bolt-action rifle now augmented by the boom of high-calibre field-guns fed by mountains of shells, and by the "rapid rattle" of machine-guns. Tanks and poison gas were soon added to the armory of war. In "No Man's Land," between trenches which, Paul Fussell estimates, ran to 12,000 miles on the Allied side alone (1975, p. 37), whole divisions collided and were blown to pieces or riddled with bullets. So many men were dismembered beyond recognition that at Verdun, one of the longest and bloodiest battles of the 1916 campaign, the French erected a monument to the 150,000 *assumed* to have died there. Indeed, one of the reasons advanced at the start of hostilities for its anticipated conclusion in weeks was the killing capacity of these machines of war. In common with all soldiers at the Front, Sassoon was required to endure this modern "Golgotha." Sassoon was lucky in that he came back from this "place of skulls" — four important English poets, Owen, Sorley, Thomas and Rosenberg, did not. But despite his charmed life, he was permanently scarred, both physically and psychologically, by the experience.

His initiation had an element of anti-climax about it. On the third of August, 1914, he enlisted with the Sussex Yeomanry, but was thrown from his horse during training. The resultant complications from a broken arm delayed his entry into the war. It was not until 24 November, 1915 that Sassoon, now commissioned, joined the Royal Welch Fusiliers in France. But he was all too soon experiencing the vagaries of trench warfare: by June his extraordinary heroism had earned him the Military Cross; a month later and in the aftermath of the Somme attack, he was in hospital in Amiens "feeling very ill. Temp 105" (*Diaries*, 22 February, 1916, p. 99) with a dose of "trench fever" (as much a portmanteau term as "shell-shock"), that necessitated his evacuation to England and an Oxford hospital. Back at the Front early in the following year, he found himself in Rouen, being treated — bizarrely — for German measles, his "brain pitifully confused by the war" (*Diaries*, 22 February, 1917, p. 133). Less than two months later, when fighting in the morasses of the Arras sector, he was wounded in the shoulder "and was no good for about a quarter of an hour," but continued, as his diary laconically records, to "deal with the show with about seventy men and a fair amount of bombs, but no Lewis-gun" (*Diaries*, 16 April, 1917, p. 155).

Again invalided back to "Blighty," he fired off his celebrated "Protest" against the war before being sent home to Weirleigh to recuperate. By now many of his best friends were dead; he himself, having narrowly avoided a court-martial or worse, was declared a victim of shell-shock and sent to Craiglockhart War Hospital near Edinburgh. Only in March 1918, now apparently recovered in body and mind and desperate to rejoin his front-line comrades, was Sassoon posted to Palestine and thence on to France with the 25th Battalion of his old regiment, the Royal Welch Fusiliers. His stay at the Front was brief. Wounded in the head by one of his own men on 13 July, the poet ended up in hospital at Lancaster Gate, London, in a state of "sleeplessexasperuicide." Now on indefinite sick-leave, Sassoon did not return to the trenches. On 12 March, 1919, he resigned his commission. *Picture Show*, Sassoon's last collection of war verse, was published in June of that year.

Sassoon's experience, both as officer and poet, was in some ways exemplary. To begin with, he embraced the "Great War for Civilization" as fervently as Brooke, Newbolt, Henley and the rest of the artistic establishment. "Absolution," his first war poem of 1915, with its reference to "fighting for our freedom, we are free," prompted the later remark: "People used to feel like this when they 'joined up' in 1914 and 1915" (WP, p. 15). Though he was older — almost 28 as opposed to Sorley's more usual 19 when the war broke out — he was the product of a privileged public-school and Oxbridge environment, a background shared by so many young officers in 1914. One estimate is that 75 percent of the university-educated war poets went to either Oxford or Cambridge (Parfitt, 1990, p. 14). Moreover, Sassoon was a subaltern, as were most of his fellow artists and most of his personal friends (one early poem is actually entitled "A Subaltern"). His personal rite of passage was not so different from that of other survivors. That he missed death by millimeters, that he was twice wounded, that he suffered several bouts of "trench fever," and later from what was called, with an equal lack of concern for its individualized manifestations, "neurasthenia," were fairly typical; that he was constantly desolated by the death of close friends was an equally common experience; so too was the growing conviction — shared by veteran campaigners — that the conflict was being incompetently conducted and mendaciously reported both by politicians at home and by "brass-hats" behind the lines. The trench soldier was not a conventional hero — in this kind of war he could not be — but a long-suffering victim.

Posterity should be grateful for the fact that Sassoon was, in other ways, far from being stereotypical. He came as close as anyone to being an authentic hero in an essentially unheroic war, an officer who led by dashing example, and who was worshipped by his men. Not for nothing was he affectionately nicknamed "Kangar" and "Mad Jack." They adored him for other reasons. In the trenches or back in England, he showed a conspicuous concern for the well-being of his fusiliers. Writing to Roderick Meiklejohn, he characteristically insisted: "As you know, I do all I can to make their lot as happy as possible" (letter from Sassoon to Meiklejohn, 2 June, 1918, ULUT). If that meant sending boxes of kippers or even a gramophone to the "boys," then he was happy to oblige. When *The Old Huntsman* came out, it was soon being read "up the line" where, recorded Cottrill, "the boys are enjoying it" (letter from Cottrill to Sassoon, 29 June, 1917, IWMP).

But his double role was difficult to maintain. Sassoon, we recall, was a man who, before the war, had wanted to combine the apparently antipathetic roles of aesthete and athlete; to enjoy a "double life" which required one half of him to be "hunting-field and the other ... gentleman writer" (WY, p. 208). Now an enforced version of this double life again necessitated the assumption of conflicting stances: that of the soldier-poet, conscious of the tensions created by his position as company-commander — where he needed to be hard-headed and efficient — and the mercurial demands of the artistic temperament. As he reflected during his last spell at the front line: "One cannot be a good soldier and a good poet at the same time. Soldiering depends on a multitude of small details; one must not miss any of the details. Poetry depends on wayward moods and sudden emotions" (*Diaries*, 15 June, 1918, p. 271). His friend Julian Dadd put it more bluntly: "I suppose it is not reasonable to combine the characteristics of a poet and champion bomber with the constitution and nervous system of a horse" (letter from Dadd to Sassoon, 29 March, 1917, ULUT).

The problem was exacerbated by Sassoon's growing conviction that the "Great War for Civilization" was anything but civilized; someone *must* make a public denunciation of what had become, in his view, no longer a war of "defence and liberation," but one of "aggression and conquest." In making his courageous stand, he was, he declared, protesting on behalf of "those who are suffering now," against the "political errors and insincerities for which the fighting men are being sacrificed" (*Diaries*, 15 June, 1917, p. 174). It is significant that the epithet "suffering(s)" appears three times in the brief "Protest," the word "agonies" once. That Sassoon was now, to all intents and purposes a pacifist poet, that he had what his analyst Rivers would label an "anti-war complex," meant not only an intensification of his revulsion to xenophobic attitudes, but an obsessive sympathy for the ordinary fusilier. Ironically, that obsession would feed his sense of guilt at being apart from his fellow martyrs and eventually drive him "back to grope with them through hell" ("Banishment"). The politicians might predictably reject his manifesto; the men at the Front assuredly did not. His quarter-master, Joe Cottrill, warmly congratulated him: "I endorse all you say about the politicians —

'the swines of profiteers,' the hypocritical parsons (The Church has been the biggest failure of the war) and the 'callous complaisance' of those viewing from afar" (letter from Cottrill to Sassoon, 11 July, 1917, IWMP) .

This polarized perspective — fury at establishment attitudes alternating with compassion for the "fighting-men," and allied to the compulsive desire to document front-line conditions, demanded a new kind of poetic utterance for which neither traditional "tub-thumping" war poetry nor existing Georgian models were appropriate. As Johnston observes:

> the characteristic qualities of Georgian poetry — its blandness, its decorum, its homogeneity, its simplicity of attitude, its preoccupation with rural themes (rather than with "nature" as the Romantics understood the term) — all reflect the decline of a once powerful imaginative vision. The Georgians expressed themselves through what Daiches calls the "static lyric," a kind of poem in which there is no movement of ideas and no enlargement of emotions [Johnston, 1964, p. 8].

This *is* an over-simplification of Georgianism, the kind of pejorative view anticipated by Eddie Marsh, whose introduction to the last edition averred that "those who have graced these collections look as diverse as sheep to their shepherd," adding that he "would *deny with both hands*" the notion that "insipid sameness is the chief characteristic of this work" (Prefatory Note to *Georgian Poetry*, 1920-1922). But it is true, particularly of the mainstream contributors, that the verse was generally lyrical, formally conservative and imbued with a sense of the English countryside.

In 1914 such poetry had its appeal for Sassoon, if less so than verse which reflected a more aureate Romantic-Victorian sensibility. But neither was a remotely adequate vehicle to convey the starkly different circumstances of trench warfare. Sassoon's early efforts would see him attempting to model his verse upon some of these precursors — witness the decasyllabics of "Absolution" or "To Victory." Almost reflexively, when short of inspiration, anxious to escape the hell of the front-line, or moved by the mute martyrdom of his troopers, he would return to such procedures. But the negative impact of the war increasingly insinuated a poetic response that not only divested it of any potential for "glory," but concentrated instead on its victimizing capacity, its destructive and dehumanizing nature.

That politicians, parsons and parents, indeed most of "Blighty" as far as Sassoon was concerned, seemed blissfully unaware of the war's actual character meant that the revelations needed to be more rather than less shockingly veracious: It forced on Sassoon the conviction that such events demanded a flexible and direct language capable of highlighting the pitiable degradation of the slain, or of denouncing the incompetence of the establishment. That Sassoon followed his instincts, using two very different poetic modes to express his feelings — both evocative documentation *and* pithy epigrammatic verse — makes him a significant poet of modern war. If there is a downside, it resides in the familiar criticisms of Sassoon: that his poetry is too often negative and even splenetic, that his insistence on the particular means a failure to encompass universal issues or sustain a prophetic vision, an inability, in Johnston's words, to "elevate it much beyond the level of vivid reportage" (1964, p. 20).

These strictures are a matter for conjecture. What is not a matter for debate is the war's role in force-feeding the poet: without immersion in its travails he would have remained an accomplished but minor versifier — a status to which both his pre- and post-war achievement entitles him. For Sassoon did revert to more traditional modes after a holocaust that remained, as for other writers who did not survive its embrace, "his one authentic subject." As Bergonzi not unfairly attests: "When Sassoon attempted to write straightforward poems on subjects remote from the war, he dwindled to the stature of a minor Georgian survival: the bulk of his later poetry, sententious or laxly pastoral, is carefully written and overpoweringly dull" (Bergonzi, 1965, p. 108).

Sassoon, then, was probably destined to remain an accomplished but limited poet, temperamentally disposed to write in lyrical or pastoral modes and operating in a fine frenzy of aureate unreality — until war's horrors impacted on him. His friend Robbie Ross's opinion of Sassoon's innocuous "pre-war pamphlets" was that "They rather remind me of the delicious teas of many years ago" (SJ, p. 19). Nonetheless poetry, in some shape or form, *was* his destiny. There were artistic genes in his make-up; significantly, he had grown up in an aesthetic environment. On the Thorneycroft side, Uncle Hamo (after whom Siegfried's brother had been named) was a celebrated sculptor; on the Jewish side, his aunt Rachel had been an accomplished composer as well as editor of the *Observer* and the *Sunday Times*. In the genteel and all-too-relaxed atmosphere of Weirleigh, Sassoon's mother, herself an artist, had encouraged such aspirations in her sons. While his public-school stay at Marlborough had been uneventful and undistinguished, it was there that he rediscovered the allure of poetry in the form of Thomas Hood's "Bridge of Sighs," a poem whose "word music" gave him "gooseflesh" and "brought tears" to his eyes (OC, p. 218). At Marlborough he also developed a life-long enthusiasm for sport, especially cricket. Summers and winters spent in a village community provided opportunities to indulge these sporting predilections: in addition to cricket, Sassoon developed a passion for fox-hunting (the household had stables and a resident groom) and, as an accomplished horseman, for point-to-pointing. In *Siegfried's Journey*, he would describe how the writing of the early poems of *The Old Huntsman* was an attempt to transform his "hitherto insensitive fox-hunting self into someone more aware of the beauties and complexities of life" (SJ, p. 20).

But there were dissonances as well as harmonies in Sassoon's upbringing that tend to be glossed over by commentators. Patrick Quinn, for example, argues, like Bergonzi, that there was little in the background to suggest "a potential rebel and defier both of public opinion and military authority" or indeed the "socialist crusader" of post-war years or "metaphysical companion of Herbert or Vaughan" (Quinn, 1980, p. 149). I am not entirely convinced by this line of argument. It is true, and particularly on the evidence of the *Memoirs of a Fox-Hunting Man* and the pre-war verse, that little appeared to ruffle the surface of his Edwardian idyll. But Sassoon was never quite part of the establishment; indeed he would later pour scorn on his vastly richer cousin Philip's attempts to climb the greasy pole of political preferment and to ingratiate himself into the most exalted echelons of society. Moreover Siegfried realized early in puberty — and both the powerfully oedipal relationship with his mother and his experience of boarding at public-school must have contributed — that he was homosexual. Such a realization distanced him from conventional upper-class attitudes, which were, on the fairly recent evidence of the Oscar Wilde trial, still rampantly homophobic. To excel at sport as well as cock a snook or two at the conventions of class — his friendship with Richardson the groom is a case in point — made him somehow more manly and potentially more attractive to young men who might themselves be questioning received opinions about their sexual orientation. Since stereotypes suggested there was more than a whiff of the effete about homosexuals, then the public persona of cricketer, race-rider, golfer and huntsman needed to be assiduously cultivated. If Sassoon wanted to explore his hidden emotional life in verse, then he needed to do so by operating within the codes and conventions of homoerotic verse — by the deployment of classical allusion, the adoption of mythical persona, and the employment of an utterance so poeticized as to disguise any manifest eroticism.

Sassoon's genetic inheritance was extraordinary. His mother's side was quintessentially English, landed gentry from the rural rides of Cheshire; on the other hand, his father's stock was oriental Jewish. Not poor immigrant Jews, the Sassoons, originally from Baghdad, were one of the richest families in England. The effect of this, apart from infusing Sassoon with plenty of "hybrid vigour," was the creation of a tension — the more recent and much discussed example of Sylvia Plath's Aryan/Jewish genetic inheritance comes to mind — that was fecundating to him as an artist. Patrick Quinn aptly quotes Robert Graves (who knew all about this!) on the subject of poets. They were, Graves argued, made by

> some peculiar event such as marriages between people of conflicting philosophies of life, widely separated nationalities ... likely either to result in children hopelessly struggling with inhibitions or to develop in them a central authority of great resource and most quick-witted at compromise [Graves, *On English Poetry*, quoted by Quinn, 1994, p. 149].

He probably had himself in mind when writing this; nonetheless the general point is a valid one and applies with equal felicity to Sassoon. For warring voices would appear in his poetry: the Georgian pastoralist at odds with the documenter of destruction, the pacifist versus the insensate killer, the prophet of doom at odds with the gentlemanly writer of memoirs. In all this Sassoon's Jewishness cannot be discounted. Writing in old age to Dame Felicitas Corrigan, he remarked: "you have got it right about my Jewish blood.... As a poetic spirit I have always felt myself—or wanted to be—a kind of minor prophet ... the idea has always been very strong in my mind and found utterance in the war poems of course" (Corrigan, 1973, p. 21).

Yet for most of his life and certainly during the war, Sassoon was at pains to suppress — as he suppressed so much else — his Jewish background. We should remember that he not only went to public school, a quintessentially English institution, but also and crucially, that his father left the family home when Sassoon was five. Almost never mentioned by the adult Sassoon, it is as though he tried to expunge his father's memory by denying his own Jewish connection. When his father died (Sassoon was still only eight), the young Siegfried became obsessed with death; on one level Alfred Sassoon's passing seemed to furnish additional proof of the erasure of his own Semitic origins. It is significant that the infrequent references to Jews in the war diaries are invariably pejorative — on one occasion he refers to "awful conversations in Pullman carriage by Jew profiteers" (*Diaries*, 19 December, 1917, p. 197)—and that the only allusion in the war poems, in the private verse-letter to "Roberto" Graves, refers to himself in the traditional role of usurer (he had lent the impecunious Graves some money): "Why keep a Jewish friend unless you bleed him?"

Sassoon's youth, then, was not as blissfully secure as the sanitized autobiographical writings would have us believe. Nonetheless Sassoon's pre-war poetry is nothing if not anodyne. As Thorpe observes, "Verbal facility came early, but his reading in the pre–Raphaelites, Swinburne and the dim magazines of his youth, coupled with his provincial, relatively cosseted life, served only to prolong into his late twenties a callow, youthful romanticism" (Thorpe, 1966, p. 3). Melody was the key ingredient in these early effusions. In *The Weald of Youth*, Sassoon affirmed:

> For me piano-playing and writing have always been closely connected. Most of my early verse was vague poetic feeling set to remembered music. Unintellectual melodiousness was its main characteristic. Rich harmonies and lingering sonorities induced a relaxation of the nerves, and acted on me like soothing and stimulating oxygen [WY, p. 111].

Indeed sound was assuredly more important than sense; poetry should aspire, after the pronouncements of his beloved Pater, to the condition of music.

When he did seek advice from the pre-war London literary establishment, he went to his "oracles," to Edmund Gosse and to Edward Marsh, the editor of *Georgian Poetry*. Both encouraged Sassoon, but in ways that insufficiently stimulated the development of a distinctive poetic voice. Marsh's advice was sound enough, though predictably based on Georgian precepts. In concentrating on Sassoon's sonnets and lyrics, Marsh emphasized their musicality: "I think it certain that you have a lovely instrument to play upon and no end of beautiful tunes in your head," but added that "sometimes you write them down without getting enough meaning into them to satisfy the mind." More trenchantly he observed that Sassoon's "sonnets contained far too much of the worn-out stuff and garb of poetry" (WY, p. 139). Edmund Gosse's taste was more traditional. Significantly, "To Victory," one of the most conventional trumpet-pieces of Sassoon's war, would be dedicated to Gosse. But something more cataclysmic than the comments of critics would be required to force a radical change of artistic direction. Reminiscing to S. C. Cockerell in 1932, Sassoon said of his antebellum versifying: "The odd thing is that I felt more of a poet than I do now" (*The Best of Friends*, 1955, p. 44, quoted by Keynes, 1962, p. 25).

In circulation by the outbreak of hostilities, these modish pieces were contained in slim, privately printed volumes, with Sassoon's predilection for the sonnet much in evidence, and with his favorite verses putting in repeat appearances: *Orpheus in Diloeryum* (1908), *Sonnets* (1909), *Sonnets and Verses* (1909), *Twelve Sonnets* (1911) and *Poems* (1911), *Melodies* (1912), *Hyacinth* (1912), *Amyntas* (1912), *Ode for Music* (1912) and anonymously in 1913, *The Daffodil Murderer*.

Orpheus in Diloeryum was, according to Sassoon, "an unactable one-act play which had never quite made up its mind whether to be satirical or serious" (WY, p. 15). It is a parody of "pseudo-artistic" attitudes, a potpourri of literary echoes expressed variously by Epicurio, an aesthete, Discordias, a musician, Dorgrelian (shades of Dorian Gray), a poet, and Glypticos, a sculptor. Finally and appropriately, Orpheus sings an eloquent hymn of praise to the natural world and the dilettantes are all put to flight by satyrs. In *Sonnets* (1909), the preciosity of the language is all *too* seriously intended, replete with precisely those archaisms to which Marsh would later object. The opening of "Perilous Music" ("Whence comes this dreamed embassage with low / Strange luthany to woo thee in such wise") is so strained as to be risible. *Poems* (1911), a slim volume of 12 offerings, preponderantly in the favored pastoral mode, also contains a pair of dream poems ("Processions" and "Ambassadors"), which Eddie Marsh regarded later as "almost meaningless" (WY, p. 139). *Melodies* (1912), again preoccupied — as the title implies — with mellifluous effects, shows some progression in technique. Though Sassoon, ever the trenchant self-critic, had scribbled in the (British Library) copy, "several of these are very inferior," they are generally closer in rhythm and cadence, despite their continuing preoccupation with shepherds and pastoral paraphernalia, to the first war poems. In 1912, Sassoon published *Hyacinth*, a prose play with the Platonic epigraph, "Not all love nor every mode of love is beautiful, or worthy of commendation, but that alone which excites us to love worthily," and another one-act piece, printed but never published, entitled *Amyntas: A Mystery*. The following year saw the appearance of Sassoon's verse satire, *The Daffodil Murderer*.

It is tempting, along with their perpetrator, to dismiss most of these efforts as poetic effusions. After all, the usual critical view, largely endorsed by the writer, is that little of this pre-war material — *The Daffodil Murderer* excepted — amounted to much. But there are plenty of intimations of the mature Sassoon manner; indeed it is difficult to resist the presumption that the trench poet quarried these poems for the occasional epithet. *Orpheus in Diloeryum*, for instance, gave early notice of Sassoon's capacity to operate in a parodic, quasi-satiric mode and, on the evidence of his spokesman's pantheistic outburst, in an idiom not so different from that employed for purposes of contrast in a number of the war poems. *Sonnets* (1909), a collection which reveals the vestigial influence of Keats and Clare, contains one maverick poem, "Villon," whose imagery of "matted hair" coincidentally prefigures the opening wasteland of "Counter-Attack," and another, entitled "A Masque," whose figure of "Wan Despair / And Folly from base deeds," echoes a similar personification in "Conscripts." In the 1911 poems, "At Daybreak" consists of two stanzas, beginning "I listen for him through the rain, / And in the dusk of starless hours," that seem to have provided the inspiration for the pantheistic conclusion to "A Last Meeting." *Melodies* (1912), pointedly prefaced by a Swinburnian epigraph — "The silence that thrills with the whisper of secret streams" — is, with its invocations to Arcadian shepherds, and such lines as "There stands the lad your eyes were seeking ... Hie to him quick and say you love him," suffused with homoerotic sentiments. Such feelings, already hinted at in many of the romantic statements of earlier volumes, would reappear in the very different context of the war poems.

Homoerotic feeling is at the heart of *Amyntas: A Mystery*. In personal terms the "mystery" is the poet's own homosexuality; in dramatic terms it resides in the mysterious crushing to death of the would-be poisoner of Amyntas by a marble statue of Apollo. The personal resonances in the one-act play are barely concealed by the allegory. Amyntas, we learn, is a feminine man ("small stomach has Amyntas for such things as best befit a man"), afraid not of death but of immersion in life. All he desires is a reciprocated love, not from all men but from one young beloved who can offer "a pity more human; eyes that can answer mine, arms that shall hold me fast" (p. 19). Couched in symbolic terms and probably owing some of its impetus to his recent acquaintance with the works of Edward Carpenter, the play explores the poet's secret dilemma. His homoerotic impulses are noble; all he yearns for is a tenderly reciprocated affection. But the real world is awash with prejudice, a place where death seems preferable to living the lie of conventional existence, a world in which Virgilius typifies its homophobic dimension. Only in the miraculous microcosm of the play can Apollo, the god of poetry and song, triumph over the reality principle. After the defeat of Virgilius, Amyntas, symbolically clad in the white of purity, vanishes. Walter, a young man, permanently changed by witnessing these epiphanic events, gives his "conversion" to the cause of Amyntas a religious dimension when he confides: "I am blind; I have looked too close into the sun" (p. 25).

Amyntas was an important personal document, too revealing to be published or used as a model for future allegories. In 1913 Sassoon attempted something totally new, perhaps in part as a consequence of his perceived need to eschew the cloyingly personal, to focus on the real world of which Virgilius had been a horrid intimation. The ballad-like directness of Masefield would seduce Sassoon into a poetic manner that would have considerable implications when the war came along. Sassoon himself recognized that in *The Daffodil Murderer* were premonitions of something very different. An attempt to parody Masefield's *The Everlasting Mercy*— and Sassoon had, on the evidence of his letters to Max Beerbohm and a number of unpublished epigrams, a gift for parody he should have explored more — the poet felt he was onto something new:

> After the first fifty lines or so, I dropped the pretence that I was improvising an exuberant skit. While continuing to burlesque Masefield for all I was worth, I was really feeling what I wrote — and doing it not only with abundant delight but a ... descriptive energy quite unlike anything I had experienced before.... Never before had I been able to imbue commonplace details with warmth of poetic emotion.... In other words ... I was at last ... writing physically [WY, p. 125].

Sassoon was not alone in sensing the poem's importance as a benchmark of his artistic development. No less a judge than Robert Graves, having dismissed the earlier stuff as "a few pastoral pieces of eighteen-ninetyish flavour," referred to *The Daffodil Murderer* as "a satire on Masefield which, halfway through, had forgotten to be a satire and turned into rather good Masefield" (GTAT, p. 154). The traditionalist Gosse, who did warm to the poem, chose to ignore its parodic element and demotic vigor and instead damned it with faint praise, seeing it as a "tale of rustic tragedy ... told with real pathos and power, only — exactly as Masefield would tell it. The end is extremely beautiful" (WY, p. 134). Of course both the capacity for satire and an ear for the nuances of direct speech would become hallmarks of the war verse. Yet it would be all of three years after this exercise, 18 months into the war and six months after Sassoon's commission in the Royal Welch Fusiliers that, inspired by working parties at Festubert, he would chance his first colloquial line: "O Christ Almighty, now I'm stuck!" and then break into realism by introducing his "Muse to the word 'frowst'" in "Good Friday Morning." Not until "The Poet as Hero" (published in the *Cambridge Magazine* of December, 1916) would Sassoon acknowledge that he had bid "Goodbye to Galahad" and the fine language that went with him.

The *Daffodil Murderer* was an artistic watershed in all sorts of ways. It certainly did, as Gosse noted, reveal a newfound capacity for compassion, for sympathizing, Wordsworthian fashion, with the misfortunes of the common man. And while Housman is a key influence, it is the atypically robust world of "Terence, This Is Stupid Stuff" that has infiltrated the poem ("Out there I laboured from a lad / And lived and found it none so bad"). Indeed it is not only the proletarian world of the ballad, but its device of montage with its sudden shifts of perspective which underpin the poem's animated narrative. There are also premonitions of other poetic preoccupations: the attack on clerics, the solace afforded by a natural world ("as they lead me to the gallows / I'll think of peewits on the fallows"). All through the long days and nights in the trenches and awaiting his own end, Sassoon would console himself with such memories.

Chapter 2

The Progress of the Poet

In *Siegfried's Journey*, Sassoon alluded to the successive molts of style in his war poetry. Noting the presence in the early verse of the typical self-glorifying feelings of a young man about to go to the front for the first time, he went on to describe his growing dissatisfaction with such effusions and the perceived need to write "poems aimed at impersonal descriptions of front-line conditions ... the first things of their kind" (SJ, p. 17). These new 1916 poems were no longer a legacy of his delight in word music or a perfection achieved through a distillation of imagination. Instead they were dictated by a "resolve to record (his) surroundings," and based, to ensure their authenticity, on firsthand notes. Later these pieces would be joined by what Sassoon called "his successes in condensed satire," of which "'Good Friday Morning,' a jaunty scrap of doggerel versified from a rough note in my diary" was an important precursor (SJ, p. 17).

This crude division into aureate trumpet-pieces, trench poems based on firsthand observation, and anti-war poems, often of a satiric or epigrammatic cast, says something, however simplistic, about Sassoon's scope and development as a war poet. He began tentatively enough. "Absolution," three quatrains of "too nobly worded lines" and his first war piece, was one of four poems written in 1915. Of these only "The Redeemer" (which was in any case revised in the following March) attempts a degree of documentary realism, with its snatches of direct speech and allusions to the "muck" and "mirk" of the trenches; it was, as Sassoon allowed, his "first front line poem" (WP, p. 17). But the treatment of the Christ-like soldier veers, as so many pre-war male portraits do, towards the sentimental; his pre-war life is still, as Caesar reminds us, seen through "an upper-class lens" as some kind of idyll (1993, p. 71).

The other 1915 poems, all suffused in a romantic glow, are "To My Brother," in which Brookean poeticisms disguise Sassoon's very real sense of grief, and "The Prince of Wounds." Similarly the first 1916 poems exhibit little progress towards documentary realism: they consist of the mannered "A Testament," in which the poet is "crowded with the triumphant dead," "To Victory" (suitably dedicated to Edmund Gosse), and "The Dragon and the Undying," where war, personified as a mythical beast and thus conventionally linked to a Christian tradition, lusts to break not flesh and bone but "the loveliness of spires."

But by February 1916, in the mud of Morlancourt, the trench poet was being made. "In the Pink" shows Sassoon re-absorbing the lesson learnt in creating *The Daffodil Murderer*, that of "writing physically." It had been an important lesson. Late in life Sassoon recognized in the 1911 poem intimations of his realistic manner. It was, he reflected, "the first sign of my being capable of writing as I did during the war, and the first time I used real experience" (Corrigan, 1973, p. 68). Now by empathizing with his working-class Welch Fusilier and his vision of a rural Eden turned to a nightmare of "stodgy clay and freezing sludge" (his Sussex farmhand is similarly separated from simple country pleasures in the 1913 poem), he produced the first of his "outspoken" war poems. Indeed it was too "outspoken" for the *Westminster* whose editor refused it on the grounds that it "might prejudice recruiting" (WP, p. 22). Though the working-class soldier is again close to being sentimentalized, the reality principle dominates, for there is no doubt in the speaker's mind that "soon he'll die."

Though the unspeakable conditions of trench life and Sassoon's growing awareness of the hypocrisy of the "Home Front" were eroding the poet-officer's idealism, the pre-Somme pieces still veer uneasily between the May "aureate unreality" of "France" and the March realism of "A Working Party," an incipient veracity enhanced by the poet's growing but still tentative use of trench-speak, and his soldier's cussed questioning of Christian values. As Sassoon remarked, conscious that his poetry was becoming more gritty, he "broke into realism by introducing (his) Muse to the word 'frowst' in "Good Friday Morning." But it is not just the vocabulary — and the use of "syphilitic" in "They" would represent another "first" — that is becoming less poetical; the very subject matter is gaining in explicitness. Rats put in appearances in three March 1916 poems ("Golgotha," "A Working Party" and "A Subaltern"), appropriate denizens of a man-made hell "ankle deep" in "sludge." Moreover, a mute inglorious death, merely presaged in "In The Pink," becomes, in "A Working Party" a reality, a "startled life" "split with lead." But as yet, there are no detailed descriptions of war's horrid physical manifestations; they are suppressed or at best given cursory treatment. Even in "A Night Attack," the first of Sassoon's battlefield corpses is still invested with a certain heroism: "his sturdy legs ... bent beneath his trunk."

There *is* a steady progression towards a more naturalistic manner in Sassoon's poetry up to the events of the Somme; nonetheless, a few poems do cut across the grain; for example "France," the product of an idyllic spring interlude at Flixécourt with Marcus Goodall as companion, and the pantheistic elegies to David Thomas. Sassoon's actual immersion in the drudgery of trench life was one benchmark; the demise of "Tommy," shot through the throat, was another. Indeed, of all the formative experiences of the poet's war, David Thomas's death was perhaps the most significant. Sassoon's final memory of the "angel with the light in his yellow hair" was of him reading Sassoon's "last poem." Now he was no more (*Diaries*, 19 March, p. 45). That such an idealized love could be destroyed — at a single stroke — was ineradicable proof of war's murderous bestiality, a bestiality Sassoon's love had sought to transcend. The loss produced two quite contrasting reactions: one, an unbridled thirst for revenge — "Since they shot Tommy I would gladly stick a bayonet into a German by daylight" (*Diaries*, 1 April, p. 52) — a feeling which finds poetic and (homoerotic) expression in "The Kiss"; two, a romantic and consolatory impulse that issues in the elegiac "The Last Meeting" and the escapist "jingle" to Graves entitled "A Letter Home."

Faced with the unbearable, traumatized by grief, Sassoon thus reverted, as he sometimes would in 1917, to visions of a natural paradise and a spiritual optimism based on pantheistic renewal. "The Last Meeting" thus seeks an epiphany in which the departed spirit is rediscovered amid "the rapture of dark pines" and the heady blossoms of May. As Thorpe points out, "The Last Meeting" is an odd poem, the more so since its note of "facile optimism" was chosen by the poet to end *The Old Huntsman*, "a collection that contains such poems as 'Blighters' and 'The Hero'" (Thorpe, 1966, p. 28). But the critic's remark should be treated with caution. Sassoon probably wanted to round off the collection with a piece that clearly carried deep personal significance.

The personal disaster of Thomas's death, the worst because the first of such losses, was followed, all too inexorably, by the mass carnage of the Somme. The campaign, begun on 1 July, 1916 — Sassoon had just been awarded the Military Cross for conspicuous bravery — was another watershed in his war. It brought the incipient pacifist poet to the fore. "Died of Wounds," one of Sassoon's first post–Somme poems and written from his feverish hospital bed, focuses, as his front-line bulletins increasingly would, on the plight of the common soldier, not in this instance a close friend like David, but an anonymous victim of the annihilation at Mametz Wood. In foregrounding the dying youth's ravings, Sassoon's greatest war poem to that point achieves an uncomfortable directness and raw pathos that earlier verses can only aspire to. Graves proudly referred to its middle verse as "the best stanza in this book, probably in any book of war poems.... It knocks me more every time" (letter from Graves to Sassoon, 22 April, 1917, IBI, p. 72). Moreover it makes use of a technique as yet barely tapped by Sassoon, that of ironic juxtaposition, with an unexpected switch of emphasis in the last line. Though the subject matter owes nothing to "Blighty" conditions, the poem's organizational procedures anticipate the "Home-Front" satires yet to be written.

While recuperating at Amiens, Sassoon also heard of the death of the man who had briefly replaced "Tommy" in his affections — Marcus Goodall. Another scarcely endurable loss, it prompted a vision of the "discontented slain" thrown into "shallow pits," a Gothic vision so grotesque and haunted that it could not be considered for publication. The deaths, even of heroes, were not heroic; still less the ghastly details of their unseemly burials. Such obscenities must remain in the private realm.

The Somme campaign resulted in other poems that prefigure less dramatic directions Sassoon's verse would take: "A Night Attack" moves both towards a greater naturalism with its concentration on "the rank stench" of bodies, and an even-handed humanitarianism in its sympathetic account of a German soldier's death; "Christ and the Soldier," much underrated by an older poet anxious to play down his anti-religious war stance, demonstrates his "increasing disillusioned and rebellious" attitude towards the "Churches" at home (WP, p. 47).

"Christ and the Soldier," both trench piece and satire, encapsulates in one poem the twin impulses behind Sassoon's subsequent output. Now back in "Blighty" and convalescing at Somerville College, Oxford, the poet's anger was fanned to white heat, not by German "atrocities" but by the intransigence of public attitudes. The result was a series of "performances" that "had the quality of satirical drawings ... deliberately devised to disturb complacency" (SJ, p. 19). A trial run for these satires took place in the privacy of his notebooks where three brief epigrams ("For England," "The Stunt" and "Via Crucis") reveal Sassoon sharpening his satiric barbs. At Somerville and then at Weirleigh, Sassoon also wrote, with a "Blighty" readership in mind, "The One-Legged Man," "The Hero" and "Stretcher Case." Unfortunately he gave the game away in the title of the first of these poems, a fact which tends to vitiate the impact of the ironic conclusion ("Thank God they had to amputate"). But both this poem and "The Hero" tackle highly contentious themes and show that Sassoon was no longer disposed to mollify opinion at home. That this was indeed a born-again poet, angrily protesting his re-entry into a world awash with cant and humbug, is reinforced by the confessional piece, "The Poet as Hero," in which Sassoon renounces his "old silly sweetness" in favor of the "ugly cry" of the satirist and documentor.

The distaff side of a war that revealed all this home-front hypocrisy, cowardice and war hysteria, inspired some of the most memorable of these satires—"A Ballad," "They," "The Tombstone-Maker," "Decorated," "Arms and the Man"—all composed in the late autumn of 1916 while Sassoon was still convalescing at home. It is important to remember that Sassoon's three extended evacuations to "Blighty"—1916 (Oxford, Weirleigh), 1917 (London, Sussex, Craiglockhart) and 1918 (Lancaster Gate, Lennel)—produced three separate bursts of satiric writing. The reasons are not difficult to divine. Sassoon's creative impulse thrived on instant stimulation: in England he might be guiltily distanced from the Front, but with time on his hands and bursting with things to say, he was now everywhere reminded of the hypocrisy of those unwilling or unable to risk life and limb.

Of these epigrams, "They" was Sassoon's favorite, "the most quoted by reviewers both adverse and favourable" (SJ, p. 29). Surprisingly it was, he recalled many years on, his first diatribe against the "patriotic pietism" of the Anglican church (Corrigan, 1973, p. 80), a satire which extended (particularly through his contentious use of the word "syphilitic") his experiments in non-poetic language.

To Eddie Marsh, editor of *Georgian Poetry*, it was, predictably, "altogether too horrible" (WP, p. 57). The other satires directed volleys at targets he would return to: civilian materialism and insensitivity; a class divide now exacerbated by war; and worse, the craven and undignified behavior of soldiers "in extremis." Sassoon knew full well that no one wanted to accept these uncomfortable truths. Such pieces provided "a thoroughly caddish antidote to the glorification of 'the supreme sacrifice,' possessed the quality of satirical drawings" and "were deliberately devised to disturb complacency" (SJ, p. 19). Much of their power derives from a method that Sassoon later maintained was accidentally arrived at: "I merely chanced on the device of composing two or three harsh, peremptory, and colloquial stanzas with a knock-out blow in the last line" (SJ, p. 29).

But if Sassoon's anger knew no bounds, neither did his compassion for his fellow sufferers. Though "The Death-Bed" *does* attack "cruel old campaigners" — an increasingly frequent target — it is, first and foremost, an eloquent and impassioned entreaty to "save" yet another innocent victim of war. Of course, the young victim does not survive. In the light of such distressing events, Sassoon was himself finding it more and more difficult to generate any positive feelings, especially in the grey, polluted environment of Litherland where he found himself in late 1916. In his diary he wrote: "the year is dying of atrophy as far as I'm concerned, bed-fast in its December fogs ... newspapers and politicians yell and brandish their arms, and the dead rot in their French graves and the maimed hobble about the streets" (*Diaries*, 22 December, p. 105).

Sassoon's Litherland experience of parade grounds and "bullshit," of drab urbanscapes and the drunken womanizing of fellow soldiers, spawned not only a collection of mordant "Blighty" epigrams — "The March-Past," "When I'm Among a Blaze of Lights," and the celebrated "Blighters" — but also "Conscripts," a frankly homoerotic piece in which Sassoon casts a voyeuristic eye over his "awkward" but endearing "squad." Spells away from the action invariably allowed Sassoon to indulge in some therapeutic male-gazing, a positive counter to his well-documented contempt for home attitudes, and increasingly linked to a compulsive desire to spill his spirit for and with his suffering troops.

Sassoon's wish was soon granted. He was back at the Front early in 1917, "conscious of the same spirit that brought him serenely through it last year: the feeling of sacrifice" (*Diaries*, p. 137). "Base Details," a terse piece inspired by "guzzling" officers encountered in the restaurants of Rouen, demonstrates that his capacity for satire was undiminished; on the other hand, "The Rear-Guard" shows a willingness to record the nightmarish sensations, "the sweat of horror," produced by exposure in the trenches. As Sassoon knew full well, it was his most impressive poem in that mode thus far, a model for the greatest of all World War One poems, Owen's "Strange Meeting." By the time it was written down, Sassoon was already back in England. The simmering conflict in his mind had boiled over: either he must return to the Front with all conceivable speed, or he must "make some protest against the war." Encouraged by the Garsington set and motivated not by a doctrinaire pacifism but by an unalloyed sympathy for all those suffering, dying men, Sassoon made his famous "Protest" against the prolongation of the conflict. To avoid the inevitable court-martial or worse, Graves arranged to have him whisked off to a military hospital.

The facts of the "Protest," "an act of wilful defiance of military authority," made in the belief that the war was "being deliberately prolonged by those" who had "the power to end it," focused on Sassoon's obsessive concern for his "suffering" soldiers. Psychologically, it was a key incident in his war, a watershed in his growth as a poet. Apparently out of harms way at "Dottyville" in Scotland, he could both return to a satiric mode he had never really abandoned and compose more outspoken pieces about the conduct of the war, conscious that the poetry reading public, whether it agreed with him or not, was no longer entirely unaware of his views. At Craiglockhart Sassoon extended his range of targets to include yellow pressmen ("Editorial Impressions"), do-gooders ("Does It Matter," "How to Die," "Fight to a Finish"), old men ("The Fathers"), and hero-worshipping women ("Glory of Women," "Their Frailty"). Sassoon's misogyny, hinted at in earlier poems, here reveals itself without equivocation. So too does another visible inflection, his growing concern for the German soldier. Whatever the Allied propaganda machine might churn out, things were, in Sassoon's estimation, just as bad for the enemy troops, as "Glory of Women" makes abundantly clear.

While agonizing over his "Protest" and before his Scottish incarceration at Craiglockhart, Sassoon had written two other important and technically innovative poems. "To Any Dead Officer," triggered by the death of his friend Orme, certainly empathizes with "lads left in shell-holes dying slow." Moreover, in its strident attack on politicians it also anticipates the poet's July protest. But the "hot line to God" approach of this "slangy telephonic poem" (SJ, p. 54) was too novel even for Graves; now Sassoon, who two years earlier had been criticized by his friend for writing in rather passé modes (GTAT, p. 154), was, irony of ironies, modifying his style more radically than Graves could stomach. The other poem, "Repression of War Experience," again written during the gestation of his public protest, is yet more experimental, a piece based on the processes of free association in which the day-dreamer attempts, unsuccessfully, to ward off his most insistent obsessions about the war he has physically left behind.

That Sassoon was, as the poem attests, going "stark staring mad because of the guns" was somewhat in excess of the facts, but neurasthenia *was* cited, officially, as the reason for his stay at Craiglockhart. It was a lengthy sojourn, all of five months, time enough to form two seminal friendships, one with "reasoning Rivers," his doctor, and the other with Wilfred Owen. Rivers, whom Sassoon rapidly came to hero-worship (as was his wont with men he greatly admired), did not believe that Sassoon was remotely mad; he correctly diagnosed an "anti-war complex" and sought to treat the condition by getting his patient to unburden himself of his most harrowing memories. On his "Medical Case Sheet" he laconically recorded that Sassoon recognises that his view of warfare is tinged by his feelings about the death of friends and of the men who were under his command in France. His view differs from the ordinary pacifist in that he would no longer object to the continuance of the war if he saw any reasonable prospect of a rapid decision [IWMP].

Far from being a pacifist himself, Rivers did more than even Sassoon realized to undermine his pacifist position, to convince him that his histrionic protest could not of itself end the war, and to help him expunge his abiding sense of guilt and reaffirm his fellow-feeling for his comrades by the positive act of joining his "brothers," by "going out to them again" ("Survivors"). Meanwhile Sassoon's *satiric* victims were injected with even more venom. As a consequence of Rivers's counseling, based on Freudian principles, Sassoon became convinced that his personal restoration would be helped if he gave full vent to his feelings.

The friendship with Owen also gave a new direction to Sassoon as man and artist; it offered a reconfirmation of his vocation and talent as poet and, above all, of his capacity to love other men. The intensity of their friendship can be gauged from the fact that they were in each other's company every day for three months. As Sassoon would later recall in a revealing aside: "I received his fullest confidences and realised that he could give me as much as I gave to him" (SJ, p. 63). It is significant that it was at Craiglockhart that Sassoon blurted out his homosexual feelings to Lady Ottoline Morrell. Moreover, Owen was about to set an example by returning to the Front. So too would Sassoon. In the meantime two or three longish trench poems were composed at Craiglockhart: "Break of Day" (which compares fox-hunting — more properly "cubbing" — and man-hunting), "Prelude: The Troops," and "Counter-Attack." While the first two contain little specific detail, the opening stanza of "Counter-Attack," based on a 1916 draft and probably inspired in part by the realism of Barbusse's *Le Feu*, is a visually evocative and disturbingly physical picture of modern war in all its putrefying horror.

Other poems which would appear in *Counter-Attack* were written in the congenial environs of southern Ireland. Their tone is predictably less strident, less intense. Fox-hunting had, temporarily, become a realizable passion again; the rest of the time at Limerick was spent in the low-key business of training recruits — twin diversions. But as "Invocation" and "Memory" lyrically, and "Remorse" and "Suicide in the Trenches" realistically, remind the reader, the war was still going on. Sassoon desperately wanted to be there. Eventually, by way of Egypt and Palestine and courtesy of the German spring offensive of 1918, Sassoon would be briefly back in the lines. Meanwhile *Counter-Attack*, with its red and yellow cover, incidentally symbolic of the red-blood of war and the yellow press of "Blighty," was with Heinemann, to be published on 27 June.

Predictably, few "Blighty" satires remained in Sassoon's armory: the meditative diary poems from Egypt and Palestine reveal his romantic apprehension of a foreign but beautiful landscape. On the other hand, "Reward" and "I Stood

With the Dead" reassert, as the Craiglockhart poem "Sick Leave" already had, Sassoon's compulsive desire to be with the "lads" at the front line. Enormously moved by the compassion of Duhamel's *La Vie des martyrs*, the only "reward" Sassoon now seeks is to suffer and die with his fusiliers; his only "triumph," not without its sado-masochistic side, will be to partake of this bloodbrotherhood, and to witness the ultimate pleasure of his victorious men, their faces etched with triumph, returning from their exertions. Fulfillment of this kind was all too fleetingly achieved. Sassoon managed five days on the Western Front before being shot in the head. He was invalided back to England for a third time, where exultation rapidly gave way to despair: in the throes of "sleeplessexasperuicide," he wrote a "wobbly-witted" verse letter to Graves, uniquely confessional in tone. It is the most revealing of all Sassoon's war pieces. In it the old tensions surface again: the wish to fight gloriously is set against the terror of confronting masticating "five-nines"; the need to be loved abroad and recognized at home as "the topic of the town" is contrasted with the wish for oblivion and the regret that "the bloody bullet missed its mark"; the hopelessly guilt-laden hospital case is juxtaposed to the wished-for image of the "gallant ... lyrical soldier." That the verse letter's publication a decade later by Graves was more or less terminal to an already ailing relationship, is scarcely to be wondered at. Worse, the "bloody bullet" effectively ended Sassoon's war. He reverts, as he always did when trapped in "Blighty," to penning satirical epigrams, of which "Memorial Tablet," a combination of anger and compassion, is about the best, and finally manages to bring together the twin obsessions of war and cricket in a very un–"Vitae Lampada"–like way in "A Last Word." It was not quite Sassoon's "last word" on events: in "Vicarious Christ," he would again disparage "gung-ho" clerics; in "Return of the Heroes," hero-worshipping women; in "Devotion to Duty" the questionable ethics of a monarch exploiting war widows. His final, and disturbingly prophetic, satire would offer an ironic comment on the bloodless efficacy of poison gases.

Chapter 3

Frail Women and Glorious Boys

A product of a public school education, a member of a privileged and patriarchal society whose initiates immersed themselves in pastimes more or less denied to women, Sassoon had little time for the other sex as friends, none as lovers. When young women did express an amorous interest in the dashing officer, he did his best to discourage it. It was only because of his "love for Bobbie" (Hanmer) that Sassoon allowed Hanmer's sister to entertain prospects of marriage. But in a revealing diary passage, he admits to the folly of the idea:

> When war ends I'll be at the crossroads; and I know I must go out into the night alone. No fat settling down; the Hanmer engagement idea was a ghastly blunder — it wouldn't work at all. That charming girl who writes to me so often would never be happy with me. It was my love for Bobbie that led me to that mistake [*Diaries*, 16 July, 1916, p. 94].

Later in the war he confessed that he was worried by "the lady in the case" (unnamed) "as it can't lead to anything — if only I could persuade one of my handsome and impecunious young friends to compete!" (letter from Sassoon to Meiklejohn, 15 September, 1918, ULUT).

Though Sassoon's antebellum world was a domestic one dominated by his mother, the only woman during the war that Sassoon ever got close to, apart from his mother (and she is metamorphosed into Aunt Evelyn in the *Memoirs*), was Lady Ottoline Morrell. An exotic and an aristocrat (half-sister to the Duke of Portland), and a generous patron of artists, she developed an admiration first for Sassoon's poetry and then for the man. In her memoirs she confided after an early meeting: "I find Siegfried very sympathetic and attractive, and my instinct goes out to him for he seems so intimate to me, as if he were a twin brother" (Morrell, 1975, p. 152). They corresponded regularly throughout the war and Sassoon became a familiar presence at Garsington Manor. Later Sassoon was proud to acknowledge a friendship that had existed for twenty years.

Nonetheless he was at first suspicious of her motives. Having sent Ottoline the poem "Morning Glory" after their initial meeting, he wrote in his diary: "this morning comes her reply, full of superlatives. Does she really admire my things as much as all that?" (*Diaries*, 12 June, 1917, p. 118). But Sassoon, though capable of behaving inconsiderately to her, especially when he suspected that she was physically attracted to him, warmed to her eccentricity as well as her hospitality; she was after all outrageously unconventional in ways that Sassoon dared not be. More important, she (and her Liberal politician husband Philip) actively encouraged Sassoon's pacifist sympathies, and though Philip advised against a public manifesto, they stood foursquare behind him during his "Protest." Ottoline even came to visit him for several days at Craiglockhart. Despite the odd hiccup, the friendship endured; their extensive correspondence is testimony to that. Other women remained outside the charmed circle.

On the subject of Sassoon's misogyny (and I do not think we can call it otherwise) the diaries are revealing. Bored by the dreary scenery and rituals of Litherland, the poet admitted to himself that "the only merit of this hut-life is that there are no women about" (*Diaries*, 20 December, 1916, p. 104). Later, when quizzed by a Ceylon tea-planter as to "why there are no women in my verse," the poet famously retorted: "I told him they are outside my philosophy" (p. 106).

The tea-planter, whose name happened to be Owen, was not quite right about the absence of women in the verse. Certainly in the early war poetry they are more or less invisible — the women pathetically lining the verges in "The Road" (written five months before Owen's question) remain, by a process of authorial transference, beyond the male gaze of soldiers who apparently "never see them." "The Hero," also written in August 1916, and the first of his war poems to adopt a mother's viewpoint, had stressed the disparity between her hubristic sentiments ("we mothers are so proud / Of our dead soldiers") and the grim reality. Her "glorious boy" was nothing more than a "cold-footed useless swine" who met an appropriately ignominious end. Out of touch with war's reality like the old toddlers of "The Fathers" or the "Bishop of Byegumb," mothers were, in Sassoon's estimation, more culpable because they allowed their maternal love for their sons to become confused with absurdly romantic notions of heroism. In "Supreme Sacrifice" they make the world a "silly sort of place / When people think it's pleasant to be dead." Even a "war widow" (in the unpublished poem of that name), prepared to denounce the conflict as senseless, is trivialized as an "empty head," apparently more preoccupied with her bejeweled appearance than the fate of others. The poet cannot accept that women, even from the upper classes, are anything more than repositories of unbridled "lust" and exaggerated emotionalism.

Clearly Sassoon felt that women not only fell victim to the heroic fallacy, but that their emotionalism did have a sexual dimension. Writing in his notebook just after his protest, three weeks after composing "A War Widow," the poet made no bones about it, demanding that returning soldiers should "ask their women why it thrills them to know that they, the dauntless warriors, have shed the blood of Germans. Do not the women gloat secretly over the wounds of their lovers? Is there anything inwardly noble in savage sex instincts?" (*Diaries*, 19 June, 1917, p. 175).

But Sassoon's own notebook questions do beg other ones. Is there not an element of Freudian transference here? Is not Sassoon transferring his own "savage instincts" as well as his own sado-masochism ("secret gloating over wounds") onto women? The poet would later use very similar language about his own sexual proclivities. And were women so culpable? True, they were not allowed to fight, but women undertook dangerous jobs in munitions factories. Some, moreover, did give public expression to pacifist feelings. Not all of them who ventured into verse espoused the view that it was "sweet and fitting to die for your country."

Nonetheless, in the two Craiglockhart poems about "mothers, wives and sweethearts," Sassoon returns to the attack. The ironically entitled "Glory of Women" again targets their refusal to accept the unpleasant truth about a conflict that does not accord with female notions of chivalry, and pours scorn on their limitless capacity for adulation; "Their Frailty" concentrates on women's inability to see things in perspective: female "frailty" is a consequence of a narrowly egocentric vision that embraces only the fate of their loved one — "they don't care / So long as he's all right." Come the Armistice nothing has changed: "Return of the Heroes" focuses on a female bystander in the crowd of well-wishers; "enthusiastic, flushed and proud" of these parading "brass-hats" who "did for" so many ordinary soldiers, she is impressed only by the glitter of their ill-gotten rows of medals. This is hero-worship of the most insidious kind as far as Sassoon was concerned.

It is, of course, easy, perhaps facile, to link Sassoon's expressed contempt for women to his own sexual preference for men. After all, he did share the impatience felt by his friends Owen and Graves for the patriotic rhetoric that "little mothers" and a "certain poetess" foisted on a "yellow press" (Owen dedicated early drafts of "Dulce et Decorum Est" to Jessie Pope; Graves would quote a "little mother" letter in *Goodbye to All That*). In Sassoon's pre-war idyll, young women had rarely entered the frame, apart from embracing a role as necessary social appendages — the occasional "demure little girl in a pink dress" as partner in a Viennese waltz (*Memoirs*, p. 38). But however hard Sassoon tried to repress what he later referred to disparagingly as his "sex-fever," these feelings do appear in various and often sublimated guises in the war poems. True, this affection is often transmogrified into a generalized love for suffering soldiery and especially a haunted compassion for the ordinary fusilier that can tip over into sentimentality, but at least it exorcises any sense of clandestine guilt. Sometimes displaced from the text, the higher emotion — often associated with specific comrades — generates pantheistic outpourings in which the love object is associated with the good vibrations of the natural world. In poems such as "Invocation," the depth of his feelings for some individuals goes far beyond the homosocial bonding established between comrades in arms.

In a way the deprivations of war were worse for a man who had no "brown-eyed Gwen" to remind him of domestic and sexual bliss awaiting him at home. For Sassoon the pattern was different: a case of forming deep if platonic attachments to "lads" or "comrades" which were, with a hideous finality, all too often sundered by death. For there is no doubt that he did fall in love with fellow-soldiers (and I do not consider the expression inappropriate) on a number of occasions. His expressed feelings for Bobbie Hanmer, David Thomas, Marcus Goodall, and later Jim Linthwaite and "handsome boy Jowett," are evidence of that. The effect on the poet was two-fold. On the one hand it provided, as did his contemplation of the unspoilt French countryside or his memory of an English one, a sense of emotional and imaginative release, an escape from the blundering machine of war. On the other hand it exacerbated feelings of anger and guilt that were never far beneath the surface, feelings which increasingly could only be assuaged by the brotherhood of the front line.

In her memoirs, Lady Ottoline Morrell recalled a walk with Sassoon at Craiglockhart in which he unburdened himself of his guilty feelings about his sexual orientation:

> He had been engaged to a girl at the beginning of the war, "felt he ought to be as all his brother officers had a girl," but soon found it impossible, as he really only liked men, and women were antipathetic to him. He told me about his early youth and how much he had suffered when he found he could only like men. Tortured and worried he would roam the country all night in despair. At last he spoke about it to one of his brothers, who laughed at him and said he was the same himself [Morrell, 1975, p. 230].

Patrick Quinn, in an interesting reading of this confession, sees it as "evidence" that

> at least a part of his motivation to return (to the Front) was due to homosexual guilt. Sassoon was transforming his suppressed homo-erotic interest for Owen, Graves (who had just announced his decision to marry Nancy), Bobbie Hanmer, and others into a more generalised and acceptable form of love: a loyalty to those men who served with him [Quinn, 1994, p. 193].

While the specifics of this interpretation must remain a matter for conjecture, the general argument is, on the admittedly less emphatic evidence of the poetry as well as this disclosure, a conclusive one. In "Banishment," a Craiglockhart poem, Sassoon wrestles with a "love" that "drives me back to grope with them through hell"; the similarly dated "Sick Leave," though lacking the erotic overtones of "Banishment," emphasizes the compelling appeal of a "blutbruderschaft" in its final and self-accusatory question:

> When are you going out to them again?
> Are they not still your brothers through our blood?

This preoccupation is persuasively explored by Adrian Caesar in *Taking It Like a Man*. He sees Sassoon's post-protest response to the war and the shift from "anti-war complex" as a way of expunging his guilt and of sublimating the unconventional demands of his sexuality: "Part of Sassoon's escape was surely from the demands of his libido and the guilt arising from its direction, into an arena where close relationships between men were the norm, and were 'ennobled' by the idea of sacrifice for each other" (Caesar, 1993, p. 70).

Such shifts of attitude occurred in 1917, after Sassoon's protest and during his friendship with Rivers and Owen at Craiglockhart. By then the poet was less reticent about feelings which, while they still could not enter the public domain as his pacifism had, are traceable in the palimpsest of certain poems. In the earlier war pieces such private emotions are expressed in more conventionally acceptable ways. As Paul Fussell has observed, there was a flourishing tradition of homoerotic literature — Housman's *A Shropshire Lad* is merely the best-known — that was given a fresh impetus by the conflict. Fussell cites a number of stimuli: the erotic language of military attack ("assault, impact, thrust, penetration"), the association of "exhibitionism with the fears and excitements of infantry fighting," the irruption of sexual desire attendant on deprivation, and above all the youthful all-male camaraderie occasioned by the death-in-life existence of the trenches (Fussell, 1975, pp. 270-1). As "The Kiss" implies, eros and thanatos are close bed-fellows. In *The Age of Anxiety*, Auden would describe it thus: "In times of war even the crudest kind of positive affection between persons seems extraordinarily beautiful, a noble symbol of the peace and forgiveness of which the whole world stands so desperately in need" (Auden, 1947, p. 111, quoted in Fussell, p. 270).

Such idealized "affection" is there from the outset in Sassoon's war poetry. If it derived in part from this literary tradition of idealized love between men, it also stemmed from his pre-war questioning of his own sexual proclivities and his discovery of the writings of Edward Carpenter. Carpenter's privately printed *Homogenic Love* (1894) had been a revelation; it had, as Sassoon's discussion with his brother had more flippantly revealed, gone some way to convincing the poet that homosexual love was not only common and part of an artistic tradition from classical Greece to Persia and beyond, but inherently superior. Its practitioners ("urnings"), like Sassoon's own creation, Amyntas, were "often of a refined, sensitive nature ... including ... a great number highly gifted in the fine arts, especially music and poetry ... and many persons of high literary distinction." Carpenter went on to declare that "while bodily congress is desired, the special act with which they are vulgarly credited is in most cases repugnant to them" (Carpenter, 1894, p. 20). Where the embrace was physical, it emphasized "endearment" (*Ibid.*, p. 15). Such pronouncements were food and drink to Sassoon: he began a correspondence with Carpenter, enthusing: "I cannot say what you have done for me. I am a different being, though of course the misunderstanding and injustice is a bitter agony sometimes," adding, "I am old enough to realise the better and nobler way and to avoid the mire" (letter from Sassoon to Carpenter, 27 July, 1911, quoted by Caesar, 1993, p. 66).

The "nobler way" is most clearly manifested in his loving concern for the young soldiers under his care, a concern which not only pervades "The Redeemer," his "first front-line poem" (WP, p. 17), but is still abundantly evident in the 1917 diary poem "Foot-Inspection." The "redeemer" is in fact a "simple chap," idealized as a blessed Christ-figure who purifies the foul atmosphere of war by his fortitude and capacity for martyrdom. Even here though, the poet's sympathy is intensified by erotic tonings in the odd description of his servant as "an English soldier, *white and strong*" (emphasis added). In other early poems, such feelings find objective correlatives in non-human phenomena: in the transferred epithet of "spires of green rising in young-limbed copse" ("To Victory"), or in the flurry of pastoral poeticisms that characterizes "The Last Meeting," Sassoon's first testament to a departed loved one. For here is an elegy which sublimates his overwhelming anger and sorrow in order to concentrate on positive emotions.

Such sublimation was not always easily achieved. On 1 April, 1916, two weeks after "little Tommy" had been hit by a stray bullet, Sassoon's grief had temporarily given way to sadistic impulses. "I couldn't kill anyone in this war; but since they shot Tommy I would gladly stick a bayonet into a German by daylight.... Now I've known love for Bobbie (Hamner) and Tommy ... and hate has come also, and the lust to kill" (*Diaries*, 1 April, 1916, p. 52).

Literature is full of examples of avenging lovers who seek redemption, like the lover of *Maud* or the protagonist of "Locksley Hall," through the greater good of a patriotic cause. Sassoon's attitude at the time was less equivocal; he simply wanted to get his own back. Already possessed of an extraordinary courage, the despair engendered by the loss of loved ones gave his fury an edge that verged on the manic. Not for nothing was he known as "Mad Jack" by his admiring men.

Sexual frustration and guilt as well as "hate" may well have been motivating agents at the time. Certainly the word "lust" is often redolent not only of blood lust, but of emotions felt towards beloved but now expired comrades. In "The Poet as Hero," Sassoon angrily exclaims that "lust and senseless hatred make me glad." A strange erotic energy also pervades "The Kiss." Much discussed in terms of whether it is an exercise in irony or an enthusiastic endorsement of the art of the bayonet, the poem is also shot through with repressed sexuality. After all, Sassoon's *title* owes nothing to Major Campbell's lecture on the bayonet, and its controlling metaphor, preceded by the calculated oxymoron of "good fury" (*c.f.* the "stabbing tenderness" of "Foot Inspection"), derives its force from the equation of the "downward darting kiss" of the weapon — earlier described as "naked, cold and fair" — with phallic penetration. Like a lover establishing physical contact, the soldier "may feel the body ... quail" as his bayonet enters the other man's flesh.

David Thomas, whose "yellow head was kissed / By the gods" ("A Letter

Home") and whose untimely death provoked such a tumult of mixed emotions, was the first but by no means the last comrade-in-arms to be eulogized and elegized by the poet. In the grim aftermath of the Somme came the intensely private "Elegy: For Marcus Goodall"; later still, there were poems to Gordon Harbord and "Colin" (Dobell). But David, perhaps because he was the first of Sassoon's loves to be killed, is accorded the most extended treatment in the war poetry. Also the subject of "Goliath and David" by Robert Graves, he features in no fewer than three of Sassoon's early poems. One, "A Subaltern," written before his untimely demise, does no more than essay a sympathetic portrait in which the initial meeting of eyes triggers memories of a cricket match. On the other hand, "The Last Meeting" and "A Letter Home" are extended elegies to "my little Tommy." The first of these, which has all the intensity of a love poem, is a pantheistic vision in which the soul of the dear departed returns with the burgeoning spirit of spring. The language is elevated, the setting pastoral ("I knew him him crushed to earth in scentless flowers"), and draws heavily on the imagery and cadences of pre-war poetic effusions such as "Daybreak" (*Poems*, 1911). Nonetheless, its very conventionality of utterance barely masks an intensity of feeling that borders on the erotic. When the speaker admits he has "slaked / the thirst of my desires in bounteous rain" or is "filled with molten power," the imagery hints at profoundly personal emotions and a physical attraction that underlies the sense of spiritual affirmation, feelings "lit by love" as the young man's body is transcendentalized into "the magic of the world." As the poet confides in the tactile figure of the conclusion, his death has "touched my lips to song."

The escapist diction of these early love poems — it takes the form of a Gravesian pastiche in "A Letter Home," where David reappears "like the prince in fairy story"— is less in evidence in the notebooks. Admittedly Sassoon refrained from making explicit allusions to his homosexuality until the postwar journals, where idealistic comrade love gives way to homosexual affairs and the private expression of remorse attendant upon its practice: "this cursed obsession of sex cravings" (*Diaries*, 29 September, 1921, p. 86), and the harassment of "sex fevers" (*Ibid.*, p. 74). But in any case a private prose record is likely to be more candid than a poem intended for a public certainly aware of a tradition of homoerotic literature, but in essence homophobic. Of his "urning" affection for Bobbie Hanmer he could declare: "I fell in love with his kind eyes and ingenuous looks ... he would be a good person to die for." Earlier he had written in similarly romantic terms of "little Tommy," remembered as looking "like an angel, with the light in his yellow hair" (*Diaries*, 19 March, 1916, p. 45).

It is significant that Sassoon kept his most intimate expressions of feeling, whether in the form of prose or verse entries, in notebooks that would not be published in his lifetime. In the verse, even in 1917 and 1918, subjective responses that might get out of hand are often swathed in innocuous poeticisms or transplanted to rural landscapes. "Together," a sonnet composed after a good day's hunting, brings back insistent memories of a friend's "hand ... upon the mud-soaked reins," an imaginary companion "with me on my way home"; the Limerick poem "Invocation," with its altogether more fulsome plea to the beloved to "come down from heaven's bright hill, my song's desire," renders a still deeply felt loss in terms of an aureate pastoralism and studied homoerotic diction that echoes "The Last Meeting," written nineteen months before.

But such innocuous reversions to a pastoral-erotic mode do not tell the whole poetical story. More confident in his role as poet, less worried about his public persona, perhaps encouraged by his friendships, especially with Wilfred Owen and Dr. Rivers in 1917, Sassoon did begin to allow homoerotic impulses to surface in his verse by employing a language more personal and not just drawn from pastoral, to encode his feelings. He was helped by the fact that some of these poetic procedures were already in currency, particularly in so-called "Uranian" writing — for example, the expressions "boy" and "lad." Paul Fussell observes that *A Shropshire Lad* could have furnished Owen — and by implication, Sassoon — with a "whole set of tender emotions about young soldiers, their braveries, their deaths, their agonies, and even their self-inflicted wounds" (Fussell, 1975, p. 293). Sassoon was already, on the substantial evidence of his pre-war poems, an admirer of Housman's nostalgic verses — the poetic expression of an impossible love — and more than willing to incorporate some of his characteristic epithets in his own verse. The word "lad," for example, is present in seven Sassoon poems written between May 1917 and May 1918, perhaps most reminiscently in the Housmanesque "O lad that I loved, there is rain on your face" ("I Stood with the Dead"). The word "comrade" undoubtedly carried similar coded associations, at least for Sassoon. "Absolution" concludes with a plea to all believers:

> Now, having claimed this heritage of heart,
> What need we more, my comrades and my brothers?

More prosaically, the names "Dick" or "Dickie," with their similarly erotic associations — Graves's public-school lover was always referred to as "Dick"— are present in "The Effect" and "Died of Wounds." In the *Memoirs*, Sassoon, for once forgetting himself, looks admiringly at "Dick" (Tiltwood), thinking "what a Galahad he looked."

Frequently there is alluring eye contact between officer and fellow soldier: in two poems, both written in June 1918, the exchange of glances indicates the existence of an unspoken emotional bond. "From their eyes I hoard my reward" is the recrudescent message of "The Reward"; similarly, in the unpublished "Foot-Inspection" the poet meets the eyes of his exhausted men (and especially Morgan) with feelings of "stabbing tenderness," an ambiguous oxymoron which reminds one of the "good fury" of "The Kiss." While this bonding through a blood brotherhood of suffering informs such late poems as "Banishment," "Reward" and "I Stood with the Dead," there are other poems in which the focus on "lads" and their eyes extends to other parts of their anatomies — to golden hair (the "yellow head" of David Thomas "kissed by the gods") and especially to young limbs. The dead German of "A Night Attack" has "sturdy legs," the poet-instructor's "young fusiliers" are "strong-legged and bold." Alluded to most memorably in "The Dug-Out," a poetic reverie inspired by memories of his sleeping friend, "handsome" Jowett, the description of his huddled legs and especially the arm across his "exhausted face" that the watcher wishes were his own, carries erotic connotations that would not be lost on all of his readers.

Sassoon's references to dying, while linked to the poet's guilty wish to join the increasing band of brothers killed in action, sometimes hint — after the fashion of Jacobean drama — at a sexual consummation devoutly to be wished. "How glad I'd be to die, if dying could set him free" is the officer's unspoken wish in "Foot-Inspection," an expression, it seems, of both selfless love and erotic fantasy.

It is the case then, that Sassoon occasionally transgresses traditional modes and resorts to personal strategies in order to reveal private emotions. Nonetheless the pastoral framework, usually a positive gauge against which to measure the mad frenzy of war, is often still a repository of personal feeling. In this regard Sassoon's use of the epithet "whispering" is significant. Evidence of a collusive pact between the poet and a natural world in tune with his most intimate feelings, the adjective is frequently applied to trees, as in for instance "The Last Meeting," "Before the Battle" and "Invocation." In "Sick Leave" his dead friends "whisper" to the poet's "heart"; in "Thrushes" the same heart is a "haunted woodland whispering"; in "The Triumph" the "whisper of leaves" acknowledges the speaker's private desires. This last poem, an apparently innocuous exercise which, through its anapests, reverts to a pre-war, incantatory manner, carries, in its brief eight lines, resonances which express a tormented frame of mind. For the contemplation of "Beauty," a beauty which is initially associated with nature and conclusively with soldiers, must inevitably be an isolating experience ("a bird's lone cry") that can only be whispered to initiates; only in the public business of the "fight" can this suppressed eroticism, alternately taking sadistic and masochistic forms, find socially acceptable expression:

> I was cruel and fierce with despair; I was naked and bound;
> I was stricken: and beauty returned through the shambles of night;
> In the faces of men she returned; and their triumph I found.

Once away from the pressure-cooker atmosphere of the Front, Sassoon could unburden himself of such highly wrought feelings in more prosaic terms; given an innocuous setting — and "Conscripts" provides one — he dares to take a sly, humorous look at his own sexual proclivities. Drilling recruits on the parade ground, the poet has time to indulge his male gaze, to fantasize — "love" is mentioned three times — by using arch personifications ("young Fancy — how I loved him") and a kind of dismissive casualness ("many a sickly, slender lord who'd filled / my soul long since with lutanies of sin") about the imagined sexual orientation of the young men under his command.

Predictably, the poet was invariably disappointed when young officers displayed too much interest in women. Writing from Palestine, he complained of "subalterns" who "seem to have absolutely no inner life except when they take out a note case for a look at a girl's photograph" (letter from Sassoon to Meiklejohn, 25 February, 1918, ULUT). For once, in "Conscripts," Sassoon is prepared to treat his private yearnings in a jocular way; even such parapraxes as "Press on your butts!" or "Joy was slack," seem to accord with the tone of sexual innuendo which informs both the parade ground and the poetic exercise.

Of course Sassoon was most likely to be attracted to fellow officers that he could meet on an equal footing. When Sassoon did experience affection for the ordinary fusilier, he was rarely identified by name. Conversely, his most antipathetic feelings were ageist ones, directed at the old men of the war, be they "brass hats" or civilians. It is worth reminding ourselves why. In one respect the answer is obvious enough; they were the ones who sped "glum heroes up the line to death," the ones who preached about heroism and patriotism without risking their own skins. The prospect of getting his own back on these old fogies, if only on the cricket pitch, was immensely appealing ("A Last Word"). But there is another dimension to all this. In Sassoon's estimation, old men were deficient in other ways: they lacked the idealism of young comrades-in-arms, they knew nothing of the blood brotherhood that ennobled the sacrifice of soldiers, they had none of the "faun-like good looks, innocence, vulnerability and charm" that characterized young subalterns (Fussell, 1975, p. 272). As the poet knew only too well, it was always the young ones who were bled white by war. To Roderick Meiklejohn, he confided: "O these young men, they wring my heart, they make me like being at the war, because I don't want to be away from them. And then they get killed" (letter from Sassoon to Meiklejohn, 16 May, 1918 ULUT). Worse, from Sassoon's point of view, these old men were, in his estimation, obsessed by sex of a debased and heterosexual kind that the poet found distasteful anyway, and especially when boasted about openly. In a 1916 letter to Sassoon, Graves complained of the CO who maintained that "there should be only one subject for conversation among subalterns off parade," adding ruefully, "I leave you to guess it" (Graves to Sassoon, 15 March, 1916, IBI, p. 44). Such old men were also prone, in Sassoon's estimation, to homophobia. Late in the war, Sassoon betrayed his fury at Pemberton-Billing's witch-hunt against the homosexual community and voiced his concern that Robbie Ross, once a lover of Oscar Wilde, was getting all too ensnared in its machinations. "What a disgusting show the Billing affair is!" he complained to Meiklejohn (2 June, 1918, ULUT), adding, perhaps a little naively, that "decent public feeling must surely be all against P-B and D."

Sassoon's abhorrence for such attitudes is demonstrated in a number of poems, most strikingly in "Repression of War Experience" where the poet is unable to contain his disgust for "old men with ugly souls / Who wore their bodies out with nasty sins." Such lines hardly constitute a balanced artistic response, but at least the source of Sassoon's prudery is easy enough to identify: a compound of his own sexual proclivities, his reading of homoerotic literature and his perception of the role of these "old men" in The Great War for Civilization, "ghouls, insatiable in their desire for slaughter, impenetrable in their ignorance" (*Diaries*, 19 June, 1917, p. 176).

Chapter 4

"O World God Made!" Pacifism, Pantheism, Self-Sacrifice

As Sassoon grew more incensed by the conduct of politicians and what he saw as the prolongation of the conflict by an entrenched establishment, his attitude towards the enemy changed. The death of close friends, especially that of David Thomas so early in the war, produced two reactions: a lust for revenge, and a consolatory optimism linked to pantheistic renewal. Increasingly such impulses were overtaken by a third: a guilty desire to join his dead comrades by actively courting his own death. At Litherland he confessed to an incipient preoccupation with "the feeling of self-sacrifice — immolation to some vague aspiration — whether our cause be a just one or not" (*Diaries*, 21 January, 1917, p. 122).

That Sassoon's "lust and senseless hatred" increasingly gave way to feelings of guilt and self-sacrifice was linked to the realization that *everyone* at the front was a victim and that the German soldier merited his compassion as much as the Allied trooper. The real enemy was not on the other side of "No Man's Land," but across the English Channel, back in "Blighty." If Sassoon, persuaded by his experience of the trenches, came to this conclusion later than doctrinaire pacifists such as the Morrells and Bertrand Russell, there was no mistaking its force when it surfaced. As Lady Ottoline Morrell later deduced, it was less the product of a considered philosophical position than a humanitarian sympathy for all suffering soldiers. In her eyes this devalued his pacifism. After meeting Sassoon at "Dottyville," Ottoline noted that his mood was bleak, not just because now he felt that "his protest had apparently failed" but because he "now felt the only thing he could do was to go back and rejoin his regiment." She added, "I see now that he was not a thoroughgoing pacifist, but had been moved to protest against the continuation of the war by sympathy for his men" (Morrell, 1974, p. 229). She was right; once his opening salvo against the war's deliberate prolongation and the "political errors" and insincerities of the establishment had been delivered, the theme of suffering soldiery took over in his "Protest":

I have seen and endured the suffering of the troops, and I can no longer be a party to prolonging those sufferings for ends which I believe to be evil and unjust. I am not protesting against the military conduct of the War, but against the political errors and insincerities for which the fighting men are being sacrificed. On behalf of those who are suffering now, I make this protest against the deception which is being practised on them. Also I believe that it may help to destroy the callous complacence with which the majority of those at home regard the continuance of agonies which they do not share and which they have not sufficient imagination to realise [*Diaries*, 15 June, p. 174].

In this conspiracy of silence aimed at entrapping the "soldiers who return home," Sassoon singled out for vilification two of his favorite targets — young women and old men: women who "gloat secretly over the wounds of their lovers," and old men "like ghouls, insatiable in their desire for slaughter" (*Diaries*, 19 June, pp. 175–6).

Conversely, his compassion for his men and his awareness of their "huge sacrifices" was only intensified by events. "It is obvious," he reflected a week later, "that nothing could be worse than the present conditions under which humanity is suffering and dying" (*Diaries*, 21 June, p. 177). Sassoon's pacifism was becoming more inclusive. If "sympathy for *his* men" had been there from the start of his frontline experience — a concern which sometimes threatened to tip over into sentimentality — an even-handed commiseration with the German soldier's lot was now central to his moral stance. Indeed, it had been explored in the *poetry* for at least a year. "A Night Attack," written in July 1916, had been its first expression in verse. Here the stereotypical attitude to the Hun, xenophobic and very British ("the bloody bosche has got the knock"), gives way to the assumption of a "Prussian" perspective, as the poet recalls a handsome young soldier now squalidly dead, and empathizes with him in his last, confused moments as the "damned English" swarm into his trench and shoot him in the head.

It is hardly a matter for surprise that Sassoon felt compelled to exercise restraint: in 1916, "A Night Attack" was too contentious by half for home consumption. Indeed he never published it in his own lifetime. "The Stunt," written a month later, suffered the same fate. The poem's speaker, having killed "three men ... outright," "wounded several more and been awarded the D.S.O.," is fulsomely praised by his "Blighty" connections before Sassoon concludes with an ironic rejoinder:

> How splendid. O how splendid! his relations said,
> But what the weeping Saxons said I do not know.

Such prejudices were, if anything, hardening between 1916 and 1917 in the national consciousness. Ottoline Morrell, reflecting on the situation at the time, recalled that she did what she could "in helping an excellent society called 'Friends of Foreigners' ... as spy mania grew, they (so-called 'enemy aliens') were herded into vast concentration camps — like cattle — and their wives and children left at home" (Morrell, 1963, p. 261).

These mental postures did not commend themselves to Sassoon who would soon "openly allude" to "German soldiers who were loyal and brave" ("Reconciliation"), conscious that by then the reading public was aware of his "Protest," even if it did not necessarily approve of its sentiments. "Decorated" makes the point that only the dubious morality of war renders heroic the killing exploits of "Corporal Stubbs, the Birmingham V.C." In January 1917 and sick of the company of "conscripted humbugs ... paid to propagate inefficiency," Sassoon's thoughts were focusing more and more on the hapless German soldiery and on his own exacerbated feelings of guilt. "Enemies," for example, attempts a visionary rapprochement with the poet's dead victims; in a discarded and splenetic Litherland poem, he confesses he "would rather shoot one General Dolt / than fifty harmless Germans" (*Diaries*, 15 January, p. 119). By the end of the year, Sassoon has even grudgingly extended his sympathies to include the female sex: "Glory of Women" shows a poet who, while still critical of women's addiction to the opiate of heroism, is at least able to identify with a German mother about to learn of her son's death:

> O German mother dreaming by the fire
> While you are knitting socks to send your son
> His face is trodden deeper in the mud.

More often though, a disaffected Sassoon continues to single out those "General Dolts" who were unable to see the enemy as other than despicable murderers. "The Optimist" is literally and metaphorically scarred by his experiences; his wish to see the Huns "getting hell" is treated with heavy irony by the poet. Equally mordant is the poet's treatment of the mindless jingoism of "The Fathers" ("The Huns intend to ask for more"), and the dotty behavior of General Currycombe who is petitioning his neighbors to boycott all German merchandise ("Trade Boycott") in a display of prejudice that recalls the "spy mania" described by Lady Ottoline Morrell. In the last analysis such anti–Boche attitudinizing is seen by the poet for what it is — absurd posturing by people who should know better. And such posturing did not go away. On his last visit to the Western Front, Sassoon, appalled to discover that one of his commanders was a "professional soldier of the Prussian type," complained that "He always addresses us as 'potential killers of Germans' and in one speech to the Battalion openly avowed that 'he was out to get a Division' — over our dead bodies I suppose!" (letter from Sassoon to Meiklejohn, 22 June, 1918, ULUT).

Such vituperation should not blind us to Sassoon's innate spirituality: that he was possessed of a fundamentally contemplative nature is beyond doubt. No one should be surprised at his late "conversion" to Roman Catholicism. For what we witness, especially in the early war verse, is a profoundly religious sensibility attempting to come to terms with a hellish world which God seems to have spurned; a world in which the Christian notion of the ultimate sacrifice, everywhere demonstrated not only by the deaths of young soldiers but gruesomely reinforced by the ineradicable presence of their shattered and putrefying bodies, has become a pointless martyrdom without any redeeming "glory," or any evidence of moral salvation for mankind.

Sassoon demonstrates this religiosity in a number of ways. One procedure involves seeking God in the world of nature rather than through conventional Anglicanism, by celebrating the numinosity of the English landscape rather than its institutions, by recharging his spiritual batteries with memories of rural Sussex or the Weald of Kent. When Sassoon focuses his unblinkered gaze on the harrowing events of the war in 1916 and 1917, he frequently reacts to such injections of nightmare reality by producing a contrasting poem that may find him expressing a positive sense of kinship with the living or the dead, but more often allows the pantheist in him to escape the denatured world of the trenches and worship at nature's shrine. "The Redeemer," a trench poem, is thus followed by "To My Brother" and a vision of the dead man's "laurell'd head"; the road "dark with blood" of "The Prince of Wounds" is succeeded, less than a week later, by the nostalgic evocations of England's "blossomed slopes" and "spires of green" in "A Testament" and "To Victory." In March and April a sequence of frontline poems gives way to the burgeoning May landscape, now located in Flixécourt, of "France" and "The Last Meeting."

This last poem is pivotal to my discussion. Here Sassoon, mourning the loss of a dear friend, not only returns to the pastoral mode, to a world where the natural and the numinous coalesce, but in an epiphanic moment, encounters the very spirit of his friend David in the French woods. Personal spiritual revelation here fuses with Sassoonesque pantheism ("His hushed voice may call me in the stir / Of whispering trees") in an elegy in which the profound sense of loss is ameliorated by the conviction that David's soul lives on in the natural world. Dawn breaking in the gardens of Chapelwood Manor provided a more somber epiphany. A ghostly apparition of a friend still at the Front provides a horrid intimation of mortality; "the poor lonely ghost astray" convinces the poet that his comrade has, at that very moment, been "shot ... through the head."

If "Death in the Garden" signifies anything, it is that contact, real or imagined, with the restorative world of nature is less easily achieved as the poet becomes yet more immersed in the hell of the frontline. That the process *can* still occur — often an English landscape is seductively glimpsed before the war relentlessly erases such evocations — is a reflection of Sassoon's overwhelming need to escape the grim reality of the battlefield, and his belief, never entirely compromised, that nature will always work its miracles. But it is a tough assignment. In "Repression of War Experience," one of the most confessional poems of Sassoon's war, even the garden at Weirleigh, lovingly recalled as a haven of "blossomed slopes" in "A Testament," is now a threatening place where the "breathless" air connotes menace and suspense and ghosts wander among the trees.

Already conventional religion has provided scant consolation for a poet who later admitted that he never once prayed during the conflict. Even in the earliest poems, his trumpet of faith is giving forth uncertain sounds. In "The Redeemer," Christ is transmogrified into an ordinary soldier; in "The Prince of Wounds" the question is asked, "Is he a God of wood and stone?" By the time Sassoon came to write "The Dragon and the Undying," God had been supplanted by a frontline dragon: now only an expression of pantheistic sentiments provides any solace for the observer of war's "darting fires." "Via Crucis," a fine poem inexplicably omitted from later collections, compares the ignominious end of "jolly soldier-boys" to that of a Christ-figure who at least "had a purpose for his pain."

One measure of the rejection of conventional religion is afforded by the introduction of potentially blasphemous expletives. "The Redeemer" carries the final line, "O Christ Almighty, now I'm stuck"; "A Subaltern," "Good God! he laughed..."; "Stand-To: Good Friday Morning," "O Jesus, send me a wound today." Such expressions operate on two levels, both as blasphemous curse and as futile prayer to a savior who assuredly will not save. Later Sassoon would directly attack the "Bishop Byegumbs" of the Anglican establishment; in the spring of 1916, his use of the demotic language of the frontline is a way of exposing the fatuous irony inherent in any misguided appeals to the Almighty.

"Stand To: Good Friday Morning" was considered "blasphemous" by Graves of all people — and a failure. He added: "I knew it was a very obstinate poem but you could have solved it" (letter from Graves to Sassoon, 22 April, 1917, IBI, p. 70). Sassoon did not agree, believing it anticipated his "later successes in condensed satire" (SJ, pp. 17–18), and subsequently maintaining that "soldiers say they feel like that sometimes." By August 1916, Sassoon was pulling no punches; in "Christ and the Soldier," the speaker is prepared to reject a Messiah out of touch with reality and unable to influence events or help in any way. Though he did not publish the poem and subsequently dismissed it as "an ambitious failure," an attempt to write "a potent parable" (WP, pp. 46–7), the poem did reveal that Sassoon was beginning to shift his point of attack from the Christian message itself to those who dispensed it in sermons. After all, the clerics were the mouthpieces (Sassoon later called them "Anglican gramophones") for much cant and humbug about the war. Talking with the benefit of hindsight to Felicitas Corrigan, he conceded that "behind it ['Christ and the Soldier'] was the persistent anti-parson mentality — and it *was* difficult to swallow their patriotic pietism which seemed unreal to many of us front-liners" (Corrigan, 1973, p. 80).

The post–Somme satires demonstrate the growth of this "anti-parson mentality": in "They," "Vicarious Christ" and "Joy Bells," the wartime version of the Anglican establishment comes under heavy fire. The despairing pleas to God from the ordinary soldier are heard again in "Attack" ("O Jesus make it stop!") while "The Investiture" paints a picture of an unhappy and all too clinical heaven. "Thrushes," a highly subjective piece written at Craiglockhart, finds no evidence at all of God's benevolent existence. That the spiritual longing somehow remained — to be eventually satisfied — "for the savagely annihilated joys of the past when nature and man were in peaceful harmony, for the spiritual intimacies of solitude, and for a dwelling-place for the spirit of man" (Corrigan, 1973, p. 23) is a tribute to Sassoon's innate optimism. For the present, the war and its immediate aftermath might provide moments of transcendence, but could offer no orthodox religious answers. Even the great Christian festivals — Easter in "Stand-To" and "The Distant Song," Christmas Day in "The March-Past" — provoke very un–Christian sentiments.

Sassoon's intense spirituality would nonetheless find expression in a variety of ways: in poetry and the muse, in music, in a belief in the restorative, even transcendental power of the natural world, and increasingly in the desire to suffer with his martyred comrades. If the notion of sacrifice had any meaning, it did not reside in the self-conscious glory of Christ's crucifixion but in the camaraderie of the killing fields.

Not that such sources of inspiration or solace always produced the desired effect. Even classical music, the battle-hardened Sassoon was forced to concede, could sometimes fail. It might soar "above despair": indeed in "The Elgar Violin Concerto" the poet is so elated by the music that, in the most profoundly spiritual image in the war poetry, he identifies himself with the suffering Christ on the cross. However, the message of "Dead Musicians," written a mere year later, maintains that such transcendence is out of place; music can no longer build "cathedrals in the poet's heart." Now, like the Ancient Mariner, he guiltily wears "a wreath of banished lives." Paradoxically, only the grim reality of suffering and death at the Front can provide any possibility of spiritual sustenance.

If Christian principles of the kind inculcated by his mother and now espoused by Anglican clerics failed to impress the officer-poet, the Jewish half of his background was dismissed out of hand. Admittedly Sassoon had not been instructed in the Jewish faith, and in pre-war England he had been careful to play down his Semitic origins. The war intensified such feelings. At the Front he took pains to distance himself from other Jews, to disparage what he envisaged as their materialistic motives: "Lieutenant X is a nasty, cheap thing. A cheap-gilt Jew," he wrote in his diary, adding, "they see only greasy bank-notes and the dung in the highway where they hawk their tawdry wares" (*Diaries*, 22 January, 1917, p. 123).

Yet if Sassoon was anxious in the war, both as officer and aesthete, to distance himself from such connections — the only *poetic* allusion to his Jewishness is in the private verse letter "Dear Roberto" — he subsequently came to recognize that his "Jewish blood" had been an important factor in his poetic progress. Recalling his excitement at tales of the prophets of the Old Testament in his boyhood, he declared, "I sometimes surmise that my eastern ancestry is stronger in me than is the Thornycrofts. The daemon in me is Jewish." He added, "Do you believe in racial memories? Some of my hypnagogic visions have seemed like it, and many of them were oriental architecture" (Corrigan, 1973, p. 17). It was this desire to be a "a minor prophet," to communicate his moral insights to the mass of "Blighty" unbelievers, that Sassoon retrospectively believed had triggered his decision to speak out as a conscientious objector and apologist for the ordinary trooper. Writing to Felicitas Corrigan, he remarked: "You have got it right about my Jewish blood. As a poetic spirit, I have always felt myself— or wanted to be — a kind of minor prophet. I suppose most poets aim at being prophetic communicators. But the idea has always been very strong in my mind. *And found utterance in the war poems of course*" (1973, p. 21; emphasis added).

As Corrigan reminds us, Sassoon's defiant and singular stance as conscientious objector recalls the experience of Jeremiah (38:4), for whom the princes demanded death for "weakening the hands of the soldiers who are left in the city and the hands of all the people, by speaking such words to them" (1973, p. 22). Sassoon indeed risked a court martial by "speaking such words." The decision to detain the poet at Craiglockhart constituted a hegemonic attempt to deny him that prophetic voice. Of course, this awareness of his prophetic role was retrospectively achieved and coincided with his late conversion to Roman Catholicism. After all, Sassoon deliberately erased all thoughts of conventional Christianity from his mind early in the conflict and was, on his own admission, "a very incomplete and quite unpractising Christian" (WP, p. 47). His pilgrim's progress sent him from questioning the message of the Gospels to taking issue with establishment dogma preached by "parsons beating their drums noisily to the rhythm of the Warrior-Christ" (Corrigan, p. 18). But Christian or no, the war did reveal the existence of a profoundly spiritual temper. Bishop Byegumb's muscular Christianity might prompt the response: "For he made me love religion less and less." But Sassoon's tormented pacifism, his prophetic rallying cry of anguish in 1917, his guilt at not being with his disciples — these were more than humanitarian gestures — even if the poet did not realize it at the time.

Chapter 5

Working Methods and Formal Concerns

Sassoon's working methods demonstrate the existence of creative principles which he rarely compromised: poetry was, for him, "an essentially personal experience"; it should be "direct" and "spontaneous, like the unfolding of a flower"; it should be "visual" and possess "clarified construction and technical control." All this was set down more than twenty years later, for his 1939 Bristol lecture. Nonetheless these principles inform the war poetry, part and parcel of the poet's desire to record these harrowing experiences as truthfully and vividly as possible.

In this process, the diaries were of crucial importance to Sassoon. When responding to a request for them from Lady Ottoline Morrell, he declared: "My notebooks are no good. Too inconsistent—*invaluable for my own use*—but very poor reading" (emphasis added) (letter from Sassoon to Morrell, 11 April, 1917, ULUT). If poems did not go straight into the notebook as creative adjuncts to the day's jottings—and upwards of a third of his war output did—they often captured some of the spirit of the prose record, and possess a corresponding freshness and immediacy. Sometimes it is no more than a tone of voice which is followed up: "To Victory" picks up on the fulsome "praise of life and landscape" that informs the prose entry for that day (*Diaries*, 3 January, 1916, p. 31); one year on and depressed by the "most Mondayish of Monday mornings" and posses of "bragging" officers (*Diaries*, 8 January, 1917, p. 116), the poet added to his diary the jaundiced verses entitled, "When I'm Among a Blaze of Lights."

On other occasions the nexus between notebook and poem is more explicit: diary poems become faithful if invariably more dramatic and finished verse-accounts of what is matter-of-factly recorded in the prose. The minor piece "Life-Belts" is a case in point. Sometimes, indeed, the images in the notebook are striking enough to warrant inclusion in the accompanying poem. Thus the old fogies "guzzling at the base" not only prompt the reflection, part repeated in the poetic version, that "all the really brave men were dead, or else maimed or up the line" (*Diaries*, 4 March, 1917, p. 140), but inspire the pejorative imagery of "Base

Details," one of Sassoon's most trenchant satires. Similarly, "At Carnoy," with its obsessively remembered and incongruous detail of thistles, orange sunsets and discordant mouth-organs, is very close to the facts of the notebook entry made on that fateful evening before the Somme offensive (*Diaries*, 3 July, 1916, p. 87).

Sassoon knew just how crucial the role of the notebooks was if his front-line poems were to be authentic. Recollecting his progress towards a new realism, he recalled that "the gradual process began, in the first months of 1916, with a few genuine trench poems, dictated by my resolve to record my surroundings and *usually based on the notes* [emphasis added] I was making wherever I could do so with detachment. These poems aimed at impersonal description of front-line conditions and could at least claim to be the first things of their kind" (SJ, p. 17).

That the majority of Sassoon's poems were not initially preserved in the diaries does not render them any the less important. Though there are two significantly wide gaps in the notebooks — during his extended sick leave in 1916 and again for five months after his 1917 protest — Sassoon was a compulsive recorder and correspondent, particularly during the cataclysmic events of the Somme campaign. And even in the cramped confines of a dugout or, more likely, away from the line in base-camp quarters, impressions would be dutifully recorded in Sassoon's neat handwriting, a lode that could be mined later when inspiration slackened or when the poet, now physically distanced from events at the Front, had time to hammer his thoughts into verse. Late in the war Sassoon told Roderick Meiklejohn that he was sending his "half-filled" notebook home for safekeeping, adding, "Such drivel as I write from day to day is of great value to me when reconstructing my impressions under more favourable circumstances" (letter from Sassoon to Meiklejohn, 14 June, 1918, ULUT).

The process of "reconstruction" might draw on more than one notebook entry. "The Redeemer," for example, coalesces two experiences separated by five months: Festubert in November 1916 provides the mud-clogged trench-scape, an incident involving his servant Molyneux triggered off a March 1917 revision. Surprisingly, the first draft of "The Rear-Guard" was written from his hospital bed at Denmark Hill; with the aid of his precious notebook, Sassoon was able to relive the events of ten days before when, having single-handedly taken an enemy trench in the Hindenburg Line, he had been overwhelmed by ghastly sights of dead bodies from both sides (*Diaries*, 12 April, 1917, p. 153).

While the notebooks were the primary source of instant impressions that might subsequently find their way into verse, the writing of letters — and Sassoon corresponded enthusiastically with Lady Ottoline Morrell and Roderick Meiklejohn among others — also stimulated the creative process. "My head full of hunting," Sassoon wrote from Limerick, with "evening coming on and a cold drizzle blown across the dark brown hills," sentiments and images that find an echo in "Together," a poem written three days later (letter from Sassoon to Morrell, 27 January, ULUT). And at least one war poem, the confessional "Testament" was tried out on Ottoline Morrell, in a letter of 9 May, 1918. Never published, its sentiments and procedures are characteristic enough:

> For the last time I say — War is not glorious
> Though lads march out, superb and fall victorious,—
> Scrapping like demons, suffering like slaves,
> And crowned by peace, the sunlight on their graves.
>
> You swear we crush the Beast; I say we fight
> Because men lost their landmarks in the night
> And met in gloom to grapple, stab and kill
> Yelling their fetish-names of Good and Ill
> That have been shamed in history.
> O my heart,
> Be still: you have cried your cry; you have played your part.

Chance associations inevitably brought images of war flooding back. Sassoon's early convalescences saw the embattled warrior trying, as "Repression of War Experience" makes clear, to erase the most nightmarish memories. But paradoxically, the *artist* needed to be reminded of such things. In "A Quiet Walk," Sassoon tells his reader that he has walked a recuperative three country miles past "hawthorn drifts of silver" and stately, processional clouds. Suddenly the sight of a corpse-like tramp, and more especially the stench emanating from his inert body, brings all the "old, ugly horrors crowding back." Similarly, in "The Dream" the rank but innocent smell of farmyard dung-heaps inexorably returns the poet to a trench world of sweaty boots and "filthy straw."

Generally though, Sassoon seems to have been moved to write his most effective trench pieces by the immediate impact of events. It is significant that most of the Craiglockhart poems are satires targeting home attitudes; after all, he was in contact with such views whenever he played golf or dined out. On the other hand, those "Dottyville" verses that attempt to recapture the atmosphere of life at the Front — with the notable exception of "Counter-Attack" which was originally drafted during the Somme campaign anyway — offer vaguer and more generalized pictures of "brave companions," or concentrate on the subjective emotions of a guilt-laden poet desperate to rejoin his comrades-in-arms. It is hardly a matter for surprise that while the leisurely ambiance of country retreats or even army camps allowed Sassoon to compose in relative tranquillity, his muse thrived on the adrenaline generated by battle conditions, on the inspiration of the Front: "I am getting very restless and begin to hanker after horrors and excitements again now that I've got my book finished," he confided to Ottoline Morrell from Litherland Army Camp (letter from Sassoon to Morrell, December, 1916, ULUT).

All this is not to suggest that Sassoon lacked a retentive memory, or that his most harrowing experiences of the conflict were ever effectively repressed. Sometimes a poem would gestate for weeks, even months or years, before it emerged. "Twelve Months After" coalesces two memories of recruits: one, as its title implies, twelve months old, the second a year further back. While the poet was at Litherland, the least stimulating of places, he recalled: "I've written nothing for weeks. It is nice to feel poems slowly piling themselves up inside one's head until they are ready to burst forth with bright faces or haggard exasperated eyes" (letter from Sassoon to Morrell, 26 December, 1917, ULUT).

But to dwell on past events, and paradoxically the creative act demanded such a focus, could, as Sassoon knew, be more traumatic than inspiring. An abiding problem, for Sassoon, as for all survivors both during and after the war, was how to live with its ineradicable horrors. That some pieces did "pile up" in the memory is a tribute to Sassoon's nagging conviction that he must needs confront his muse even if she appeared "haggard" or "exasperated." Indeed, fever or shock seemed to stimulate the poet's creative faculty: "Died of Wounds," "The Rear-Guard" and "Dear Roberto," three of his most intense war pieces, were composed when Sassoon was in hospital, physically and mentally distraught. Other poems, trench pieces and satires alike, were spontaneous or near spontaneous reactions to events, sensory or emotional responses that demanded immediate preservation in the notebooks. That Sassoon wrote so little poetry about the war during the twenties reflected his fear that not only would these events be "moribund — remote," but that his scarred "soul" needed to be "protected against the invading ghosts of what I saw" ("A Footnote on the War," 1926).

By comparing the notebooks and the poetry, one can see that the verse, if only because of its formal constraints, usually offers a different slant on the experience of war. After all, the poems were intended as finished works of art and usually written with an eye to publication. Yet Sassoon could be his own severest critic. He knew full well that when he lacked genuine inspiration he was liable to lapse into contrivance. "Return" was a case in point. It was "written in the train at night," and the poet recognized in the train's ghostly whispers "an example of entirely artificial emotionalism. The dead are underground all right, but they don't care whether I come back or not. This is the sort of poetry I'm always trying to avoid writing" (*Diaries*, 29 March 1917, p. 143). Some poems were deemed too confessional or too contentious to justify an appearance in print. His "Elegy to Marcus Goodall" remained unpublished in his lifetime for purely personal reasons. Others, for a variety of reasons, never got beyond the stage of first drafts. That Sassoon managed to complete so many bulletins from the battlefield is a tribute to the tenacity of his muse.

Final versions or not, the war poems have a focused human interest or subject that the more matter-of-fact diaries, written "with detachment," generally lack. Sassoon was conscious of this difference, confessing to Ottoline Morrell that "Somehow I can't get much of the human-side into my notes at the time" (Letter from Sassoon to Morrell, 16 May, 1918, ULUT). What Sassoon does capture in the best of his war verse is this "human-side," a sense of emotional intensity, whether a subjective projection of his own anger, horror or compassion, or voiced through the equally mixed emotions of his ordinary fusilier.

At root, Sassoon's creative impulse was essentially lyrical, a fact which in part explains why so many of the war poems are short, concentrated exercises, either in the epigrammatic mode or in what might be loosely described as pastoral or elegiac lyric (e.g. "France," "Before the Battle," "Reward"). Often this lyrical element is present only as a deliberate precursor or contrast to war's ugliness; sometimes the need to explore a single, brief, emotional response issues in cameo portraits of fellow soldiers such as "A Subaltern," "Stand-To," "The Quarter-Master" and "Lamentations." It is a reflection of Sassoon's attitude to poetry that 70 (out of a total of 133 in the Hart-Davis edition of the *War Poems*) consist of 14 lines or less: of these more than 20 pass muster as sonnets. Such figures are indicative of Sassoon's penchant for the concentrated effect, lyrical or epigrammatic; it is only, by and large, the documentary pieces — those "aimed at impersonal description of front-line conditions"— that seem to require extended treatment. Here the diaries were especially useful; a quarry of rough-hewn material that could be cut, polished and shaped during its metamorphosis into poetry.

Some Formal Concerns

When Sassoon gave his "lecture" (he disliked the word) on poetry to a Bristol University audience in 1939, he concluded with a quote from Browning's "Pippa Passes":

> For, what are the voices of birds
> — Ay, and of beasts — but words, our words
> Only so much more sweet?

To his listeners he added: "Is there anything for me to say after that?" and sat down. The passage, obviously an important one for Sassoon, focuses on two features of his muse: one, a belief in the restorative power of nature's music and especially bird-song; two, his conviction that poetry must have a "full and living voice" (*On Poetry*, 1939, p. 11) What most appealed to Sassoon about Housman was his music, a music which "enchants me first" (*Ibid*., p. 17).

Music had always been important to the young poet. Writing in *The Weald of Youth*, he recalled: "for me piano-playing and writing poetry have always been closely connected. Most of my early verse was vague poetic feeling set to remembered music" (WY, p. 111). The very first poem that he sent for publication in the appropriately named *The Thrush* was a roundel, a simple song with a refrain (WY, p. 13).

In the war poetry, listening to music becomes a necessary therapy: in "Secret Music," the melodies retained in his head enable him to survive the "torment" and "gloom" of the battlefield. Admittedly, by 1918, he prefers the evocative and up-to-the minute tunes of rag-time to the "great names" of "Dead Musicians"— the syncopated rhythms of the fox-trot at least remind the poet of his comrades

— but music, in whatever shape or form, retains its capacity to move and inspirit. And nothing more so than bird-song.

In the war verse, birds are a pervasive if generally invisible presence, an antidote to the blundering cacophony of war. Like "whispering trees," their trillings have a soothing effect on the shattered sensibilities of the poet. In a significant proportion of his poems, bird-song, associated with the dawn chorus or carried as a solitary melody on a gentle breeze, is a soothing presence; the fluting of blackbirds and thrushes echoes across the landscape or, retrieved by memory, serves as a reminder of nature's "harmonious hymn of being." In "Thrushes," for example, the "quavering song" reminds the "haunted woodland" of man's "heart" that these birds are aloof from man and his mindless capacity for self-destruction. The blackbird singing amid the shattered trees of "Hidden Wood" at least makes the poet aware, however incongruously, that spring has sprung. Significantly it is a "Lenten blackbird," like Keats's nightingale, that triggers a personal reverie — in Sassoon's case about the trenches — in "A Footnote on the War."

Typically, the lyrical effects are a natural consequence of Sassoon's formal procedures: a secure rhythmic sense, an unerring ear for rhyme and verbal melody, and a willingness to exploit such sound devices as assonance and alliteration. In "Before the Battle," anxious to invest the verse with an elegiac dimension, the poet resorts to the feminine rhymes of "falling / calling" to emphasize the incantatory effect of the final psalmic plea for protection; in "The Triumph," the sound of "whispering leaves" and a "bird's lone cry" similarly elevate the tone of the verses and assist the process of expressing personal anguish within the conventions of the pastoral lyric.

One of the dilemmas which exercised Sassoon as a poet of war was whether he should incorporate melodious sound textures, which his artistic temperament still yearned for, into a poetry so much of whose subject matter was necessarily preoccupied with dissonance and discordancy. Such verbal music, as Sassoon well knew, is associated with the lyric or at least with traditional modes of poetic expression. That Sassoon did not altogether dispense with mellifluous diction reflects his firmly held conviction that, since sound was a key ingredient in poetry, its harmonious effects could at least be set against the cacophony of war. When Sassoon does avert his gaze from the battlefield and nostalgically evokes scenes from an English landscape, the verse can acquire a lyrical intensity that provides a poignant antidote to the bludgeoning noise of battle. In "A Letter Home," "Soldier David" becomes a spiritual presence in a sylvan landscape, "standing in a wood that swings / To the madrigal he sings"; the musty odors of the trenches in "Break of Day" trigger memories of misty mornings spent hunting. Not that the expedient is other than a temporary one. The "horn" at the end of "Break of Day" is a bugle summoning the soldier-poet to battle. And even away from it all, the troubled past obstinately refuses to go away. "Repression of War Experience" charts the experience of a poet trying desperately to recapture a harmonious "lyric muse" that has abruptly departed, to be replaced by a "big, dizzy moth" that "bumps and flutters" in a most unlyrical way. In any case, to capture the discordant noise of battle meant that Sassoon had to eschew all pretensions to lyricism. That he was able to catch the colloquial directness of the ordinary soldiers' speech or the thunder of modern war is a tribute to his concern that his verse should at least sound authentic even if its music was a dissonant one.

It is scarcely a matter for surprise that Sassoon, of all the war poets, should most consistently appropriate the language of the trenches. "The Redeemer," his "first front-line poem," ends with a vernacular curse: most of the subsequent bulletins from the line variously describe the thud of guns, the "yells and groans" of victims, the muffled commands of subalterns ("Stand To!") or, more frequently, the audible swearing ("O Jesus, make it stop") of the trooper. "Died of Wounds" derives much of its poignancy from the all too audible ravings of a dying officer. "Christ and the Soldier" juxtaposes ecclesiastical pomposities with the practical plain-speak of the soldier. Nor did Sassoon ignore the inanities of "club-speak": "The Fathers" and "Does It Matter," for example, show how effectively Sassoon could reproduce the hearty idioms of golf-club or country-house party. So taken was the poet with the dramatic potential of direct speech that he promptly incorporated it in most of his epigrams. Adding their voices to the groundswell of debate are mothers and bishops, amputees and dead men, parade-ground martinets and quarter-masters, tombstone makers and music-hall audiences — all vocal additions to that of the trooper cursing his way through the war. The use of quotation marks is liberal. Of course Sassoon is guilty of *some* cosmetizing of the sulphurous language of his men — he had to tread carefully — but he gets as close as anyone to the vernacular of the front line. Dadd's shattered voice-box must have seemed to Sassoon the ultimate horror — his strained whispers a "message from the maimed and dead." Only Sassoon's considerable powers of aural recall enabled him to remember the old Dadd: "memory brought back the voice I knew."

Not that Sassoon's lyrical bent entirely disappeared in the noxious mud of the trenches; the sad tributes to his blood brothers at the Front show that he is still capable, even in 1917 and 1918, of a poignant and affecting music which endeavors to give some dignity to their courage and suffering.

> On the shapes of the slain in their crumpled disgrace
> I stared for a while through the thin cold rain...
> "O lad that I loved, there is rain on your face,
> And your eyes are blurred and sick like the plain."

Nonetheless Sassoon knew that while the ear was important, it was "not enough" on its own. There was also "the eye ... the faculty of inward visualization." But Sassoon went further in declaring:

> I have never been fond of ideas for their own sake. In fact they have played a comparatively unimportant part in my literary life....

> Thinking in pictures is my natural method of self-expression. I have always been a submissively visual writer [*On Poetry*, 1939, p. 19].

Such a statement needs to be taken with a pinch of salt: many of the "Blighty" epigrams are not noticeably pictorial, and there are visual aspects of trench warfare which Sassoon rarely invites his reader to visualize. The war poetry is, in any case, not devoid of ideas: it is just that the ideas, certainly as presented in the verse, are pretty straightforward.

Nonetheless, his remark is, on balance, a fair one. Sassoon's capacity to "think in pictures," as he himself attested, is evident in trench pieces that rely on his capacity to recollect the visual details of circumstances that might be hours, days, or in the case of the Craiglockhart recollections of the Front, months away. It is worth remembering that the diaries were available as a quarry that he could and did excavate at will, but the imagery of many pieces depends on Sassoon's powers of recall. What seems to be lost in the retrospective poems written months after the event or without recourse to the notebooks is the kind of documentary detail that suggests recent eyewitness experience: on the whole, the trench poems composed in "Blighty," necessarily more reliant on memory and imagination, are broader in their brush strokes. To compare "Prelude: The Troops" and "Counter-Attack" is to become aware of the latter's compelling visual catalogue of carnage, a description heavily reliant on an earlier draft and a 1916 diary note. By comparison, "Prelude: The Troops" offers a more imaginative response, atmospheric and ultimately more visionary with its allusions to "some mooned Valhalla," but overall softer in its focus and lacking the "shock-horror" imagery of the "green clumsy legs" and "naked sodden buttocks" of "Counter-Attack." To pursue the point: a poem such as "The Quarter-Master," jotted down in the notebook within hours if not minutes of overhearing the conversation between two battle-hardened campaigners, displays a Hogarthian capacity for telling caricature; on the other hand, "Memory," a Limerick poem pledged to absent friends and dependent on reminiscence, lacks immediacy and contains nothing more specific than "the faces of my friends."

It is all a matter of degree. Clearly Sassoon's powers of description operated best as a consequence of direct stimulus; left to reflect on events, the poet's own emotions tend to take center-stage. But the visual image was, on his own admission, a staple constituent of his poetry. His pronouncements about Dryden and Donne show his inability to warm to poets whose pictorial sense was, in his estimation, limited to a capacity "to make one see *words* and nothing else" (*On Poetry*, 1939, p. 20). Such ratiocinative or complex verse was not to the taste of a poet who believed that the artist should "create with his mind's eye" (*Ibid.*, p. 21). In returning to his theme of directness, Sassoon averred that "strength and simplicity always go together" and that the "imagination, instinct controlled" had the capacity, denied to "contrived thought," to eliminate the "inessential" and to achieve "breadth and intensity by transmuted perception" (*Ibid.*, p. 25). That is what is happening in a poem such as "Prelude: the Troops."

But such an authorial view does not always bear close scrutiny. While Sassoon's epigrams demonstrate that "strength and simplicity" *can* go together, that the best poetry eliminates the dross and pares away the inessential, they also reveal a capacity for creating verse that is not always imaginatively conceived. Perhaps Sassoon was aware that a poem such as "Blighters," which does take risks and does make a huge imaginative leap with its surreal visualization of tanks lurching down the stalls of a music hall, is actually less effective than "They," an epigram which derives largely from verbal recollections of an actual sermon juxtaposed to the trench-speak of the soldiers.

But it is hard to avoid the impression that Sassoon's penchant for the direct statement, for the uncomplicated visual image, does reveal the limitations of his critical position and, more important, his own practice. It was a position that both prevented him from appreciating "difficult" poetry — T. S. Eliot is a case in point — or composing it himself. On the whole Sassoon's war verse rarely ventures far beyond the complexities of the pun (often a nonvisual device anyway) and generally ignores the capacity of metaphor and symbol to yoke heterogeneous images together by an effort of the imagination. Complex imagery, especially when couched in such figurative tropes, was an obstacle to comprehension. The poet, he believed, should draw on a stock of imagery common to all poets — sensuous, natural and, by and large, traditional. It *is* enormously to Sassoon's credit that in confronting the harrowing circumstances of war he should introduce a new realism into his verse. But although he does manage it in a handful of poems, he is temperamentally reluctant to embark on the kind of gross naturalism that informs, say, Barbusse's *Le Feu*. Nor was he much interested in the possibilities of extended metaphor. "Anthem for Doomed Youth," Owen's first trench poem, derives much of its power from a series of sustained metaphors that powerfully yoke together home and overseas. There is nothing quite like it in Sassoon's war poetry.

Yet Sassoon's most consistently used and effective structural device in his poetry *is* that of contrast. If he is no advocate of the metaphorical school of verse-making, he does employ a smattering of puns and oxymorons to emphasize his sundered world: "bloody-fingered from the fight" ("The Road") is a chillingly effective instance of a pun, while "hobble blithely," "stabbing tenderness," "bitter safety" and the "good fury" of the bayonet's thrust reveal the poet's propensity for the concentrated antithesis.

More typically, the contrasts are on a broader canvas: in the more obviously subjective poems, as we have seen, one world is usually set in stark opposition to another: a landscape, and especially a dawn English landscape replete with birdsong (though "France" provides a rare exception), provides a positive antidote to the warscapes of the front line. In earlier pieces such as "A Testament" or in later reversions to such a manner ("Invocation"), the comparison is conventional enough — "drumming shafts of death" are set against a lost Eden of "whispering trees." As Silkin observes, "nature is deployed in the kind of sanative and pleasure affording mode found in Blunden; it is the repository of goodness and peace and in the greatest contrast to war" (Silkin, 1972, 1998, p. 155).

Elsewhere the contrasts are more specific and more convincingly orchestrated. Thus "Break of Day" employs the highly associative device of smell, of musty autumnal odors, to link two disconcertingly disparate events: the all too real morning attack about to happen, and nostalgic memories of "drawing the Big Wood." The two worlds clash in the equivoque of the last line. Grim reality intrudes as the sound of the bugle summons the soldier to hunting of another and altogether more menacing kind:

> Hark! there's the horn: they're drawing the Big Wood.

"The Dream" offers a variation on this theme: nature is not simply a repository of everything beautiful and reminiscent: it can also be a source of pungent farmyard smells that jog the memory into thoughts, not of hunting, but of filthy hovels and men with sweaty, blistered feet behind the front lines. Such poems show how Sassoon was inventing subtler ways of depicting these polarized perspectives. Indeed he takes pains to indicate, in "Before the Battle," just how strained any sense of harmony between man and nature — a nexus at the heart of the poet's sensibility — is liable to become in the denatured world of war. Here, in the tense moments before the assault, he prays to "low-voiced streams" and a "river of stars and shadows" to lead him "through the night."

It is in the epigrammatic pieces, though, that the device of contrast is used to maximum effect. Here, two attitudes of mind, one the complete antithesis of the other, are often presented in the same poem. The poet's own view is left unstated; it is present only by implication. What makes "Does It Matter" one of the more effective of the satires is the fact that no alternative opinion is actually offered as a counter to the inanities mouthed by the civilian do-gooder. Elsewhere, and more obviously, Sassoon uses dialogue to ram home his truths, with one opinion treated with irony while the other view, usually expressed by a fusilier, represents that of the poet. "Christ and the Soldier" and, more obviously, "The Tombstone-Maker" are early conversation pieces in this mode; "They," perhaps the most successful.

The central focus of the satires is this gap in attitudes between the "Nation at Home" and the "Nation Overseas." Ranged on the distaff side, associated with hypocrisy and cant, are the familiar targets: old men ("The Fathers"), women ("Return of the Heroes," "Supreme Sacrifice"), politicians ("Great Men," "To Any Dead Officer"), journalists ("Editorial Impressions," "Fight to a Finish"), xenophobes ("The Optimist," "Trade Boycott," "To the Warmongers"), music-hall audiences ("Blighters"), bishops ("They," "Vicarious Christ"), materialists ("The Tombstone-Maker") and the squirearchy ("Memorial Tablet"). On the positive side are the ordinary soldiers on both sides, but especially the British "Tommy," almost always depicted as a repository of plain-speaking, honest-to-goodness values who simply cannot comprehend why he is being sent to a pointless death.

In the epigrams it is the soldier who is often allowed the last word, a salutory comment that casts fresh light on all that precedes it in the poem. In "The One-Legged Man," it is the maimed victim's — to us bizarre — thought, "Thank God they had to amputate," which puts everything else into perspective. This technique of ironic reversal, usually in the last stanza or line, is a skill at which Sassoon has few peers. Encouraged in its deployment by his friend Robbie Ross, it derives perhaps from Shakespeare's sonnets, long-time favorites, or, as Sassoon himself suggested, from Hardy's satires. It quickly became a staple of his epigrammatic method — "two or three harsh, peremptory, and colloquial stanzas with a knock-out blow in the last line" (SJ, p. 29).

These "knockouts" are almost always surprising and frequently bathetic. Witness the "scarlet majors" of "Base Details," who send young men to their doom and then "toddle safely home and die" in the safety of their own beds. Moreover these coups de grâce often have a sarcastic ring: at the end of "Editorial Impressions," the "lad," recuperating from a severe wound, nonetheless has the wit to "butter up" the reporter who has been paying for his tipple: "Ah, yes but its the press that leads the way!"

The conclusion of "Memorial Tablet" is equally sardonic, as the soldier, watching the church from his redoubt in the sky, recalls the unspeakable experience of the trenches, and concludes by mocking the inane "Blighty" platitude, "What greater glory could a man desire?" In "The General," one of the most consummately crafted of the satires, the ending is so conclusive that it brooks no reply — as the cheerful, trusting tommies become just another lifeless statistic in "his plan of attack." Likewise in "Blighters," the contrast is between drunkenly sung music-hall numbers and dead men for whom such inanities "mock the riddled corpses round Bapaume." Other, equally effective blows are struck by a poet anxious to convey the inconclusiveness of so many questions posed by the war. Why, for instance, has the established church indulged in so much empty rhetoric? "They" provides no answer; only an orotund reply that reminds one of the wayside shrine's equally obfuscating response in "Christ and the Soldier."

Such ironic juxtapositions and reversals are not always reserved for the final line or stanza; they are often embedded in the main body of the poem. The roadside Calvary of an "Uplifted Jesus" in "Christ and the Soldier" is incongruously seen to have a bizarrely different function in the battle —"an observation post for the attack"; the "brave and glorious boy" of "The Hero" has, in the heat of battle, proved to be "a cold-footed useless swine." In "The Effect" a kind of counterpoint is built up by an enthusiastic sales pitch in which the *only* goods for sale by the street-trader are corpses. In other poems the very names carry ironic overtones — Captain Croesus of "Arms and the Man" is anything but rich — but such names as Sawbones, Dudster, Currycombe and Leggit are positively Dickensian in their directness. Some of these effects are too obvious, too close to caricature, the product of an anger not quite under artistic control: "Great Men" or the notorious "Fight to a Finish," in which "Yellow-Pressmen" are bayoneted, reveal Sassoon at his most vituperative. But there is never any question about which side Sassoon is on — and consequently his reader. It is impossible not to want to take sides.

Chapter 6

Literary Influences

Lecturing about poetry in 1939, Sassoon declared that "All verse is traditional, and every verse-maker has a direct or indirect ancestry" (*On Poetry*, 1939, p. 7). Nevertheless Sassoon's poetic progenitors do not exactly declare themselves. In *The Weald of Youth* he confessed to falling, as so many young aesthetes did, under the seductive spell of Tennyson, Swinburne, Rossetti and the escapist verse of the "Celtic Twilight"; his admission that "poetry was a dream world into which I escaped through an esoteric door in my mind" (*WY*, p. 28) is reminiscent of an adolescent Yeats. These honey-tongued poets remained favorites, but their *direct* influence on the war poetry is necessarily slight. After 1916 not even Swinburne gets a mention in the diaries.

The only *admitted* poetic influence from an older living generation, and then primarily on the "satirical epigram," was Hardy. In *Siegfried's Journey*, Sassoon observed: "I have never been able to ascertain that my method was modelled on any other writer, though the influence of Hardy's *Satires of Circumstance* is faintly perceptible in a few of the longer poems" (*SJ*, p. 29). Faint indeed; only perhaps in "The Hawthorn Tree," which appears, significantly, as part of a diary jotting in which Sassoon has just been applauding Hardy's honest pessimism, does the tone and subject come close to the direct unpretentiousness of a Hardy "reverie." Admittedly there is the same countryman's awareness of the sights and sounds of the English landscape. Moreover, Sassoon's own baffled search for and rejection of a God in the Western Front recalls the agnosticism of such Hardy verses as "God's Funeral" (*Satires of Circumstance*), in which the speaker stands "dazed and puzzled, 'twixt the gleam and the gloom." The poet would also have noted Hardy's penchant for surprising his readers with a sudden reversal of tone: the demotic "Good God — I must marry him I suppose" in "In the Room of the Bride Elect" might well have appealed to Sassoon's love of the unexpected conclusion. As this example illustrates, Hardy's *Satires* are a mix, generally speaking, of dialogue and observation, a combination of modes that Sassoon tellingly exploits in his own condensed epigrams. Sassoon quickly became aware that it was these poems that naturally appealed to Hardy. Writing to Sassoon in 1917, the "great man" remarked:

> I appreciate thoroughly "When I'm in a Blaze of Lights" and "Blighters" and much like the grim humour of "The Tombstone-Maker" and "They," the pathos of "The Hero" and the reticent poignancy of "A Working Party." How we realize that young man!

This prompted a perceptive reaction from Sassoon:

> I think this is all right. You see he picks out the ironic ones which are (more or less) in his favourite vein. And it would not be characteristic of him, of all men, to say pleasant easy things about the more tender poems" [letter from Sassoon to Morrell, 21 May, 1917, ULUT].

If Hardy's impact on the war poems is rarely a direct one, however much Sassoon came to admire the man and his work, his encouragement was important in convincing Sassoon of the value of irony. So too was the general impact of Hardy's vision, a vision of a beautiful but threatened rural England and what Sassoon called his "grim, wise fatalism" (*Diaries*, 21 May, 1917, p. 171). Sassoon admitted as much in a letter to Roderick Meiklejohn on 25 March, 1917:

> If you want to send me a book that will really help me through the intolerable days, send a pocket edition of Hardy's *Far from the Madding Crowd*. It brings the English landscape out here; and yet his *irony* [emphasis added] helps one to fight against the inevitable homesickness for things which really don't matter, such as comfortable rooms and blameless domesticity.
>
> I am very glad I dedicated my poems to him. He has always been more to me than any other writer, in the times I've spent out here. A thinker of crooked thoughts upon life in the sere, and on that which consigns men to night after showing the day to them [ULUT].

When Sassoon met the living legend at Max Gate in 1918, he found him a "great and simple man" capable, when saying "something profound," of contriving "to make it seem quite ordinary." Being in his presence was "the nearest thing to Shakespeare I should ever go for a walk with" (SJ, p. 91). On the evidence of the war diaries Sassoon already knew many of his works, could quote from the poetry and took "Moments of Vision" with him to Palestine. To get a "nice letter from him saying how much he liked my 'Dead Officer' poem" was the stuff of inspiration" (letter from Sassoon to Morrell, 5 September, 1917, ULUT). Of all Sassoon's contemporary literary heroes, Hardy was the most revered, "my main admiration among living writers" (SJ, p. 13). It is a credit to Sassoon's determination to sing his own songs that Hardy's music is not often heard in his verse.

Vivian de Sola Pinto argues that Sassoon did have some pre-awareness of "the hollowness of the gentlemanly paradise in which he spent his youth and a deep sympathy for the common man who was excluded from that paradise" (1939, p. 143). It is certainly the case that *The Daffodil Murderer*, a pre-war parody of Masefield's *The Everlasting Mercy*, was written not only with a new "descriptive energy" (*WY*, p. 124), but with an earthy directness and an ear for working class colloquialisms that Sassoon would later put to good use in the pithy epigrams from the Front. But whether Sassoon had much sympathy for "the common man" at the time is doubtful, granted the evidence of his retrospective prose and the fact that his groom was about the only "common man" that Sassoon knew at all well before war changed all the rules. But Masefield, and particularly the ballad versifier, did show Sassoon that the most compelling way to highlight the ordinary soldier's plight was to give him an authentic voice, to allow him to speak "in propria persona."

In this connection, a more likely inspiration, at least for the colloquial, epigrammatic pieces, ought to be Kipling. According to one poll, in the *Journal of Education*, he was the most widely read poet in 1913 and his instantly accessible verse — an appropriate medium for a public purpose — is shot through with the homely expressions of the British trooper. But there is little in Sassoon's war verse that directly echoes Kipling, despite the older man's acknowledged ability to recreate the conditions of army life and, later on at least, to target civilian insensitivity. Though Sassoon, after the manner of Kipling, does allow the soldier to be his own apologist, his fusilier seems to speak a different "argot" from Kipling's barrack-room boys. Perhaps Sassoon, who makes *no* reference to him in the war diaries, bracketed Kipling with an older and more knowing generation, a writer who, granted his awareness of the realities of modern combat, should have warned his public about what was in store. In any case, Kipling's early verse had helped to perpetuate many popular conceptions about war, to create a stereotype of the British soldier — cheery, optimistic, but ultimately "a simple chap" — which Sassoon was increasingly disposed (at least after "The Redeemer" and "A Working Party") to regard as doing no favors to his own men.

Johnston, in drawing attention to these differences, offers the view that despite certain similarities of style, the use of colloquial language and simple rhythms, Sassoon's techniques

> shrill, abrupt, discordant and shocking — were therefore calculated to be as unsettling as the older poet's were re-assuring. Only twenty or thirty years separate Kipling's Indian and Boer war verse from Sassoon's *Counter-Attack*; the contrast in attitude and technique, however, reflects the astonishing rapidity and profundity of the changes with which we are dealing [Johnston, 1964, p. 108].

Some poems do betray a tangible enthusiasm for contemporary poets. Though Sassoon was evidently not enamored of his fellow writer, Rupert Brooke's discernible influence on a handful of early "happy warrior" effusions is hardly to be wondered at. Commenting tersely on their solitary encounter, Sassoon observed: "I was only one more in the procession of people who now were more interested in him than he was in them" (Thorpe, 1966, p. 152). But like so many of his generation, Sassoon *was* bowled over by Brooke's sonnet-sequence: "Absolution," "To My Brother" and the notebook poem "Peace" are steeped in its sentiments and phrasing, in places little more than a pastiche of "Safety" or "The Dead." "To Victory," dedicated to Edmund Gosse and pandering to his wish for "idealised soldier-poems" (SJ, p. 28), is characterized by the kind of pathetic fallacy and patriotic pantheism that Brooke had exploited in "The Old Vicarage, Granchester." Such literary eclecticism was no more than a reflection of Sassoon's enthusiasms at a particular time. But Brooke's influence was as ephemeral as his life. By December 1916, "The Poet as Hero" is poking fun at the chivalric sentiments and elevated rhetoric of those early Brookean pastiches. The poet, having sought a non-existent "Grail," is now "no more the knight of dreams and show." Both Brooke's happy warrior sentiments and, apart from the odd re-surfacing phrase, the diction in which they are couched, have disappeared in the slime and mud of the trenches.

Elsewhere a few resonances of a Victorian Romantic tradition remain. It was a tradition to which Brooke himself paid some obeisance and from which *Georgian Poetry*, with its advocacy of mellifluous rhythms and pleasant, homely landscapes, its editor's insistence that poetry should be "intelligible, musical and grounded in some formal principle," seemed in some ways a logical development. Indeed Sassoon was well aware of the existence of Edward Marsh's anthology, commenting on *Georgian Poetry 1913-15* that there was "nothing new to me in it," an indication that its contents—which included Brooke's "The Soldier" and Lawrence's "Cruelty and Love" (which begins as Georgian pastiche but ends up unadulterated Lawrence), as well as much minor verse now consigned to obscurity—were already familiar to Sassoon.

Like his friends and fellow war poets Nichols and Graves, Sassoon contributed substantially to the 1916 issue of *Georgian Poetry*, the presence of eight recent poems ("The Kiss," "A Letter Home," "The Dragon and the Undying," "To Victory," "They," "In the Pink," "Haunted" and "The Death Bed"), a mark both of his friendship with Marsh and his tacit support for the kind of verse being published in the anthology. And though after the war *Georgian Poetry* lost its way and with it Sassoon's approbation (he refused to contribute to its last volume), its contents were never as homogeneous as most critics have since assumed. Such an assumption was in fact denied "with both hands" by Marsh, anxious to rebut the "allegation ... that an insipid sameness is the chief characteristic of our anthology" ("Prefatory Note" to *Georgian Poetry 1920-22*).

Of course Sassoon was a friend and admirer of some of its contributors during the war years. Moreover the traditional strain in *Georgian Poetry*—verse formally precise, pastoral in subject, elevated in tone—was a model that Sassoon approved in 1915 and, even in the later stages of the war, occasionally reverted to. He retained, for example, his admiration for de la Mare, who had no fewer than thirty poems published in the various issues of the anthology. After receiving *Motley and Other Poems* (1918), Sassoon recorded in his diary: "After tea an exciting mail came in—Walter de la Mare's new book of poems." He proceeded to read them immediately "sitting in the long grass" (*Diaries*, 2 June 1918, p.

260). Though the romantic temperament of Sassoon demanded that the spirit of Pan, particularly when nostalgically invoked from the battlefield, be accorded a music more elevated and amplified than that provided by, say, Masefield, Davies, Gibson or even de la Mare, their "Movement"-like concern for simplicity, even homeliness was a principle not lost on Sassoon. In 1914, when Sassoon met his mother's companion Wergie at the Zoo, she reminded him of their "delighted discovery" of W.H. Davies "about seven years before" (WY, p. 237). "Stretcher Case," for example, is a quintessentially "Georgian" poem which, significantly, Sassoon dedicated to Marsh. In it the English landscape unfolds before the hallucinatory gaze of the returning soldier. Then he remembers that his name is Brown and recognizes "with thanksgiving ... the railway advertisements of 'Lung Tonic, Mustard, Liver Pills and Beer'" (SJ, p. 5).

A.E. Housman, whose poetry never appeared in *Georgian Poetry*, remained a Sassoon favorite. *A Shropshire Lad* was not only quoted in the 1915 diary (7 December, p. 25), it was one of the collections of verse that Sassoon took with him to the Front via Egypt in 1918. Much later, in his Bristol lecture *On Poetry*, Sassoon would approvingly quote Housman's "Tell It Not Here" as a paradigm (in its intensity and musicality) of the lyric genre: "The tone of voice is as natural as ordinary speech, yet it is utterance lit and transfigured from within" (*On Poetry*, 1939, p. 17). "In Barracks" pays homage to that distinctive lyricism; its finale, "The bugle's dying notes that say 'Another night; another day,'" is an acknowledged allusion to Housman's "I hear my bones within me say / Another night, another day" (*A Shropshire Lad* XLIII). It might be thought odd that a 1918 poem should quote Housman, but the piece was written at Limerick and reveals a relaxed and rejuvenated Sassoon waxing lyrical about "young fusiliers, strong-legged and bold" and reverting to a poetic manner that sometimes recalls his earlier war verse.

In any case Sassoon remained an enthusiast. Housman himself believed "that the start" of *A Shropshire Lad's* popularity "was the outbreak of the First World War." Roy Fuller maintains that "doubtless he was right, for the book was on the spot (as was Rupert Brooke) to take advantage of the increase of interest in poetry, brought about by 1914" (R. Fuller, *New Statesman*, 30 July, 1971, p. 152, quoted in Fussell, 1975, p. 282). On the substantial evidence of the slim prewar volumes, Sassoon was already a disciple of Housman's verse; the war's outbreak merely rekindled his interest. But Sassoon was also aware, not only of Housman's lyrical gifts, but of his place in the pantheon of homoerotic verse. Whenever Sassoon remembers a loved comrade or, as in the poem "In Barracks," lusts after young men, he tends to fall back on the poeticisms and euphemisms of this tradition. Paul Fussell maintains that "perhaps Housman's greatest contribution to the war was the word 'lad' to which his poems had given the meaning 'a beautiful brave doomed boy'" (Fussell 1975, p. 282). It is interesting to note that in the *War Poems*, Sassoon's use of the epithet occurs mainly in the later poetry and hardly at all in the satires, testimony to his growing confidence about utilizing the "codes" of homoerotic verse and to the "bloodbrotherhood" he increasingly yearned for. The most Housmanesque poem of all is the relatively late "Suicide in the Trenches." Its simple vocabulary and uncluttered lyricism culminate in a stanza of considerable pathos:

> You smug-faced crowds with kindling eye
> Who cheer when soldier lads march by,
> Sneak home and pray you'll never know
> The hell where youth and laughter go.

That such a poem as "To an Athlete Dying Young" remained a perennial favorite is clear both from this poem and from the early "To My Brother"; on the evidence of "Disabled," it was also a favorite of Wilfred Owen's. In Sassoon's poem "your laurell'd head" is reminiscent of "that early laurelled head"; the sense of early achievement overshadowed by early and untimely death is again redolent of Housman's elegy. If few other specific borrowings reveal themselves, that is testimony to Sassoon's determination not to plagiarize other poets. The pre–Somme "France," has heavens "crowned by cloud pavilions white" in possible tribute to "the sky pavilioned land" of Housman's "Reveille." And the influence of "The Merry Guide" is discernible in the "web-hung woods" of Sassoon's "A Letter Home" (Housman has "hanging woods"). In both pieces a "happy guide" leads the poet on a rustic quest. Housman would continue to be a general source of guidance and inspiration. One might have anticipated a similar role for Lionel Johnson. After all Graves recollected that Sassoon was reading Johnson's *Essays* at their first encounter. But Johnson's influence on the war poems is slight.

Two poets, both personal friends at different stages of the war, were important catalysts in Sassoon's creative progress. One was Robert Graves, the other Wilfred Owen. Though Graves was to prove both a comrade in arms and an effective if uncompromising critic of Sassoon's poetry, initial signs were not encouraging. In his notebook of 28 November, 1915, Sassoon referred patronizingly to his first encounter with "a young poet, captain in the 3rd Battalion and very much disliked, an interesting creative and self-conscious, a defier of convention." The same disparaging reaction was accorded Graves's poetry. Though Sassoon came increasingly to admire the verse of "Dear Roberto," he regarded the first drafts to come his way as a very mixed bag, some "very bad, violent and repulsive ... a few full of promise and real beauty" (*Diaries*, 2 December, 1915, p. 21). Certainly their early poetic manners could hardly have been more different. Graves, with his idiosyncratic propensity for distinctive, quirky rhythms and outrageous rhymes, adopted a poetic method that veered from confronting the full horror of war to seeking release through myth, allegory and fairy-tale; Sassoon, on the other hand, "wanted to have fine feelings about ... the war ... terrible but not horrible enough to interfere with my heroic emotions. David, (Graves) on the other hand ... had no use for anti-war idealism" (*Memoirs*, p. 386). In *Goodbye to All That*, Graves would recollect Sassoon's pained reaction to "one or two drafts in my pocket-book" when he "frowned and said the war should not be written about in such a realistic way." But Sassoon's poems fared no better with the younger man. The opening of "To Victory" provoked a memorable reaction: "Siegfried had not yet been in the trenches: I told him, in my old soldier manner, that he would soon change his style" (GTAT, p. 146).

Graves's prognosis proved correct. In the uncongenial environs of Mametz Wood, there began an artistic and emotional rapprochement in which the fellow officers and brother poets sought not only to minimize these aesthetic differences, but to encourage the creative process by discussion and, when apart, by correspondence; to edit each other's drafts sensitively and scrupulously; to compose pieces on set subjects; to recommend each other's efforts to influential literati at home; to share their joint enthusiasms for Brooke and Nichols; and even to communicate in the form of verse-letters. It is rare for poets to engage in this kind of symbiosis, and for poets so different in terms of temperament and technique, it was little short of extraordinary.

Contributing to this creative rapport was a ghostly third presence, a former captain in the Suffolks whose war was already over, as he had been killed at the infamous battle of Loos in October 1915. His name was Charles Sorley. His youthful verse, as promising as anything written in 1915, was closer, rhythmically and temperamentally, to that of Graves, but both friends (Sassoon appears to have discovered him first) found themselves talking and writing about him in terms at once reverential and affectionate. Sorley was both absent lover and fellow soldier-poet, whose verse they could unstintingly admire. These twin images surface in their letters and notebooks. Sassoon, fellow Marlburian, quoted "When you see millions of the mouthless dead" in his Christmas Day diary entry for 1916. On the previous day, "Sorley's letters" had given him "a cheer-up" and caused Sassoon to remark in his notebook: "He was so ready for all emergencies, so ready to accept the 'damnable circumstance of death'— or life" (*Diaries*, p. 106). It was probably the letter-writing Sorley, with his praise of Hardy's *The Dynasts* (to become a Sassoon favorite), his awareness of the perversion of values and self-righteous chauvinism spawned by the war, his sympathy for the common man and the German soldier alike, his distrust of "the Georgian retreat into sentiment and sensibility" (Johnston 1964, p. 56) that spoke most eloquently to Sassoon. After all, these were attitudes that he was increasingly disposed to regard as right. Sassoon's homage to the poet is most clearly seen, however, in "A Letter Home," which takes up the marching rhythms of Sorley's "All the Hills and Vales Along," and shows Sassoon operating in a quite atypical but nonetheless effective poetic mode.

But Sorley, alas, was no longer flesh and blood. Graves was. Meeting up in Harlech after both had been invalided back home, Graves explained that they "made a number of changes in each other's verses; I proposed amendments, which he accepted, in an obituary poem 'To His Dead Body'— written for me when he thought me dead" (GTAT, 1957, p. 205). Graves was not slow to praise Siegfried's verse when he thought it was deserved. To Marsh he enthused about "A Subaltern," "a perfectly ripping one about a mutual friend of ours called Thomas"; admired "The Last Meeting"; and singled out for fulsome approbation the middle verse of "Died of Wounds" ("the best stanza in this book, probably in any books of war poems"). In a letter two months later the Graves verdict on "To Any Dead Officer" was that it was "Without doubt a great poem" (letter to Sassoon, 30 June, 1917, IBI, p. 71).

Though Graves inevitably warmed to poems closer to his own—"A Subaltern" links demotic language and anti-heroic attitudes after the manner of his "Big Words"—his critical instincts were normally right. "Died of Wounds," one of Sassoon's first Somme poems and composed in hospital, is a remarkable poem by any standards. But Graves was anxious to roughen up or naturalize Sassoon's metrics, to get him to vary the even melody of his predominant pentameter lines. Often these proposals were very specific. In the case of "To Any Dead Officer" his "tentative suggestions" concerned the poem's rhythmic impulsion: "The simple effect," he argued, "would be strengthened by a more regular sweep in the first half of each verse" (letter from Graves to Sassoon, 30 June, 1917, IBI p. 71).

Sassoon's second memorial to David Thomas showed just how far he could go in a Gravesian direction if he chose to. The ostensible subject remains the same, but "A Letter Home" is a homage to Graves by way of Sorley. Written, unusually for Sassoon at this time, in the four stressed line favored by Graves and Sorley, the upbeat rhythms accord well with the gaiety of a poem which cocks a defiant if rather facile snook at war. As Sassoon was keen to demonstrate, the audacious rhymes (often bi- or tri-syllabic), surging rhythms, and jokey tone were consciously borrowed from his friend's verse. Addressing "Robert" in the final stanza, the poet acknowledges both their complicity and Graves's likely poetic response:

> You can hear me; you can mingle
> Radiant folly with my jingle.
> War's a joke for me and you
> While we know such dreams are true!

Convalescing in a military hospital at Lancaster Gate, his war over, Sassoon did write one more verse-letter to "Dear Roberto." Its importance as a poem, despite Sassoon's mental confusion at the time, has been overshadowed by its notorious 1929 role in delivering the coup de grâce to a friendship long since moribund. As an old man Sassoon could reflect: "Since about 1927 I have differed from Robert Graves about almost everything, and he from me" (*Letters to a Critic*, 1966, p. 13). The pity is that Sassoon *was* trying, as in the 1916 "A Letter Home," to write in a style that Graves would approve, though, two years on, a line such as "Why keep a Jewish friend unless you bleed him?" was hardly likely to appeal to the newlywed and impecunious Graves.

Over the four years of the war, the Graves influence on Sassoon is—perhaps surprisingly — the more palpable and the more frequently articulated. Sassoon, a self-styled "Mercutio," given to extreme fluctuations of feeling and yet coming from a conservative artistic tradition, inevitably changed more radically as a poet. Graves, anti-heroic from the start, underwent no such epiphany. Sassoon would later marvel at the fact that until he met Graves in 1915, he knew "no writer of his age or anywhere near it" (Corrigan 1973, p. 63). Hardly surprising then is the fact that no one individual did more than Graves to bring the lofty Sassoon down to earth, to persuade him to capture some of the horrid reality of trench life in his poetry, to confront experience directly, or at least ruefully, in verse. It was Graves, more than anyone else who helped Sassoon eschew the sentimental stance and tone down the heroic gesture (though in action he remained the authentic hero); it was Graves who, early on, suspected Gosse and others "of being his retarding influence — 'keeping me,' Sassoon complained to Edward Marsh, 'to my moons and nightingales and things'" (letter from Graves to Marsh, 15 March, 1916, IBI, p. 44). It was Graves the poet who confirmed for Sassoon the importance of unpredictable effects, the astringent value of direct, natural expression at the expense of poetic diction, the need to leaven the mix with a dash of humour, to put some rum in the punch or some seasoning in the dish. In "A Pinch of Salt" (1916) he counsels:

> Poet never chase the dream
> Laugh yourself and turn away.

What Graves could not do was to convert Sassoon to his own brand of poetry. Sassoon never quite took to Graves's rollicking rhythms and his penchant for Skeltonics: while two-thirds of the poems in *Fairies and Fusiliers* play variations on the four stressed line (others are written in trimeter and even dimeter), Sassoon tends to prefer the more leisurely movement of the iambic pentameter. The quatrain, a Graves hallmark and a mark of his interest in the ballad, is sparingly employed in *Counter-Attack*. Moreover Sassoon avoided Graves's tendency to turn to myth and symbol, to liken war to a Roman battle or biblical event. At times an inventive procedure, it often smacked, as Sassoon knew, of escapism or even intellectual showmanship. Nor did Sassoon, lacking Graves's yearning for children, wish to explore things through the eyes of the child. In the three "Nursery Memories" of *Over the Brazier*, Graves's response to horrid experience is to leap back into infancy, to revive such memories as a way of coping, as "The First Funeral" does, with the traumas engendered by war. In this poem the unburied corpse on the wire becomes a dead dog, a smelly and disgusting memory from childhood:

> His horrid swollen belly
> Looked just like going burst.

War, Graves recalled in *Goodbye to All That*, was something he "deprecated" from the outset, "in so far as it interfered with me and failed to make the pleasurable most of itself" (p. 43). When he did face the unpleasure, he found it disgusting, grotesque, something from which he wanted to recoil, a world where "flesh decays and blood drips red" ("Dead Cow Farm"), where it is necessary to "hold your nose against the stink / And never stop too long to think" ("The Next War").

For a long time, Sassoon had even more difficulty than Graves in introducing the full ghastliness of trench warfare into his verse. But in a few late poems of *The Old Huntsman* and particularly in *Counter-Attack* (1918), Sassoon began to experiment in realistic directions that his friend did not approve. While Graves did advocate the use of "common and simple words," it is significant that he advised his fellow poet in "To Any Officer" to eliminate the "vulgarities," to "cut down the slang" and reconsider the use of the modern metaphor of "the telephone" (letter from Graves to Sassoon, 13 September, 1917, IBI, p. 83). Post–Somme it was Sassoon who began pushing the war poem in directions — satiric and otherwise — that Graves would not follow. He may have had Graves's ballad-like stanzas and comic deflections in mind as he began to deploy these ironic methods, but the coruscating satire is his own. In 1918 a Sassoon reproof about Graves's evasions elicited a touchy reaction: "As for my not 'writing deeply' blast you, you old Croaking Corbie aren't I allowed for the honour of the Regiment to balance your abysmal groanings with my feather top rhymes and songs?" (letter from Graves to Sassoon, 9 July, 1918, IBI, p. 95). As poets they had become poles apart; at Craiglockhart Graves's role of poetic confidant was taken over by Wilfred Owen.

No discussion of mutual influence can ignore the symbiotic relationship between Sassoon and Owen. If the critical consensus is that Owen, despite a creative life of Keatsian brevity, is the more achieved artist, it is evident that Sassoon's influence was, on Owen's own admission, palpable. Writing to his mother on 15 August, 1917, from Craiglockhart, Wilfred confided:

> I have just been reading Siegfried Sassoon, and am feeling at a very high pitch of emotion. Nothing like his trench life sketches has ever been written or ever will be written.... I think if I had the choice of making friends with Tennyson or with Sassoon, I should go to Sassoon [*Collected Letters*, 1968, pp. 484–5].

It is part of literary history, recorded both in *Siegfried's Journey* and *Goodbye to All That*, that Owen's admiration for the older man soon turned to adulation when the officer-poets met. In his first letter to Sassoon after leaving "Dottyville," Owen would memorably describe his feelings: "Know that since mid–September, when you still regarded me as a tiresome little knocker on your door, I held you as Keats + Christ + Elijah + my Colonel + my father-confessor + Amenophis IV in profile" (*Collected Letters*, 1967, p. 505). Clearly the influence was both personal and artistic. Sufficiently emboldened after their first meeting to show Sassoon some "old sonnets" which "didn't please him at all," Owen remembered that the older man did "pronounce" one lyric "perfect work" and exhorted Owen to "sweat your guts out writing poetry!" Posterity should be grateful that he did.

Characteristically Sassoon was soon playing down his influence and belittling his own war poetry while eulogizing the achievement of Owen. Years later, he made the generous observation that "my only claimable influence was that I stimulated him towards writing with compassion and challenging realism.... 'Exposure' is dated February 1917, and proves that he had already found an authentic utterance of his own" (SJ, p. 60). But Sassoon does propose more specific ways in which he may have helped the apprentice poet: their own joint devising of "technical dodges" and Sassoon's own "simplifying suggestions" emanating from a "technique ... almost elementary compared with his innovating experiments" (SJ, p. 60). Sassoon was also responsible for introducing Owen to the Fitzwater Wray translation of Barbusse's *Le Feu* "which set him alight as no other book had done." Most crucial of all, Sassoon suggests that Owen only began "to risk the colloquialisms ... so frequent in my verses ... after he got to know me." Sassoon's conclusion is modesty itself:

> Turning the pages of Wilfred's *Poems*, I am glad to think that there may have been occasions when some freely improvised remark of mine sent him away with a fruitful idea. And my humanized reportings of front-line episodes may have contributed something to his controlled vision of what he had seen for himself [SJ p. 60].

Siegfried then saw his role largely as technical adviser, a role which involved, as with Graves, considered discussion of each other's work. In fact, as Dominic Hibberd has pointed out, Owen also had access to Sassoon's notebook (dated October 1917) which contained most of the poems, either in manuscript or in proof, that subsequently appeared in *Counter-Attack and Other Poems* (*Notes and Queries*, August 1982, p. 341).

Some specific phrasal resonances are inevitable. In "Disabled," where both subject matter and treatment are close to Sassoon's "Does It Matter," the amputee's "He thought he'd better join. He wonders why" recalls the last line of Sassoon's bitter epigram, "And still the war goes on — he don't know why." Nonetheless the two poems highlight the distinctively different gifts of the writers. Predictably, Sassoon's poem is daringly slangy and angrily sardonic, an attack on "Blighty" attitudes painted in broad brush strokes. By comparison Owen's poem concentrates less on these hypocrisies (save in the penultimate stanza) and more on the shattered sensibilities and broken body of the wheelchair victim himself.

"The Next War" takes as epigraph the concluding lines of Sassoon's "A Letter Home," to which Owen added, in one draft, the cancelled "A Postscript to Siegfried Sassoon's letter to Robert Graves" (Sassoon, we recall, composed his Gravesian pastiche as a tribute to a friend whom he wrongly believed to be dead). Owen, now repeating the act of conscious homage — to Sassoon — adopts a similarly jaunty tone, and in the description of "He's spat at us with bullets ... he sang aloft" seems to allude to the "Rifles crack and bullets flick / Sing and hum like hornet-swarms" of Sassoon's altogether slighter offering. In a letter to Leslie Gunston, Owen enclosed a draft of "The Dead-Beat," adding, "After leaving him, I wrote something in Sassoon's style" (*Letters*, 1967, p. 485). "Anthem for Doomed Youth" bears the imprint of Owen's "father-confessor." Jon Stallworthy believes that the poem's initial impetus came from the maudlin "Prefatory Note" to *Poems of Today 1916* (1973, p. 216), but points out that Sassoon suggested a number of alterations including the change in the title from "dead" to "doomed." There are also possible reverberations of "The Dragon and the Undying." Owen's sonnet lacks the pantheistic optimism that pervades Sassoon's strained piece, but "the pallor of girls' brows shall be their pall" appears to echo "Their faces are the fair, enshrouded night" and "In their eyes / shall shine the holy glimmer of good-byes" perhaps builds on "The Planets are their eyes, their ageless dreams." Sassoon's 1916 poem lacks the haunting and discordant music of "Anthem for Doomed Youth," a power that derives from Owen's capacity to sustain — as Sassoon's poetry rarely does — a series of original and daring metaphors. Indeed this was the poem that convinced the older man that Owen was "much more than the promising minor poet I have hitherto adjudged him to be. I now realised that his verse, with its sumptuous epithets and large scale imagery, its noble naturalness and depth of meaning, had impressive affinities with Keats.... This new sonnet was a revelation" (SJ, pp. 59–60). Elsewhere in Owen's poetry there are few discernible echoes of Sassoon's verse, conscious or otherwise. But an alert reader, familiar with the work of both poets, might adduce similarities of rhythm or cadence, common structural tricks or clusters of reminiscent epithets. Jon Stallworthy points out that a phrase ("heaven of flowers") from an unpublished poem by Sassoon did find its way into Owen's "My Shy Hand," a poem that he believes offers intimations of "a new music to which Owen was then — perhaps at Sassoon's recommendation — being exposed" (1974, p. 213). In Owen's "Dulce et Decorum Est," the halting rhythms of the opening tableau which limp along like its "blood-shod" marchers, may have been catalyzed by "A Working Party" with its sodden and desensitized trench trudger. In the cloying "sludge" common to both poems, Sassoon's victim is "groping with his boots"; Owen's have already "lost their boots." Inevitably both poets draw on similar situations and experiences; after all this was a conflict in which horrors replicated themselves with a grim inevitability. Owen's depersonalized title "S.I.W." introduces a poem which makes use of the same idea — though the melancholy practice of self-inflicted wounding was common enough, as Sassoon's "A Ballad" testifies. Owen's "Mental Cases" and Sassoon's "Survivors" again share a similar subject. Both describe the shell-shocked victims of battles, but while "Survivors" may have been in Owen's mind when he came to write "Mental Cases" the following spring, no direct borrowings are apparent. Increasingly that seems to have been the case: Owen's voice, while initially honed by contact with a technically superior poet, came increasingly to be his own, a poetry, as Sassoon recognized, of "sumptuous epithets and large scale imagery" (SJ, p. 59).

A few conclusions are worth making. It is received wisdom that Owen's "superiority" as a war poet relates to his daring innovations, especially his use of consonantal rhyme, and his greater imaginative vision and sympathy. Johnston, for example, offers the questionable opinion that Sassoon was "beginning to understand the inadequacy of the brief lyric and narrative forms he had been employing" (Johnston, 1964, p. 111); Thorpe, the view that Owen, unlike Sassoon, "sought to create, not force, a change of heart" (1966, p. 27). Of course Owen was a quick learner, an instinctive humanitarian and poet. But it is instructive that Sassoon believed he helped Owen both to simplify his technique *and* to inform his poetry with a sense of compassion.

That the relationship was symbiotic in artistic terms is well documented. But it is more difficult to assess the impact of Owen on Sassoon, a poet who was not only established, but technically more conservative. On the evidence of the Craiglockhart poems, Sassoon *did* begin, perhaps encouraged by Owen's example, to experiment with less regular meters and essay some attempts at half-rhyme. "Wirers," for example, opens with the duplicated rhyme "out /out" to convey the impression of mechanically repeated orders. On the other hand "Prelude: The Troops" and "Counter-Attack" dispense almost entirely with conventional rhymes and instead promote sound textures which, by virtue of their discordancies and halting rhythms, connote echo, remoteness, the sound of battle. Here, if anywhere, Sassoon is responding to Owen's inspiration.

Both men had, by late 1917, read Barbusse. In *Siegfried's Journey*, Sassoon punningly recollected: "And didn't I lend him Barbusse's *Le Feu*, which set him alight as *no* other book had done" (SJ, p. 60). Sassoon's observation is accurate, for there are measurable imprints of Barbusse in Owen's verse. The effect on Sassoon is harder to gauge. He did read the Fitzwater-Wray translation during his first few weeks at Craiglockhart and did preface *Counter-Attack* with an inscription from the final apocalyptic chapter. That he was moved by the novel's naturalistic reportage and stirred to fury by its eloquent anti-war finale is clear from the *Memoirs* (p. 525). Sassoon, now distanced from his trench experiences, seems to have absorbed the brooding atmosphere of *Le Feu*, a "yellow" landscape (c.f. "The Effect") where the pitiless, drenching rain is unrelenting and where men are mere troglodytes, "shaped ... in shrinking files, stooping, abashed, splashing" (p. 130). The images of death and putrefaction, of soldiers more dead than alive, must have brought back appalling memories. But while Barbusse stresses horrors that Sassoon modifies or suppresses — the ineradicable odors of excretion and food, the killing slime-pools and befouled faces, men as degenerate as animals — the novel's intensely physicalized picture of war *is* reflected, if somewhat attenuated, in such Craiglockhart poems as "Break of Day," "Attack" and more especially "Counter-Attack." Indeed Barbusse's opening vision of "faces ... matted with uncut beards and foul with forgotten hair" may well, in addition to

Graves's "Dead Boche," have provided the inspiration for Sassoon's disturbing picture of "face downward in the sucking mud ... mats of hair, and bulged, clotted heads," an opening passage which has been consistently praised for its sharply focused realism. Moreover the manic frenzy of a prolonged attack, captured so vividly by Barbusse in his title chapter, informs the third and final section of "Counter-Attack" where everything is forgotten in the insane fury of battle.

Not that Barbusse was the only French chronicler of the war to affect Sassoon. Late in the conflict he encountered Duhamel's *La Vie des martyrs*, a novel written by a frontline surgeon and characterized by an extraordinary compassion for his patients. It concluded: "It is ... my mission to record the history of those who have been the sacrificial victims of the race.... Union of pure hearts for the redemption of the world" (1918, p. 215). Sassoon's enthusiasm pervades his correspondence at the time. Convinced that "Duhamel is quite equal to Barbusse" (*Diaries*, 22 May, 1918, p. 255), he confided to Lady Ottoline Morrell that "Duhamel moved me more than I can say.... The tenderness of it ... and the truth" (letter from Sassoon to Morrell, 7 June, 1918, ULUT). Two poems written at this time show Sassoon revisited by a vision of stricken "brothers." If Sassoon's overflowing sense of pity needed another literary voice to add to his own, then Duhamel supplied it.

As Sassoon was an avid reader of literature (his "Books to take to Egypt" list in 1918 included nine collections of poetry and ten prose works), it would be odd if allusions from these specified texts did not appear in his war poetry. Of the novels, only Hardy with his evocation of the English countryside and Barbusse (he had not yet read Duhamel) with his brutish images of the trenches influenced Sassoon's overall poetic vision. The collections of verse were a different matter; if Sassoon at his best was not a derivative writer, he did, like any lover of poetry, remember images from favorite poems and acquaint himself with their methods. Drawn to Romantic verse both on account of its rich imagery, its links with nature and its instinctive sympathy for the common man, Sassoon put Keats, in the form of his "delightful" green vellum edition, at the head of his Egypt memorandum. Already the "dripping heads" of roses in "Repression of War Experience" had echoed those mournful blooms in "Ode on Melancholy," already his fears of dying before completing his work ("all my store / cries for completion") had recalled Keats's sonnet "When I Have Fears That I May Cease to Be." While at Craiglockhart Sassoon began to read Shelley avidly. "Autumn," a response to a Scottish October, was catalyzed by Shelley's "Ode: To the West Wind." In both poems the central personification, the animating wind, scatters the leaves as though in murderous pursuit of them. Shelley's image is more melodramatic — his "pestilence-stricken multitudes" are metamorphosed in "Autumn" to leaves "scattered in flocks of ruin" — but Sassoon's inspiration is clearly Shelleyan, even if Sassoon characteristically extends the metaphor of victims to include "martyred youth." In another Craiglockhart tone poem, "Thrushes," nature is again seen as menacing to mankind. However its menace does not extend to birds who

6. Literary Influences 75

share its airy element; like Shelley's skylark, they are apparently "scornful of man" and of his earthbound trials and tribulations.

Sassoon's love affair with Swinburne was of longer duration. The epigram to the 1912 *Melodies* had been taken from his verse; four years on six lines from "Ave Atque Vale" were copied down in his December 1916 notebook (*Diaries*, 27 December, 1916, p. 111). Twenty-three years later Sassoon was still espousing his virtues: "Now anyone who denies that Swinburne was a 'lord of language' is, in my opinion, a crass idiot. He used words and meters with a superb virtuosity which has never been excelled in English poetry" (*On Poetry*, 1939, p. 14). Sassoon's unfettered admiration for Swinburne is interesting. After all Swinburne, as Sassoon knew full well, was hardly fashionable in 1939. But Sassoon was determined to celebrate him as a superb technician, a "lord of language." It was this aspect of the poetry that probably moved Sassoon to employ one of Swinburne's favorite meters, the anapest, in a number of latish war poems, "Aftermath," "The Triumph" and "I Stood with the Dead"— poems in which he appears to have rediscovered Swinburne's penchant for one of the most difficult meters in English poetry.

In the final analysis it was for technical virtuosity, for sound textures, for "natural vocal cadence" (*On Poetry*, 1939, p. 26) that Sassoon went to other poets — and we should include in this list Tennyson for his music, Browning for his conversational rhythms and revealing portraits, and Shakespeare the sonneteer for his surprise endings. Sassoon was never a slavish imitator, not a man to experiment with complex images or Modernist procedures. Though T. S. Eliot's first volume appeared in 1917, there is no mention of it in the notebooks or letters. Sassoon wholeheartedly approved of Max Beerbohm's later description of Eliot as a "dried bean" sitting in a "melancholy back-yard ... analysing an empty sardine-tin" (*Diaries*, 10 April, 1930, in *Letters to Beerbohm*, p. 30). For Sassoon, poetry was first and foremost about emotions and their transfusion. If war generated new experiences and unsought feelings, then Sassoon had to transmit these vibrations to the reader without being able to rely consistently on traditional models or current practice. In the heat of battle he had to forge his own style.

Chapter 7

The Poetic Achievement

One of the problems of attempting a dispassionate assessment of Siegfried Sassoon's achievement as a war poet is that unflattering comparisons are so often made with the work of his friend Wilfred Owen. Bergonzi offers what is a pretty standard judgment:

> He is usually regarded as a smaller, because less compassionate and universal poet than Owen; and this is certainly true. Satire does not reach the heights achieved by Owen's generalised lyric pity; but the comparison is not an easy one, and within the limits of his satirical mode Sassoon is a brilliant performer. In those poems, however, in which he attempts something closer to Owen's manner, Sassoon's treatment is less assured [Bergonzi, 1965, p. 96].

We will return to the matter of Sassoon's status as satirist; the point about the poet's "less compassionate" stance needs to be addressed here and now. Sassoon himself objected to a view which was already received opinion in his own lifetime:

> *The Sunday Times* says I'm "a good second to Wilfred Owen," though less compassionate which I deny, since I was bursting with it, wasn't I, when I made my famous and futile protest, which many now consider reasonable? [Corrigan, 1973, p. 86].

Sassoon's objection is valid. His celebrated "protest" referred to suffering no less than three times. Indeed Lady Ottoline Morrell intuited — and secretly regretted the intuition — that Sassoon's "anti-war complex" was less the result of a doctrinaire pacifism than an obsessive compassion for his comrades-in arms. While such sympathies made him deplore the senseless blood-letting, they also produced another response: the guilty conviction that only by returning to action and thereby demonstrating his love for his men, by ennobling himself through the act of shared suffering and perhaps by dying alongside them, could his dual role as officer and artist be vindicated.

This critical stricture may in part result from a misreading of a procedure that Sassoon tends to overdo, that of juxtaposing the weighty to the trivial. Such a technique, while aiming at an intensification of *effect*— as in the poem of that name — may appear to call in question his sympathy for his human subject. Thus the image in "The Effect" of "Dick ... Flapping along the fire-step like a fish" in his death-throes is positioned next to some street-trader banter about "nice fresh corpses"; in "Died of Wounds," the bathetic conclusion of "some slight wound ... smiling on the bed" follows hard on the delirious ravings of a young innocent, mentally and now physically destroyed by the war. Even as percipient a critic as Michael Thorpe has been taken in by this tactic.

That compassion is abundantly present in the poetry, and not merely as a consequence of Sassoon's tormented guilt at being preserved at home, cannot be gainsaid. True, he does want to share the burden of suffering, to go "back to grope with them through hell" ("Banishment"); he does seek to demonstrate his love for his fellow comrades, not only in the general humanitarian sense but also in more personal ways. Indeed I have argued that Sassoon's homosexual desires — and both "The Dug-Out" and "I Stood with the Dead" provide examples — can intensify his capacity for fellow-feeling, for brotherly solidarity with his men. Such feelings permeate his 1918 correspondence with Ottoline Morrell. Typically he confides: "O these men, they wring my heart! They make me *like* being at the war, because I don't want to be away from them. And then they get killed...." (Sassoon to Morrell, 16 May, 1918). But there are also less obviously subjective poems in which Sassoon suppresses his own reactions in order to concentrate on the voiceless victims of man's inhumanity to man. His haunting evocation of despair in "Died of Wounds," his sensitive portrait of the dying soldier in "The Death-Bed," these are intensely poignant moments. Sassoon's plea to his listeners, to "rouse him; you may save him yet," gives a tragic dimension to what Owen called a perfect piece of art. "Suicide in the Trenches," "Lamentations" and "In an Underground Dressing-Station" are harrowing pictures of the desolated victims of war.

Nor, it must be remembered, was Sassoon's solicitous gaze directed just at his own fusiliers: "Reconciliation" recognizes that everyone, even German mothers who have "nourished hatred harsh and blind," needs to be educated in the feelings, to show pity and concern for others. As the poetry attests, no one knew better than Sassoon that there were only Pyrrhic victories in war, only suffering combatants on the battlefield.

The nourishing of "hatred harsh and blind" towards the perpetrators of war was, on the other hand, something that the poet did assiduously cultivate. Perhaps the most frequently articulated criticism of his war verse is that it is too often motivated by and infused with anger, that it is consequently one-dimensional and partisan, that it savages "Blighty" values but puts little or nothing in their place. As early as 1918 the celebrated critic John Middleton Murry had declared that the poetry was unredeemed by any "triumph over experience," that it consistently conveyed a sense "that everything is irremediably and intolerably wrong" (*The Nation*, 13 July, 1918). Interestingly, Murry goes on to cite the opening of

"Counter-Attack" by way of illustration. Such a line of argument undoubtedly paved the way for a later generation of critics, but it is a thrust which has been more usually directed at the satires.

Thus George Parfitt, arguing that "ambivalence and a lack of analysis are central to Sassoon's satire," goes on to declare that "contempt and hatred are antagonistic, matching blindness with blindness." The contrasts, "usually between 'Trench' and 'Home' are too simplistic" he asserts, adding that "a satiric account which seeks to destroy Home totally (seeing all women as harlots, all fathers as secure in illusion) can only rely on Trench which isolates, corrupts and teaches violence" (Parfitt, 1990, p. 48). Parfitt seems to have taken his cue from Vivian de Sola Pinto, who felt that the satires possessed "passionate sincerity and honesty" but were "purely destructive," unable to create a myth to express the inner meaning of the conflict and the crisis of which it was a symptom (Pinto, 1936, p. 145). Admittedly, Parfitt has chosen his two examples well. I have argued elsewhere in this study that it is impossible to defend either a personal stereotype of women which amounts to misogyny, or a jaundiced perspective which is apparently incapable of seeing any virtue in an older male generation. The violent anger directed at "Yellow-Pressmen" in "Fight to a Finish" is not only sadistic, it reveals a poet prepared to abdicate all pretense of appearing to be democratic. Nor can "The Kiss," Parfitt's second example, be convincingly explained away, despite Sassoon's subsequent attempts, as a self-conscious exercise in irony.

But satire invariably runs the risk of painting black and white portraits, of over-simplifying issues. Indeed its epigrammatic mode invites the short sharp phrase, the vivid cameo, the "knock-out blow in the last line." Brevity is, we are told, the soul of wit. And if the victims do not choose to see themselves in the satirist's mirror, then the satirist can hardly be blamed for their myopia. Sassoon was trying, with admittedly limited success as a public propagandist, to expose the hypocrisy of "Blighty" attitudes; his aim was not to preach a doctrine of violence but to denounce those who allowed it to continue. "Scarlet majors," politicians, "gung-ho" bishops and the like were legitimate targets. He operated in a satiric tradition graced by Pope and Byron; it was, as Bergonzi reminds us, a much neglected poetic mode. Sassoon's epigrams, however splenetic, turned poetry back from the cul-de-sac of Georgian "lyrical introversion," injected it with some much-needed demotic vigor and gave back to poetry a "social purpose" (Bergonzi, 1965, p. 92).

In fact, the more usually accepted view is that Sassoon's epigrams, memorably described by their creator as "two or three harsh, peremptory, and colloquial stanzas with a knock-out blow in the last line" (SJ, p. 29), rank not only among his most significant achievements, but, on the considerable evidence of "They," Does It Matter," "Base Details," "Arms and the Man," and "The General," among the key poetic documents of the Great War. It is a view I would endorse. Bergonzi offers the following evaluation:

> On the whole Sassoon remained aware of his limitations and did not attempt a profundity that was beyond him: his gifts were, pre-eminently, those of a satirist, and it was in satire that he excelled; some of his epigrams have achieved a permanent status [*Ibid.*, p. 105].

There is still the sense here that satire is, "ipso facto," inferior, say, to the lyric, let alone the epic. Nonetheless the judgment is one that Thorpe endorses in the only book-length study of the poetry:

> The truth, as Sassoon presents it in his more characteristic satires, is hard and clear-cut. He had no doubt that he held a number of incontrovertible truths in his hands. He possessed the kind of certainty about this which is probably the satirist's essential attribute. For this reason, his most telling satires are short poems in which he says *one* thing with clarity and conciseness ... fierce contemptuous pieces, moments of hate that carry the reader with them at once [Thorpe, 1966, p. 22].

He continues:

> In showing the dreadfulness of the conflict, in its surface aspects, he preceded Owen and surpassed him and all English poets who had previously written of war. His satires have, quantitatively, greater bite than those of his fellow war poets and a sheer brutality of utterance that matches the reality [*Ibid.*, p. 26].

Oddly, though, Thorpe singles out for praise a handful of poems which he cherishes for a "moving directness and simplicity which eschews sentimentality ... or a morbid preoccupation with his own predicament." He cites, by way of illustration, "Two Hundred Years After," "The Hawthorn Tree," "The Dug-Out" and "Enemies," as well as, with some reservations, the longer descriptive pieces, "Concert Party" and "Night on the Convoy" (p. 32). For me, these verses are, with the notable exception of "The Dug-Out" (which incidentally narrowly "eschews sentimentality"), less effective precisely because they are less intensely conceived, occasional poems that lack the passion of the best satires and trench poems.

Sassoon's poetic instinct was in essence, lyrical. This predilection, at the heart of all his antebellum poetry, in part explains his frequent reversions to this lyrical-pastoral mode, and his preoccupation with short poems, especially of twelve, thirteen or fourteen lines. Indeed melody was not only a sought-after ingredient, it remained a necessary therapy. Talking of his early poetic effusions, Sassoon recalled that "Rich harmonies and lingering sonorities induced a relaxation of the nerves, and acted on me like soothing and stimulating oxygen" (WY, p. 111). Music and creativity went hand in hand: "Nothing magical has appeared — I lack music terribly," he confessed to Lady Ottoline Morrell from Craiglockhart (letter, 5 September, 1917). Such an authorial stance chimes with Pinto's observation that Sassoon believed that poetry should be musical, accessible and "written on some formal principle. He was in the tradition of the great Nineteenth Century nature poets"; his poetry was "conceived as the product of a craftsman who should work on traditional lines ... a pastime for the leisure of a governing class" (1939, p. 131).

Faced with the blundering cacophony of war, such traditions were inappropriate vehicles to express the shock of the new, to convey unimaginable experience or "unpoetic" emotions. Sassoon reacted in a number of ways. Some of his poetic strategies were not novel. Indeed, to give expression to his romantic and often lonely self, he returned to the mellifluous rhythms and homely landscapes of Georgian and earlier verse. Even when giving vent to his sense of outrage, and experimenting with colloquial language and sudden ironic twists, he cleaved to the octosyllabics, or more usually the decasyllabics, of his poetic antecedents. Only in a few and mainly later frontline pieces of reportage did Sassoon move away from traditional meters as well as drawing on imagery which veraciously depicted conditions.

Even then, there were unspeakable aspects of the conflict that Sassoon could not confront as, for example, Barbusse did: the stench of excrement and putrefaction and cordite, the rowdy behind-the-lines scenes in estaminet and brothel, the dismembered and rotting cadavers. These bulletins from the battlefield are a mixed bag. Part of the problem is that they often bring together, for purposes of dramatic contrast, pastoral elements and frontline impressions. The temptation is to overwork this technique, particularly when the poet lacks the inspiration of fresh material. Many of the poems composed at Craiglockhart and Limerick which attempt to recreate the atmosphere of the trenches counter its horrors with hackneyed pastoralisms, or simply lack the compelling visual imagery of a piece such as "Counter-Attack," which, though completed at "Dottyville," was based on the freshly recorded details of a post–Somme draft.

Johnston's 1964 book, the first full-length study of the poets of the Great War, offers a criticism of a different kind, directed at those documentary pieces which concentrate on the experiences of the trenches. Commenting on "Counter-Attack," which, in common with most critics, he foregrounds for its opening catalogue of "obscene details that ... shockingly summarize the war's undepicted horror," he nevertheless regrets an absence of narrative impulsion which he attributes to the poet's "obsessed mental state" (Johnston, 1964, pp. 96–7). In attempting "to depict the chaotic attempts of a British assault and an abortive enemy counter-attack," Johnston admits, the poem "powerfully conveys a sensation of irredeemable horror and confusion." But he is worried by the shift from "generalized narration to the consciousness of an individual soldier ... the action ends abruptly with the death of that soldier." In other words, Sassoon's poem exhibits "the fallacy of imitative form"; it fails to distinguish between "the haphazard continuity of actual experience and the progression demanded by the narrative mode" (p. 98). This seems to me a prejudicially formalist view. Indeed, one could argue that Sassoon is generally *too* preoccupied with formal considerations, that it is precisely when he captures this inchoate immediacy that his frontline poems come alive for the reader. As his friend Edmund Blunden observed, Sassoon, like Owen, "utterly grasped the terror of particular moments" (*Athenaeum*, 10 December, 1920, p. 807). In this regard, his discussions about poetic technique with Graves and then Owen at least encouraged *some* experimentation. If anything it is a pity Sassoon did not attempt more in this mode, and not just when dealing with the confusion of battle. "Repression of War Experience" carries conviction precisely because it captures the random interplay of reverie and conscious thought; "Dear Roberto," Sassoon's confessional verse epistle to Graves, a reflection of "nerves gone phut and failed," derives its quirky edge from its shifts of tone and mood, its fractured syntax, its Joycean telescopings. How better to express the "little inferno" of his tormented psyche. Silkin, who is generally sympathetic to Sassoon, argues — and T. S. Eliot makes the same point about our post–Jacobean divided sensibilities — that he "cannot feelingly think or reason sensuously. Thought and response suffer in isolation from each other, and the poem therefore suffers" (Silkin, 1972, p. 133). Silkin gives no examples to illustrate his assertion — it would, for instance, be less applicable to mixed-mode poems such as "To Any Dead Officer" — but it is not unrelated to Sassoon's singular distaste for metaphor. Writing in *The Weald of Youth* he remarked:

> I have always instinctively avoided the use of metaphors, except when they came uncalled-for. Indirect and allusive utterance has never been natural to me. I much prefer the poetry which I can visualise and feel to that which needs thinking out afterwards [WY, p. 112].

Owen's "The Show," with its plague-ridden vision of "No Man's Land," or poems such as "Miners" or "Anthem for Doomed Youth," replete with brilliantly sustained figurative tropes, seem to be outside Sassoon's remit. Though Murry's review does not put it in so many words, this lack of metaphor is at the heart of his criticism of the war verse. Quoting the striking lines, "The land where all / Is ruin and nothing blossoms but the sky," Murry asserts that the "last five words are beautiful because they do convey horror to the imagination, and do not bludgeon the senses" (*The Nation*, 13 July, 1918).

Of course poetry is not entirely dependent on figures of speech; while Sassoon's mastery of both "bloody" pun and oxymoron *is* frequently in evidence, the poet usually preferred the proven tactic of a direct assault on his readers' sensibilities. When he did resort to metaphor, it often seemed contrived: the "lifebelts" in the poem of that name, the bells metamorphosed into prelates in "Joy-Bells," the dragon epitomizing the spirit of war in "The Dragon and the Undying," the "poisoned birds" which now can contemplate "freedom" in "Everyone Sang." Yet Sassoon could not always deny the efficacy of the metaphorical trope. Though Graves disliked the comparison, the telephonic metaphor in "To Any Dead Officer" is crucial to the success of the poem. Interestingly, when the poet attempts to deny this associative process in "Repression of War Experience," it fails: books, candles, above all the fluttering moth insist on acquiring metaphorical resonances — to the benefit of the poem if not the poet. On this evidence at least, it is a matter for regret that Sassoon felt that such figures of speech might lessen his poetry's imaginative potency.

Adrian Caesar sees another potentially problematic area in the war poetry. His recent study argues that "Sassoon felt sacrificial love between comrades to be the principal positive of the war." It was only "in France that the aesthete and the sports man could happily co-exist ... where anxieties about his homosexuality could be allayed by 'manly heroism'" (Caesar, 1993, p. 90). Such a persuasive reading, though borne out by the autobiographical record, does not invalidate the poems qua poems. Indeed the tension was often a creative and fecundating one; an erotic energy does pervade certain poems, despite the poet's attempts to mask or sublimate such emotions. "Conscripts" would be a less complex poem without its homoerotic sub-text, and the best of the elegies to departed comrades have an intensity which transcends the conventions of mere friendship. On the distaff side, his homosexuality seems to have prompted a powerful strain of misogyny, all too visible in the verse, and a prudish abhorrence of (hetero)sexual activity, especially when indulged in by "old men" — another source of prejudice — who seem hell-bent on wearing out "their bodies with nasty sins" ("Repression of War Experience"). Moreover, and this is not an unrelated point, several early poems such as "The Redeemer" and "A Working Party," as well as such post-protest poems as "I Stood with the Dead," seem to sentimentalize the ordinary soldier; even to idealize him, to celebrate "an idea of manliness" which Caesar believes to be "inextricably bound up with military values" (Caesar, 1993, p. 82). Of course Sassoon did applaud "manliness": it not only possessed a strong personal appeal, it was a required attribute of the efficient frontline soldier. But there is almost nothing in the poetry written after the Somme which celebrates patriotic military values and a great deal that questions such attitudes.

Caesar goes on to argue that Sassoon's verses, "for all their supposedly anti-war feeling, in fact express ideas which excite young and unwary readers and covertly support war by providing positive consolations based on the idea that suffering is good" (p. 98). It is certainly the case that Sassoon sought to expunge a sense of guilt engendered both by his homosexual feelings and his extended "Blighty" remissions by partaking in the shared experience of frontline suffering. That many of the poems which espouse such a view are post–Craiglockhart pieces indicates, if nothing else, the impact of his discussions with Rivers. But if there are a number of moments in both the letters and the verse, especially after his cathartic protest, when he yearns for the "bloodbrotherhood" of the trenches, the overwhelming impact of the poetry is one of unmitigated horror at what war can inflict. To want to *share* the burden of pain is not the same as saying that "suffering is good."

In fairness to him, Sassoon was too immersed in events to be able to adopt an oracular position with any consistency: his Mercutio-like temperament could induce wild fluctuations of feeling and attitude in the verse. He subsequently maintained that he hated poetry of ideas anyway, and never presumed to provide an objective or balanced account of the conflict. On the other hand, he was convinced that the most effective way of offering a personal critique of the war was by describing actual conditions and by satirizing those groups and individuals who refused to accept their existence.

It is probably the case that Sassoon's lack of interest in complex ideas, in the subtler issues of the war and its aftermath, or at least in the belief that they could be transmuted into poetry, is what prevents him from making a more visionary response. He is less preoccupied than Owen with what Blunden rightly called the "war's effect on the spirit of man" ("The Real War," *Athenaeum*, 10 December, 1920, p. 807). While "Enemies," with its Dantesque vision of "a queer sunless place," anticipates the ghostly confrontations of "Strange Meeting," it stops short of Owen's bardic prophecy of an insistent "trek from progress." Similarly, there is no poem like "The Show" with its omniscient vision of a conflict in all its "Protozoic obscenity" (*Ibid.*). In two poems which do view the Great War from a future perspective, "Two Hundred Years After" and "Song Books of the War," only in one line, "to cleanse the world of guilt," does Sassoon attempt an oracular pronouncement about the conflict and its likely impact on events yet to come.

Judgments will continue to be made about the merits and demerits of Sassoon's war verse, but the poet was insistent about one thing—that his verse was an exploration of self, a record of his progress as man and artist. Talking late in life to Felicitas Corrigan, he declared:

> My real biography is in my poetry. All the sequence of my development is there. For me, it is the only thing that matters, and was my only path in the bewilderments and inconsistencies of existence [Corrigan, 1973, p. 15].

Sassoon was, of course, referring to a creative life which, as far as he was concerned, had only fully "developed" after his conversion to Roman Catholicism. But his *accelerated* growth as a poet occurred in those four intense years from 1915 to 1918. The artistic evidence provides irrefutable evidence of that. Admittedly he can, without warning, revert to a mannered pastoralism. For while one response to the Armageddon of the trenches is to savage those unwilling to face up to its realities, another, understandably, is to repress its horrors, to escape to an Edenic world ("Invocation"), or to seek refuge in a romantic vision of a war ennobled by mutual suffering ("Reward"). But the poet's progress is, despite these Mercutio-like shifts, tangible enough. Temperamentally opposed to the unpoetic in any shape or form, Sassoon nevertheless succeeded in repressing these antipathies: he captured not only the trench-speak of the trooper but the "Blighty-speak" of bishops, "little mothers" and retired colonels, confronted recalcitrant subject matter in his satires, and, far from repressing all his "war experience," produced, in a handful of post–Somme trench pieces, images altogether more harrowing than anything yet produced by the circumstance of trench warfare.

Without question Sassoon is one of the two great English poets of World War One. Like Owen, Sorley, Blunden and Rosenberg, he had, in Hemingway's phrase, "been there"; severely mauled, like his friend Graves, he was fortunate enough to survive the experience. In comparison with Owen, whose war started later and ended tragically just before the Armistice, Sassoon wrote much more — 150 poems or so — about the conflict. Less experimental than Owen, he nonetheless essayed a number of different manners; styles that veer from romantic, even confessional, to Augustan and aphoristic. Indeed, his best efforts are not restricted to one mode. The outstanding verse satirist of the war — and that despite the frequently-leveled charge that his tone of voice is too strident — Sassoon left several trench-poems of the first rank, of which "Counter-Attack" and "The Rear-Guard" are the most successful. As Edmund Blunden asserts: "It was his triumph to be the first man who ever described war fully and exactly; and had description been all that he did, the feat would have been distinguished" (Blunden, 1930, p. 20).

But Sassoon did much more than document conditions in the trenches. He also composed a number of deeply moving elegiac pieces — for example, "To Any Dead Officer," "Died of Wounds" and "The Death-Bed" — and some genuinely innovative poems which have received much less than their proper due. Of these, "Repression of War Experience" is a "tour de force," and "Dear Roberto," rightly dubbed by Graves "the most terrible" of Sassoon's war poems, powerfully encapsulates a whole gamut of conflicting emotions. Preoccupied with war's mental accumulations as well as its physical manifestations, Sassoon was concerned to chart its impact on other men's minds as well as his own. It cannot be denied that Owen's poetry has, at its best, a brooding tragic sense and "an emotional depth" — his friend's words — that is less evident in Sassoon's verse (SJ, p. 62). On the evidence of such pieces as "Futility," "Dulce et Decorum Est," "Spring Offensive," "The Show," "The Parable of the Old Man and the Young," "Apologia pro Poemate Meo," and "Strange Meeting," there is both a sensuousness of language and a mythic awareness, a large-scale vision of catastrophe that is more-or-less absent from Sassoon's verse. On the other hand Sassoon, who must take much of the credit for inspiring Owen's extraordinary burst of creative activity, was already taking war poetry off in directions it had never gone before; if the old antebellum mannerisms occasionally returned, the main direction of the verse was towards "a mood of anti-heroic revolt," expressed with such "fervour and harsh wit" that it struck "a new and incisive note in the literature of war" (Bergonzi, p. 107). It is these satires, along with the best of the bulletins from the battlefield and the empathetic elegies to the victims of the conflict, that ensure Sassoon's preeminent place in the pantheon of First World War poets. In bidding "Goodbye to Galahad" after the Somme, Sassoon opened the dug-out door to the poet of modern war.

Part Two

Chapter 8

1915–1916: "War Is Our Scourge; Yet War Has Made Us Wise"

Between 3 August, 1914, when Sassoon enlisted as a cavalry trooper in the Sussex Yeomanry and the bombardment that announced the Somme campaign almost two years later, Sassoon composed about 20 war poems (from "Absolution" to "Before the Battle"), three of which appeared only in the notebooks ("The Quarter-Master," "Peace," "The Giant-Killer"). For a quarter of this period, from October to April of 1915, Sassoon was convalescing at home, victim of his own impetuosity when he had tried to jump a blind fence and been rolled on by his horse. In *Siegfried's Journey*, he describes this period of enforced physical inactivity:

> I experienced a continuous poetic afflatus, of which I took the fullest advantage, regarding it — not unnaturally — as my final chance of being visited by the Muse. This productiveness had indeed been almost like a recovery of the vernal raptures of my juvenilia, but I had been conscious of a newly-acquired technical control, while pervaded by an exultant sense of verbal freshness [SJ, p. 17].

Sassoon's "main performance had been a poem of nearly two hundred blank verse lines ... vigorously impersonating an old huntsman remembering better days..." (*Ibid.*). The poem was "The Old Huntsman," later to become the title piece of Sassoon's first major collection. Containing a number of "war-oblivious lyrical pieces" (*Ibid.*), the volume would also feature many of the early frontline poems when it finally appeared in May 1917. "The Old Huntsman" is assuredly *not* a poem about war — Sassoon had as yet no experience of it — so it does not merit detailed discussion here. Suffice to say that the speaker, an old whipper-in, now "old and bald and serious-minded," contemplates, like Wordsworth's Simon Lee, the adventures of his long-departed youth. In *Amyntas*, the aesthetic and homoerotic side of Sassoon's nature had been foregrounded; here the old man, recalling the checkered events of his sporting past, mirrors the sporting element in Sassoon's personality. Like Sassoon, he regrets his earlier imperviousness to the delights of vernal woods; his obsession with hunting has rendered him blind and deaf to the inspiring sights and sounds of nature. More ominously, he now relives a recurrent nightmare from his youth, in which Hell, "thick with captains," was "the coldest scenting land" he'd known. As Thorpe persuasively attests:

> In this brief respite before going to war, Sassoon realised his dilemma — that he was a man potentially of both worlds who had so far cast himself only in one: as in the old huntsman there is a mixture of coarseness and unsatisfied sensitivity, so in him it seems that only the less significant side has had full scope — and now the other may never do so [Thorpe, 1966, p. 14].

Absolution

After this "continuous poetic afflatus" which had produced "The Old Huntsman" and a "dozen war-oblivious lyrical pieces" (SJ, p. 17), Sassoon, now recovered from his broken arm, was sent to Litherland for officer training with the Royal Welch Fusiliers, where, he recollected:

> While learning to be a second lieutenant, I was unable to write anything at all, with the exception of a short poem called "Absolution," manifestly influenced by Rupert Brooke's famous sonnet sequence. The significance of my too nobly worded lines was that they expressed the typical self-glorifying feelings of a young man about to go to the Front for the first time. The poem subsequently found favour with middle-aged reviewers, but the more I saw of war the less noble-minded I felt about it [SJ, p. 17].

The admission is candid but scarcely surprising. Sassoon found nothing at Litherland to write about, or at least nothing tailor-made for his brand of poetry. The best he could do in response to a remote conflict — since he did not want to write, as poets in World War Two would, about the "bullshit" of training camps — was to offer a pastiche of Brooke, a poet now so famous that his sonnet "The Soldier" had been read out in St. Paul's by Dean Inge on Easter Sunday. What Sassoon's poem does show is the pervasiveness of an earlier tradition of prophylactic war verse and, in particular, of Brooke's sonnets. Specifically, "Absolution" echoes the rhythms, cadences and sentiments of "Safety"; the caesural pause and antithesis of "War is our scourge; yet war has made us wise" recalls the celebrated Brookean paradox of "safe where all safety's lost; safe where men fall." The Georgian personification of "Time's but a golden wind" is a device similarly employed in "Safety"; the conviction that the negative emotions of "Horror of wounds and anger at the foe … all these must pass" echoes the throw-away message "But only agony, and that has ending of "Peace."

The sentiments are those of happy warriorism ("we are the happy legion"), of kindred spirits united in a common cause that will ennoble a world in which pain and anger will prove only transient obstacles in the progress to heavenly grace. It is easy to pour scorn on such piety. Silkin, for example, attacks encomiastic poems such as "Absolution" that apostrophize war as "the agent of nobility" and espouse the outmoded "paradox" of "life-through-death" (Silkin, 1972, p. 134). Nonetheless, we should remember that Brooke, through the very expression of these views in verse, had already achieved a kind of immortality. Whether Sassoon had completed the early version of "Absolution" before hearing of Brooke's death at sea on 23 April is a matter for speculation. Certainly his enthusiasm for Brooke's poetry was never more fervent. He wrote in his diary: "Rupert Brooke was miraculously right when he said 'Safe shall be my going, Secretly armed against all death's endeavour; Safe though all safety's lost.' He described the true soldier spirit — saint and hero like Norman Donaldson and thousands of others who have been killed and died happier than they lived" (*Diaries*, 1 April, p. 52).

Adrian Caesar offers a revisionist reading of the opening verse. It is, in his view, an early illustration of Sassoon's belief that war will be the harbinger of a "beauty" that will absolve sexual guilt. He sees in war's "scourge," "which is going to make us free," the promptings of a masochistic belief that "the sufferings of war will absolve the soldier" (Caesar, 1993, p. 68). While this preoccupation with brotherly suffering will surface again, and especially in the post-protest verse, we should remember that the main impulse behind this poem is Brooke, not Sassoon. The poet's later reaction to the poem provided a different emphasis. While he recognized the ephemeral nature of such feelings ("people used to feel like this when they 'joined up' in 1914 and 1915. No one feels like it when they go out again"), he also recognized that the poem anticipated the human capacity for irrational nostalgia, the queer craving for "good old times at Givenchy," adding, "But there will always be 'good old times,' even for people promoted from Inferno to Paradise!" (WP, p. 15).

The Redeemer

"To My Brother" was Sassoon's first poem to be composed in France, but as yet he had seen no action. Nonetheless, as his diary attests, he was all too aware that "Armageddon" was "going on" all around him. "The Redeemer," the second product of Sassoon's war, was, as the poet stated retrospectively, "my first frontline poem." Originally composed in the last week of November ("inspired by working-parties at Festubert, Nov. 25 and 27"), it was "revised and re-written March 1916...." (WP, p. 17).

His first bulletin from the battlefield, "The Redeemer" is a key poetic document. While some of the realized details which render the poem so different from "Absolution" were only incorporated in the final version, its authenticity and power derive from first-hand observation. There are clear intimations of the mature Sassoon manner: in particular the steady effacement of poetic diction for an utterance which begins to reflect the facts of trench experience. Here a blackness, experienced both physically and mentally, dominates: images of "clay-sucked boots," "blanching flare" and "floundering in mirk" convey the grim business of "inhuman forms going to and from inhuman tasks" (*Diaries*, 27 November, 1915, p. 20). The diary is now a quarry to be mined in the cause of poetry; the metaphor of the "windowed sky" probably derives from the same entry where "The moon shines through matchwood skeleton rafters of roofs." There are further characteristic moments in the poem: the contrast between life in the trenches and a land "when peaceful folk in beds lay snug asleep," the unexpected shaft of irony ("the distant wink of a huge gun"), the Sassoonesque intimation of a Christian salvation only occasionally glimpsed in "Hell's unholy shine."

Moreover the terse and ironic conclusion, couched in the direct speech of an ordinary soldier's expletive, sees Sassoon's verse partaking, for the first time, of a poetic strategy that will become a hallmark of the trench verse. Yet the bathos of the soldier's curse, "O Christ Almighty, now I'm stuck!" is rendered all the more effective because it contrasts with the unlike visionary experience that is at the heart of the poem (and which the relevant notebook entry makes nothing of). For the "Redeemer" of the title conflates two separate memories: one, where the men, Christ-like, carry "hurdles up the communication-trenches about three-quarters of a mile" (*Diaries*, 25 November, p. 20); two (and the reference to "Lancaster on Lune" would seem to confirm this), his servant Molyneux (Flook in the *Memoirs)* "who had been a railway signalman in Lancashire," and who, on a subsequent occasion, "blundered in at the door with a huge sack of firewood, which he dropped on the tiled floor with a gasp of relief" (*Memoirs*, p. 254). That the poem was rewritten on 16 March allows the poet to amalgamate these two memories. The recognition of Christ-like qualities in his suffering, burdened and doomed men, of the ennobling power of sacrifice, was not a poetic stance peculiar to Sassoon. The sacrificial theme, already invested with homoerotic implications, is found elsewhere in the literature of the war. Sassoon's friend and fellow poet, Robert Nichols, now forgotten but the most popular during the later phases of the conflict, wrote of "the soldier's cup of anguish, blood and gall" and of men whose "feet, hands and side / Must soon be torn, pierced, crucified" ("Battery Moving Up to a New Position from Rest Camp: Dawn"); and Owen, in a justly famous letter, would write movingly of his recruits: "Teaching Christ to lift his cross by numbers.... With a piece of silver I buy him every day, and with maps I make him familiar with the topography of Golgotha" (Owen, *Letters*, p. 562).

The poem has its detractors. Sassoon's verses have been described, by Caesar, as "both condescending and sentimental," the product of an upper-class view that presumes that his hero is "simple," "unjudging" and "content to die." Without doubt there is some idealization here and perhaps, as Caesar suggests, an undue emphasis on passivity: "volunteers are not merely enduring suffering, but also likely to be causing it as well" (Caesar, 1993, p. 71). Nonetheless the intensity and surprise created by the symbolism give the poem real dramatic force, particularly at the epiphanic moment of recognition, captured in the arresting spondaics of "I say that He was Christ." That Sassoon is also able to sustain the analogy by denying any straining at biblical coincidence — "No thorny crown, only a woollen cap"— and by envisaging the inevitable suffering of this soldier-Christ, blessed only with his savior's concern for others, reflects a compassionate progress.

To My Brother

Of the 35 poems on the subject of war in *The Old Huntsman*, about a third are written in a spirit of modern knightliness. But the sustenance of these emotions, however infectious on the evidence of the *Memoirs* where, as Sassoon reflected later, "war-weariness had not yet been heard of" in May 1915 (p. 236), was soon to be tested by shattering tidings, the news of his brother Hamo's death in battle. Originally entitled "Brothers" (that he retained the deliberate impersonality of the title on initial publication is instructive), and included in his diary as the solitary 18 December entry, Sassoon's verses constitute the only poetic acknowledgment of his brother's demise. They were first published two months later in *The Saturday Review* of 26 February, 1916.

By a curious irony, both Hamo Sassoon and Rupert Brooke perished in the Gallipoli campaign, but this Brookean piece makes no reference to a tragic coincidence that Sassoon was probably as yet unaware of. The homage to current literary values is evidenced by what Thorpe accurately identifies as a tone of "sombre exaltation" (Thorpe, 1966, p. 16) in lines which, by suggesting the cathartic effects of heroic sacrifice, recall Brooke's 1914 sonnets, and in the epithet "laurelled head" the impact of Sassoon's undiminished enthusiasm for Housman's "To an Athlete Dying Young." Grief is here distanced, rendered remote by literary convention. Now his brother is in the company of "ghosts of soldiers dead," but his ennobling death constitutes a victory that will encourage the soldier-poet to continue to fight the good fight.

The Prince of Wounds

"The Prince of Wounds," the last poem Sassoon wrote in 1915, returns to the same theme of Christian sacrifice that he had exploited poignantly, if sentimentally, in "The Redeemer." At first Christ promises to be a reassuring presence, a reminder that suffering ennobles the sufferer. But the poem takes a didactic turn as the speaker questions the point of renouncing those proven favorites, "music and colour and delight," for an atoning death on "warfare's altar" and wonders whether a Christ who can allow the "Spirit of Destruction" a pointless triumph on the bloody battlefield is anything more than an unfeeling effigy of "wood and stone." This is a theme memorably explored by Wilfred Owen in "The Parable of the Old Man and the Young," where Abraham's imminent sacrifice of his son, stayed by the hand of a benevolent God in the biblical version, is contrasted with the mindless slaying of "half the seed of Europe, one by one" by the old men of the war.

For some reason Sassoon omitted "The Prince of Wounds" from all published collections of his verse. It is a slight enough piece — the line "Guarding immitigable loss" is a horror — but perhaps the exhortation that "we ... can no longer worship Christ" was considered too sacrilegious to be risked on an Anglican establishment. In 1915 such advocacy more than hinted at an irreligious stance that Sassoon was not yet publicly prepared to divulge.

A Testament

"A Testament," written a mere five days after "The Prince of Wounds," again explores the idea of sacrifice in battle, and shows Sassoon wrestling with its moral and spiritual implications. For here the bitter conclusion of the earlier poem is replaced by a tone that is elegiac and exultant by turns, a reminder that when Sassoon reminisces about an Edenic pre-war England, he is still, early in 1916, all too capable of reverting to the worst excesses of an overwrought manner. Yet the immediate inspiration for the poem was not English but French, a deserted château that he had passed on one of his rural rides at Montagne (the poem was written there on 1 January, 1916):

> I would pass a grey-roofed château with its many windows and no face there to watch me pass. Only a bronze lion guarding the well in the middle of an overgrown lawn and the whole place forlorn and deserted.... But even then it wasn't easy to think of dying [*Memoi*rs, p. 255–6].

Such a vision of dereliction and loss probably rekindled memories of his childhood at Weirleigh and another "house that once was full of songs." Three weeks earlier Sassoon had recreated that idyllic atmosphere in sonorous prose:

> Lovely now seem the summer dawns in Weirleigh garden. Lovely the slow music of the dusk, and the chords of the piano-music. Loveliest of all, the delight of weaving words into verses; the building of dream on dream; Oh the flowers and the songs now so far away. The certainty of my power to touch the hearts of men with poetry — all faded now like a glorious sky.... Goodbye to life, good-bye to Sussex [*Diaries*, 17 December, p. 26].

Two disparate experiences, one recent and troubled, the other affectionately recollected, appear to coalesce in the poem. For the theme is death and in particular the poet's anticipated end. The nostalgic vision of a lost rural innocence recalls a tradition of minor Romantic verse, perhaps more paradigmatically expressed in Thomas Hood's "I Remember, I Remember," but the overriding conviction that the artist's death will come all too soon and "when all my store cries for completion" echoes Keats's early sonnet, "When I Have Fears That I May Cease to Be," and in particular the line, "Before my pen has gleaned my teeming brain." That this was inevitably a common feeling among soldier-poets is borne out by Graves's poem, "The Shadow of Death," also written in 1916, in which he alludes to "my songs never sung / And my plays to darkness blown!" Memories of a fulfilled boyhood where the aspirant writer's "home was safe among the slender trees" both heighten the sense of impending loss and furnish the soon-to-be-silenced poet with an uncharacteristic metaphor of self ("Hushed is the house that once was full of songs").

The "forlorn château at Montagne," the "cold" days to come at Weirleigh, these sad premonitions of loss, remind the poet of the approach of a "tempest" that, like a bird of prey, "stoops to bear me hence." The masochistic note is not sustained, the verses end on a positive note in which personal fears are subsumed in the pantheistic vision of a greater good. In a hymn-like conclusion, Sassoon asserts his kinship with the "triumphant dead," with the enduring forces of nature, and echoes the Brookean platitude that individual sacrifice will be crowned with collective victory.

This is not a poem that has attracted much attention. Indeed, Sassoon omitted it from the *Collected Poems* and it was left to Rupert Hart-Davis to rescue it from oblivion. It is, on the face of it, a conventional trumpet piece and, on the evidence of the odd three-line second stanza and the clumsy rhythms of line two, probably never completed to the writer's satisfaction. Nonetheless, in its blend of recent experience, past recollections and Keatsian feeling, it casts a revealing light both on Sassoon's poetic strategies and on his literary progenitors. On a personal level it also reveals the tension between the artistic self, luxuriating in life and the soldier anxious to be embroiled in the annihilating storms of battle. Nonetheless, it is the public persona of a poet conscious of the demands of his early 1916 readers that informs the verses.

To Victory

If the conclusion to "A Testament" panders to public sentiment, the whole of "To Victory," written a mere four days later and dedicated to Edmund Gosse, echoes his oracular friend's preference for "idealised soldier-poems when first-hand evidence was forthcoming from the Front" (SJ, p. 28). Sassoon clearly had both Gosse and a wider audience in mind; the poem was dispatched to *The Times* and, stage-managed by Gosse, printed anonymously in the edition of 15 January, 1916. There it was read by Lady Ottoline Morrell. She felt sufficiently moved to write to the poet. Thus began a friendship which would be of enormous benefit to Sassoon, especially during the troubled months before and after his "Protest" against the prolongation of the conflict.

Such biographical matters give the poem an importance hardly merited on artistic grounds. It is, above all, an exercise in tone poetry composed for a sentimental reader, a painterly effort in which the gardens, which are not only burgeoning and colorful but also eroticized in "spires of green / Rising in young-limbed copse," are contrasted with the denatured world of the trenches where the only noise is that of "angry guns," where the red of "living roses" now stains the bodies of "men slain." The Swinburne-like anapests of the final stanza return the poet to a consolatory world of harmony and "brightness," to a pastoral paradise replete with "blossom" and the compensations of a "blithe wind" now imbued with the "uplifted voice" of the poet.

In the Pink

Sassoon was aware that "In the Pink" broke new ground. Just how new can be adduced by comparing it with his previous piece, "To Victory." It is surprising that they come from the same pen; that they were written only five weeks apart is a measure of Sassoon's fluctuating attitudes towards poetry and the war. Admittedly he had now encountered Graves, the most significant flesh and blood artistic influence on him at the Front, and though initially he did not approve of this "defier of convention" (*Diaries*, 23 November, p. 21), his down to earth approach to life and poetry was already beginning to rub off on the older man. Looking back, Sassoon remembered "In the Pink" as the "first of my outspoken war poems":

> I wrote it one cold morning at Morlancourt, sitting by the fire in the Quartermaster's billet, while our Machine-Gun officer shivered in his blankets on the floor. He was suffering from alcoholic poisoning and cold feet, and shortly afterwards departed for England, never to return. Needless to say, the verses do not refer to him but to some typical Welshman who probably got killed on the Somme in July, after months and months of a dog's life and no leave. The *Westminster* refused the poem, as they thought it might prejudice recruiting!! [WP, p. 22].

Outspoken the poem certainly is. Even so, Sassoon is careful not to sail too close to the actual circumstances. Reference to alcoholics at the Front would not have gone down well in "Blighty" and would have lessened the impact of the piece. Instead, and for the first time in verse, Sassoon is able to empathize with the plight of the ordinary soldier and to do so in a colloquial language that, while sanitized, does begin to approximate the slangy "argot" of the trenches. The soldier has the first hopeful and last hopeless word ("he don't know why"); it is the trooper's simple recollections of home that the poet endeavors to recreate. As in "The Redeemer," the enterprise is not entirely convincing: the picture of "brown-eyed Gwen" is stereotypical, and the reference to the simple, silly things she liked to hear," early evidence of Sassoon's dismissive attitude towards women. Nor is the poet yet able to give full vent to what Rivers would describe as the soldiers' "picturesque" or "sulphurous language" (1923 passim); while Davies can write and reflect in his own way, the working-class soldier is not yet allowed to swear and curse out loud. But the poem does achieve a convincing verisimilitude: here, in imagery that echoes "The Redeemer," one can envisage the sheer physicality of "stodgy clay and freezing sludge," and remark the irony inherent in the ordinary soldier's attitude, at once keen to soothe anxieties at home and uncomprehending of the terrible violence that is being done to him. For the first time, the contrast between a bucolic past of innocent "Sundays at the farm" and the horrid exigencies of the present are conveyed, not through the subjective vision of the officer-poet, but by the homespun words of a Welch Fusilier.

The Dragon and the Undying

Though the element of comparison and contrast is a key structural device in most of his war poems, Sassoon's poetic touch turns rarely to figurative language. However, in "The Dragon and the Undying," his second February 1916 effort, he cannot resist the temptation: the dragon, who has replaced the more abstract "Spirit of Destruction" of "The Prince of Wounds," becomes a metaphor for a war machine hell-bent not on breaking limbs but on annihilating traditional sanctities, lusting to "break the loveliness of spires / And hurl their martyred music toppling down." The counterpoint of the second stanza offers the now familiar pantheistic response where, in a rare extended metaphor that in part anticipates the imagery of Owen's "Anthem for Doomed Youth"—a poem that will bear a Sassoonesque imprint—the "homeless slain" leave their visual impress both on night ("planets are their eyes") and day in the pathetic fallacy of "dawn-lit trees, with arms up-flung," a figurative trope that has more than a hint of homoerotic longing.

The poem provoked varied reactions at the time. In *The Atheneum*, the reviewer, apparently fixated on traditional versification, inquired why the writer bothered to compose "fourteen line iambic decasyllabics ... without investing them with the gracious form of the sonnet" (Thorpe, 1966, p. 16n). On the other hand, Sassoon's new poet-comrade Graves wrote in a May letter that "the dragon one ... was very nice in the middle" (letter from Graves to Sassoon, May 1916, IBI, p. 49).

Golgotha

The preoccupation with the mythic dimension of war reasserts itself in the next poem where the trenches, for the first time, are likened to Golgotha (the Aramaic word for "the place of Skulls"). The piece appears to have been written in response to protracted broodings about the death of loved ones (brother Hamo and "Tracker" Richardson are both mentioned by name in journal entries at this time) and, above all the 19 March death of David Thomas, a personal catastrophe baldly alluded to — "And Tommy's dead" — in his 27 March diary entry. The atmosphere at the Front, an objective correlative to Sassoon's own desolate mood, does nothing to assuage the overwhelming sense of loss: its manifestations are of a "sky ... pitch-black with pale blots ... when the flares went up beyond the hill the sky was inky at the edge" and of a "gloomy" ground relieved only by "sandbags bleached and weather-worn."

The personal elegiac note is reinforced by the nocturnal visions of battle: even the sounds — "mimic thunder" and "mirthless laughter" — seem somehow hellish, a reminder that this was, as he later remembered, "a place ... like the end of the world" (WP, p. 24). In such a Hell, only the resourceful can expect to survive; in a characteristic "volte-face" in the last line, Sassoon observes the "nimble scavengers." In this atmosphere redolent of death and decay, only the rats thrive.

A Subaltern

If the "unmentionable odour of death" (W.H. Auden, "September 1st, 1939") hovers above "Golgotha," in "A Subaltern" it carries specific resonances. The author's note (WP, p. 25) is self-explanatory: "D.C. Thomas, killed on March 18. I wrote this about ten days before when he'd been telling me how my sage advice had helped him along." While "The Last Meeting" and "A Letter Home," both written in May, are more substantial and considered pieces to "Tommy," this sonnet records, in ways that "To My Brother" does not, a sense of personal kinship with a frontline mate which the poem's impersonal title (*c.f.* "To Any Dead Officer"), its light-hearted banter and deliberate refusal to sentimentalize the portrait, barely conceals. The self-deprecating admission of the final couplet, which echoes the poet's own unassuming reference to his "stale philosophies," is a characteristic Sassoon ploy for defusing the intensity of a recollection that might tip over into sentimentality. The colloquial last word is soldier David's:

> "Good God!" he laughed, and slowly filled his pipe,
> Wondering "why he always talks such tripe."

The sonnet, typically framed around the tension between a bucolic past and denatured present, shows Sassoon veering between the poles of two poetic manners: the first, with its allusion to "summer days" to "twenty runs to make, and last man in," is a clear echo of Newbolt's "Vitai Lampada," and recalls the nostalgic tone of much pre-war verse; the second, closer to the authentic voice of the trench poet, draws both on the lived experience of "squeaking rats that scampered across the slime" and on the slangy idioms of the Front.

The Quarter-Master

Another vignette of a fellow officer of a very different breed followed a week later. In his diary for 16 March, Sassoon recorded the gist of a conversation between his transport officer and quarter-master. It did not pull any punches. Castigating "the selfish hogs" back in England, the T.O. accused them of "clinging to their old easy ways of life ... reading the war-news and sucking in all the fabrications that suit their hopes of a speedy end to it, and hell and extinction to the Huns." The Q.M. agreed, "They're the b — — rs I'm after!" and added that the war was being carried on by "the blue-blooded upper ten and the crowd that some silly b — — r called the 'the submerged tenth,'" with "all the others ... making what they can out of it and shirking the dirty work" (*Diaries*, 16 March, p. 43).

Such battle-hardened attitudes were too indelicate for Sassoon's poetic persona in March 1916, but before long these "shirkers" at home would become sitting targets for his satire. For the moment the encounter produced a verse cameo of the quarter-master with a scarlet face "to match his breast of medals." But there is much affection in the portrait. It reflects both Sassoon's genuine personal admiration for Joe Cottrill, Q.M. with the First Battalion and the subject of the cameo, and his growing sense of identification with such frontline attitudes. Here is a career soldier who lives for his battalion and who does his bit to ensure the men's well-being, a plain-speaking man who hates "humbugs" and who, despite his rank of captain, still retains the common touch that Sassoon so valued and sought to emulate. There is even an odd absence of irony in the observation that he recruits in "swarming cities" and offers "fresh fortune and freedom from injustice" to his volunteers. That of course was a practice that the poet would soon enough realize was deeply suspect. Indeed the final stanza barely avoids sentimentality as the poet, hoping — and not for the last time — to be accepted as one of the "roaring lads," craves an emotional kinship with a fellow captain who, on the face of it, shares his rank and little else. He concludes: "It's meeting men like him that makes me glad."

A Working Party

On the substantial evidence of "A Working Party" and it is his longest war poem to date, Sassoon's verse is getting ever closer to the grisly facts of a campaign that is now numbingly cold as well as murderous; exposure in the trenches is providing a constant reminder of the unremitting nature of individual pain and suffering. The poem — littered, like Owen's "Dulce et Decorum Est," with deliberately clumsy verbs — is set against the shadowy world of what Patrick Quinn appositely calls "blurred images" and "disembodied voices" (Quinn, 1993, p. 173), as soldiers grope towards the front line under cover of darkness. It is still primarily a vision of sucking mud and aching cold rather than a world, as yet unimagined, of putrefying bodies.

A comparison of the verses with the diary jottings of the time again offers an insight into Sassoon's working methods. Hardly the product of "emotion recollected in tranquillity," the poem nonetheless draws heavily on prose accounts written two or three days earlier, which refer to the paraphernalia of an increasingly impersonal conflict. The image of "glimmering sandbags, bleached with rain," recalls the entry of 28 March in which Sassoon describes "a silver glimpse of mounded sandbags bleached and weather-worn" (*Diaries*, 28 March, p. 47), the "little weasel" of the prose account is metamorphosed into a "nimble rat" (the third successive poem in which rats appear), and the imagery of "frowsty ... fumes of coke" and "snoring weary men" of the penultimate stanza recalls the 27 March journal reference to "the gloom of the steel dug-out, like being inside a boiler" (*Diaries*, p. 46).

As a quarry these detailed prose recollections are obviously invaluable. But if much of the poem's authentic power stems from its felt experience, painfully recreated, the drama of the piece resides in its singular human dimension — the unsentimental account of the "civvy" life of a Midland soldier, a thoroughly "decent chap" now bizarrely reduced to a "jolting lump" "beyond all tenderness and care." Through the accumulation of such details, the poem foregrounds and dramatizes an unsung human tragedy in ways in which the diaries rarely do. Clearly it allows fuller expression to what was very much on Sassoon's mind: the death of David Thomas twelve days before and the unbearable sense of loss it engendered. That loss, the sorrow and impotent rage it triggered off, and the actual physical sensation of being shot in the head as Thomas was, and as Sassoon increasingly felt he would be, are feelings that the poem attempts to confront.

Peace

"A Working Party" produced one kind of reaction to the war; "Peace," written two days on, quite another. Sassoon was still experiencing, as he was all too aware, almost daily fluctuations in his attitude towards the war. After the realistic treatment of the previous piece, "Peace" opens lyrically, as befits its Brooke-like title, with elevated thoughts of peace, of an "anger grown tired of hate." But Sassoon was still smarting with righteous fury at the death of David Thomas, as his diary reveals:

Now I've known love for Bobbie and Tommy and grief for Hamo and Tommy, and hate has come also, and the lust to kill. Rupert Brooke was miraculously right when he said "Safe shall be my going, Secretly armed against all death's endeavour; Safe though all safety's lost...." He described the true soldier spirit ... thousands ... who have been killed and died happier than they lived [*Diaries*, 1 April, p. 52].

The reference to Brooke's poetry is more than coincidental. Sassoon's poem seeks identification not only with the concluding warrior-like sentiments of Brooke's "Peace" but also with "Safety," another sonnet in the sequence, where death is viewed not only as an inevitable consequence of the heroic gesture, but actively sought. Death and peace are synonymous; in the punning "stoop to me like a lover when the fight is done" ("stoop" implies both tenderness and the predatory descent of a falcon), Sassoon seeks a peace that death in battle alone can provide. Only in the contrasting middle stanza, where war is seen as a site of bleeding, maimed bodies and where his anger surfaces in the shape of "bitter lust" that "chuckles within me unashamed," does Sassoon move out of the shadow of Brooke and come close to finding an individual voice. Unsurprisingly the poem's unbridled ferocity was not something Sassoon was ready to commit to the public gaze; the poem stayed within the pages of the diary.

The Giant-Killer

"The Giant-Killer," part of a notebook entry for 14 April, deals with the altogether less painful topic of Sassoon's general attitude towards the war. It is one of a number of poems — "The Poet as Hero" will show the process significantly advanced — which explore his changing perceptions about the conflict and its outcome. The poem's fairy-tale treatment was probably inspired by Graves — Sassoon had already read a number of his whimsical poems in manuscript — and the theme recalls "Goliath and David," a piece written by Graves for their mutual friend, David Thomas. On the other hand the title is pure Sassoon, a deliberate echo of his nickname of "Mad Jack." But Jack is already questioning his role as a "Giant-Killer in a story" that seems to be undergoing some undesirable alterations to its setting and plot. While in stanza two he still pictures himself as a crusading "paladin," the notion of knight-errantry is now anachronistic; the bleak parapets are trenches, not mediaeval castles; the poet-soldier's craving for romance and music cannot be satisfied while this carnage continues. Indeed it is unlikely he will survive it anyway; in this remorseless conflict at least, "the Giant-Killer ... is learning / That heroes walk the road of no returning."

Stand-To: Good Friday Morning

Increasingly aware of his poetic destiny, "Stand-To: Good Friday Morning" is, even by Sassoon's standards, a watershed poem, both in terms of style and substance. While it again records the unpalatable facts of trench life — "deep in water I splashed my way" recalls the experiences of "A Working Party" — it also reveals Sassoon's newfound capacity to act as the satiric spokesman for his fellow officers. Later on he would acknowledge its significance as "the only one (of the early 1916 poems) which anticipated my later successes in condensed satire...," adding, with uncharacteristic immodesty, that "it summarized the feelings of thousands of other platoon commanders and I consider it one of the most effective of my war productions" (SJ, p. 18).

Its thirteen lines are included in the notebook for 22 April, "a jaunty scrap of doggerel versified from a rough note in my diary" (*Diaries*, p. 56). That the day was Good Friday, the occasion of Christ's crucifixion, gives the poem its "raison d'être." The secular spokesman is Sassoon, praying for neither immunity or glory but for a "Blighty" wound. Such an outcome will not only parody Christ's crucifixion, in that the craven poet will survive his personal "martyrdom," but will be the only way of convincing him, as only tangible evidence *can* convince serving soldiers, that Christ really did die for mankind. Only then will the poet be able to accept the symbolism of "Your bread and wine" and receive Christian absolution. His "bloody old sins," finally "washed white," contribute powerfully to the poem's satiric intensity. Here, as elsewhere, the "double entendre" of "bloody" — at once swearword and literal fact — contributes to a tone that is, for the first time, openly irreverent. That the occasion was Good Friday renders the poem's message the more obvious; it forced on Sassoon the realization that the poem might well be construed as blasphemous, as indeed it was when published six years later in a New Zealand socialist newspaper (SJ, pp. 17–18)). Sassoon had now taken the path of no return: he had expressed, in verse which brooked no argument, his growing disillusion with Christian principles. Already more than hinted at in "The Prince of Wounds," they are here given mordant and unqualified expression. In the trenches of Morlancourt, Sassoon was indeed summarizing the unheroic and heretical feelings of "thousands of other platoon commanders" (SJ, p. 18).

That Sassoon "here ... broke into realism" is undoubtedly true; that he did so by "introducing my muse to the word 'frowst'" is less accurate. In fact the human smells ("frowst") and sounds ("snore," "swore") had already put in an appearance in "A Working Party," written twenty-two days earlier, a poem which had prefigured another crucial inflection in Sassoon's writing, towards detailed documentation of the sheer physical drudgery of frontline existence. Nonetheless these epithets show just how committed Sassoon was to the cause of veracity, to the conveyance of the sense of a living hell in which even the lark's song, "discordant, shrill," fails to reassure.

Not everyone has shared Sassoon's view of the poem. Graves, already Sassoon's chief poetic confidant, wrote disapprovingly to him: "My only regret is 'Stand-To: Good Friday Morning.' A blasphemous poem must be frightfully good to hit it and you hadn't the patience to work this right. I know it was a very obstinate poem but you could have solved it" (IBI, 1988, p. 70). Silkin's objections are more specific: he dislikes the "crude" antithesis of "*They* seemed happy; but *I* felt ill" and the inconsistency of the invocation "O Jesus," since it "represents a proper cry for help, with the contingent faith wanting" (Silkin, 1987, p. 142). But that surely is the point: the speaker can indulge his crass wish in the certain knowledge that it will not be answered. Sassoon's "faith" has finally vanished in the hell of the front line.

The Kiss

On 23 April, Easter Sunday, Sassoon escaped from the knee-deep mire of the trenches. He had survived eighteen days. To him the contrast between trees "like ashen smoke" and a Flixécourt landscape like "Paradise" was enough to raise his spirits; the fortunate circumstance that he was in the company of Marcus Goodall made him ecstatic. Writing in his diary he enthused: "his is the only face I shall remember with any interest — of all the two or three hundred I've seen since Easter" (*Diaries*, 20 May, p. 63).

The landscape was in harmony with his emotions:

> At Flixécourt ... I refused to worry about the future. The world around me was luminous and lovely; I was filled with physical gratitude for it; and I strove to express that vision with spiritual exaltation. My dreams were mine and even the rigorous routine of infantry warfare instruction could not dispel them. Alone with my Concise Oxford Dictionary when the long day's work was done, I became as much a poet as I have ever been in my life, though how I had the vitality to do it is now one of the mysteries associated with the superabundant energy of youth [SJ, p. 18].

It was in this upbeat frame of mind that he wrote "The Kiss" and "France." Both commemorate his stay at the Fourth Army School, but in very different ways. "The Kiss" amalgamates two contrary emotions: one, the enthusiasm engendered by listening to a "great brawny Highland Major ... talking of the bayonet" (*Diaries*, 25 April, p. 59); the second, Sassoon's deep feelings for Marcus Goodall, now allied to the premonition that he would suffer a terminal separation from him after Flixécourt. Three weeks later he would voice these fears in his notebook, wondering if he would "ever see him again after tomorrow" (*Diaries*, 20 May, p. 63).

For the moment though, Sassoon recalled, Major Campbell, though jokey and ferocious by turns, spoke "with homicidal eloquence." His chilling words "battered on the poet's brain" and impelled him to record the catalogue of grisly imperatives in his notebook. The date was 25 April, 1916:

> The bullet and the bayonet are brother and sister. If you don't kill him, he'll kill you. Stick him between the eyes, in the throat, in the chest, or round the thighs. If he's on the run, there's only one place; get your bayonet into his kidneys; it'll go in as easy as butter.... Quickness, anger, strength, good fury, accuracy of aim. Don't waste good steel. Six inches are enough ... when he coughs, go and find another [*Diaries*, 25 April, p. 60].

Part of the same diary entry, "The Kiss" was Sassoon's creative response to Major Campbell's tirade. Consisting of three quatrains, the poem is written in brisk octosyllabics, and couches its exhortations in language — when describing the male bullet's progress — that veers abruptly from the romantic afflatus of "He spins and burns and loves the air" to the ferocious realism of "And splits a skull to win my praise." In contrast, though the "female" bayonet dispenses a cold "glitter," she is reassuringly companionable, part of the soldier's visible equipment all through "the coldly marching days." When dispensing death this affinity is bizarrely heightened: "the downward darting kiss" evokes a climactic shudder in the victim that is transmitted to the bayoneteer via his weapon.

Such fluctuations of tone give the poem an ambivalence that has led to a diversity of critical interpretations. Is "The Kiss" an undeviating glorification of butchery or is it invested with heavy irony? Or was it intended to be read either way? Robert Graves set the cat among the pigeons by offering the view that "Siegfried's unconquerable idealism changed direction with his environment; he varied between happy warrior and bitter pacifist" (GTAT, p. 226). Implying that the poem was *conceived* as a candid response, he went on to say that "Later, Siegfried offered it as a satire." Recent commentators have generally agreed. Thorpe accepts the possibility of a plural or dual reading, but adds: "There seems no doubt that its purpose was originally straightforward: the romantic vocabulary applied to the bayonet is not the kind of language Sassoon was likely to use ironically in 1916." In adducing evidence from his likely poetic source, Thorpe points to W. E. Henley's "Song of the Sword" as an exercise in the mode entirely without irony, "a chilling paeon" to the virtues of cold steel that Sassoon had certainly read (Thorpe, 1966, p. 17). Silkin agrees, remarking that "however ambiguous" "The Kiss" may seem, it is "a ferocious poem," perhaps retained to "complete the record of his responses to the war" (Silkin, 1972, 1998, p. 137)

Such views now seem too unequivocal. In 1966 Sassoon himself finally scotched the direct interpretation, remarking to Thorpe that he was "tired of telling people that 'The Kiss' was intended as a satire on bayonet fighting, which I loathed. Graves's statement is one of his many inaccuracies. Campbell's lecture was an absolute horror" (Sassoon, 1976, p. 17).

Perhaps Sassoon was unwilling to admit the truth of Graves's assertion, borne out by the poetry and notebooks of 1916–7, that his "idealism changed direction with his environment." Yet only two months later and in the aftermath of the Somme, he was ready to acknowledge this mercurial side to his nature: "For I'm never my old self—always acting a part—that of the cheery, reckless sportsman, out for a dip at the Bosches" (*Diaries*, 16 July, p. 94).

Sassoon was hardly likely, late in life, to vindicate the sentiments of a poem that, if taken literally, openly encouraged sadism. But it remains unlikely, for a number of reasons, that the poem was ever intended as a straight glorification of skull-splitting or stabbing, even if the euphemism of "nobly marching days," and the romantic personification of "She glitters naked cold and fair" do hint at modern knightliness and the glamour of a hand-to-hand combat granted the female bayonet if not the male bullet. For contrary to Thorpe's view that the poem predates such experiments, it is clear from "Stand-To: Good Friday Morning," a piece written three days before, that Sassoon was already quite capable of operating in an ironic mode. As the poet said, it "anticipated my later successes in condensed satire" (SJ, 1945, p. 17).

Moreover, the poet's initial response to Campbell's lecture was not one of unbridled enthusiasm. Troubled by what he had heard, mindful of the dangers of a "gung-ho" reaction, Sassoon wandered off to seek an "impulse from a vernal wood" (Wordsworth, "The Tables Turned"). Listening to the trees, he found that they silently echoed his concerns—"they hate steel, because axes and bayonets are the same to them" (*Diaries*, 25 April, p. 60).

This critical debate, important though it is, has overshadowed another, equally fascinating aspect of the poem—its erotic sub-text. Admittedly the gendered apostrophizing of "Brother Lead and Sister Steel" derives from Campbell's opening salvo. But much of the imagery is Sassoon's own invention. It was his decision to entitle the poem "The Kiss," and to invent a weapon both "naked" and "fair" to deliver a "downward darting kiss."

On a conventional level, the ironic title—and Sassoon had already tried the procedure in "In the Pink"—simply alerts the reader to the misplaced attitude that can glorify (as Campbell's "bullish" rhetoric had) the art of killing. But the title also invests the verses with erotic undertones that may well say something about Sassoon's repressed emotions at the time. Thus the kiss becomes a symbolic act, a sexual euphemism for a moment of physical contact that has gratification, not murder, as its objective, a "naked" six-inch penetration that causes the recumbent body to "quail," not in anticipation of an all too real death, but in anticipation of the "petit mort" of sexual climax. The oxymoron of "good fury" may have been an attempt to justify the emotion required to stab the enemy—Sassoon's diary suggests it was used by the major—but its ambivalence hints at wish fulfillment of a homoerotic kind. The final quotation encapsulates emotions very different in kind from the lust for killing Major Campbell expected to arouse. Instead, the urge is for a physical intimacy that, despite the gender of the bayonet, takes place between men.

In April 1916, Sassoon was not willing to declare his sexual preferences, but his love for David Thomas, killed a month before, couched in idealistic, even transcendental terms in "The Last Meeting," may be obliquely expressed here in the symbolism of a bayonet, its "darting kiss" the response it evokes in the recipient. The poem's sub-text offers up evidence of a sort about the poet's state of mind — a state in which consummation is linked, Jacobean fashion, to death and dying. By this token the "fury" of killing is "good" because it will bring to mind an act of love denied but desired by the speaker.

Such a Freudian reading is hardly one that Sassoon would have accepted — any more than he was willing, in old age, to accept a view of "The Kiss" as incitement to murder. But Major Campbell's talk, with its crude personifications and cruder descriptions of penetration, does seem to have provoked a response in verse that allows Sassoon to explore, through the use of symbolism, tabooed areas of personal feeling.

France

The stay at the Army School helped Sassoon to recharge his emotional batteries; the respite from battle, the companionship of Marcus Goodall, the brilliant French spring which the friends could both share, all these contributed to a "last day" at Flixécourt which culminated in a drive past "green expanses of country on each side, rolling away into the hot hazy distance ... lovely glooms of sun-glinted woods, vivid patches of clover-red, silver of daisies in lush grass, and yellow glory of buttercups" (*Diaries*, May 20, p. 61).

It is hardly surprising that such a landscape should evoke in Sassoon all his old love of the countryside and provoke a recrudescent blend of Georgian pastoral and happy-warrior sentiments where even such extravagances as "cloud pavilions white" seem appropriate. The opening apostrophe to the spirit of France partakes of the quality of an Impressionist painting ("where sun and quivering foliage meet"). The mood of optimism, both generated by and reflected in a springtime atmosphere of love and hope, is palpable, perhaps for the last time.

The Last Meeting

Though "The Last Meeting" is placed after "France" in Hart-Davis's edition of *The War Poems*, the internal evidence of "a golden day at April's end" suggests that it was in fact written earlier on, during Sassoon's four-week interlude at Flixécourt. By mid–May, Sassoon was finding considerable consolation in the companionship of Marcus Goodall: both the elegiac tone of "The Last Meeting" and the imagery of stanza two (which strikingly recalls Sassoon's early impressions of Flixécourt in his diary) point to an earlier date.

It is, by some distance, the longest of Sassoon's war poems, if one can categorize it thus. In part the poem's length is a consequence of its narrative structure, for the ongoing quest, enunciated at the outset, is to "find the face of him that I have lost." As one might expect, Sassoon, like the Tennyson of *In Memoriam*, seeks a reunion with the departed in a natural setting, far from the anger of the guns. The quest begins as the traveler wends his way through a French village, past the "dripping mill-wheel" (in the diary of 23 April it is "a mill with water sluicing and broken wooden wheel") and up the hill towards the "empty house." Groping in the darkness as he passes from room to room, he calls out the name of his friend and, in an admission of the intensity of his feelings, refers to "the love / That strove in vain to be companioned still."

When the visionary moment comes, it declares itself, appropriately enough, not amid the Gothic appurtenances of the deserted mansion but in the spring woods. Like Coleridge's Ancient Mariner disappointed by the failure of his conscious attempts to pray, but redeemed when he blesses the natural world "unaware," the searcher is only rewarded when he "blindly" seeks the woods, there to commune reverentially with Nature amid the "awakening green." The ghost of David then announces his presence in a series of romantic affirmations. Like the dead soldiers of "The Dragon and the Undying," he has become part of the cycle of nature, as "dawn and sunset flame with my spilt blood." In a series of poetic gestures that are always pantheistic and imbued with a sensuousness that borders (in such images as "molten power," "thirst of my desires," "kiss me while I slept" and "dying" "youth that ... touched my lips to song") on the homoerotic, the spirit offers a triumphant vindication of his abiding presence. "Whispering trees," to become a recurrent and coded presence in a number of love pieces, here appears for the first time in the war poetry.

The final section, which appears to borrow from Sassoon's pre-war verses and in particular "At Daybreak," returns the poet to the realization that his friend is "lost among the stars." The mourner's consolation is that the vibrant sights and sounds of nature will always remind him that his friend's spirit lives on in the "whispering trees" and in "the joy of brooks" that "leap and tumble down green hills."

A Letter Home

Sassoon followed up "The Last Meeting," his initial elegiac response to the loss of David Thomas, with "A Letter Home." Since both in style and tone the poem represents a radical departure, we might consider why. In part Sassoon was, as the diaries attest, more relaxed when he composed the poem; well into his sojourn at Flixécourt away from the battle, where from his "quiet attic room" he could imbibe the good vibrations of a French landscape "fledged with forest." On a personal note his friendship with Marcus Goodall was helping to alleviate the profound sense of loss he had experienced in March. Talks with Robert Graves had not only reconfirmed Sassoon in his role as poet and given him a renewed sense of his worth as an artist, but suggested new directions that his verse might profitably take. Indeed one could argue that "A Letter Home," despite its ostensible subject, is less a memorial to David Thomas, more a "hommage" to Graves and to a lesser extent the Charles Sorley (both poets were ardent fans) of "All the hills and vales along." It would not be the only verse-letter Sassoon would send his fellow poet-in-arms; later in the conflict "Dear Roberto" would arrive in the post from a "wild and wobbly witted sarcastic soldier-poet" incarcerated in hospital at Lancaster Gate. But "A Letter Home" would be the only poem of Sassoon's war to subscribe wholeheartedly to Gravesian poetic principles.

Of course it could be argued that the poem's jaunty tone is in part a final attempt to write his profound sense of personal grief out of his system; better then to employ the semi-jocular rhymed tetrameters of "A Letter Home," after the manner of Housman's "Terence, This Is Stupid Stuff" or Graves's "To an Ungentle Critic," than to operate once more in the overwrought and aureate mode of "The Last Meeting." That may in part be the case. As Sassoon confides in the final couplet:

> War's a joke for me and you
> While we know such dreams are true!

Certainly his fellow poet would have understood the therapeutic virtues of the "Jingle"; Graves too had been at the burial of David Thomas — "beside me," as Sassoon remembered, "with his white whimsical face twisted and grieving" (*Diaries*, 19 March, 1916, p. 45).

Graves's own reaction to the carnage was one that frequently involved a regression to the rhythms of nursery rhyme or ballad. But what most impressed Graves was the skillful nature of Sassoon's pastiche, the fact that here was an older and more established poet willing to "take on board" his poetic principles, even to ape some of his effects. Writing to Sassoon on 27 May, Graves remarked: "Your jingle letter was quite one of the nicest I've ever had: you *are* a dear. One of these days I'll try a reply" (IBI, p. 51). He did. In his "Letter to SS. From Mametz Wood" he predictably seeks to outdo Sassoon in a pacy piece replete with outrageous rhymes and exotic place-names.

Sassoon's own effort progresses from sardonic dismissal of the opposition ("Back to Hell with Kaiser send it") to a vision of Graves — whom Sassoon always insisted was odd and who had already written a poem called "Faun" — in his strange fairyland of "web-hung woods" and "hornbeam alleys." In section three the poet waxes nostalgic as he reminisces, in homoerotic terms, about "one whose yellow head was kissed / By the gods," before he is reborn, pantheistic fashion, in the hills and valleys of his native Wales. Wars continue — "Everywhere men bang and blunder" — but ultimately, Sassoon asserts, "dreams" will "triumph" as the creative principle vanquishes the spirit of destruction.

It is easy to take issue with Sassoon's optimism — Thorpe calls it "facile" — but we should remember that, written as it was during a happy interlude away from the front, it is a consciously lighthearted attempt to match the insouciant poetic mannerisms of his friend.

Before the Battle

As the title indicates, life had now become deadly serious. This brief poem was written in anticipation of the Battle of the Somme, intended as the key action of the war, and ushered in with a massive artillery barrage which Sassoon recorded in his diary on 1 July. The device of feminine rhymes ("falling / calling") adds a somber note to the poem, though nature is characteristically viewed as a repository of "radiance," replete with the restorative music of birdsong and "whispering trees." The second stanza, asserts, in contrasting vein, the truculent response of a soldier-poet anxious to demonstrate his "scorn" for the coming fight. Nonetheless the prayer-like refrain of both stanzas is a plea to nature to safeguard her own:

> O river of stars and shadows, lead me through the night.

At Carnoy

Judging from Sassoon's scrupulously kept diaries for that fateful first week of July 1916, the poet had an overwhelming premonition that the war was about to enter a crucial phase. Scribbling in his notebook at precisely 10:50 a.m. on the opening day, he recorded the scene: "Just eaten my last orange. I am looking at a sunlit picture of Hell. And still the breeze shakes the yellow charlock, and the poppies glow below Crawley ridge...." (*Diaries*, 1 July, p. 83). The Somme campaign had begun, as planned, that very morning. "At Carnoy" is part of a diary entry two days later that describes the massing of the battalions "in an open grassy hollow south of the Carnoy-Mametz road, with a fine view of the British and (late) Bosche lines where the 91st Brigade attacked on Sunday, about six hundred yards away" (*Diaries*, 3 July, p. 86). Though the tone of the entry, as befits the initial success of the brigade, is upbeat, the poem's "knock-out" line, "To take some cursèd Wood ... O World God made!" conveys an exasperation that will be reiterated in the verse with increasing frequency as events unfold. That Sassoon's worst fears would be borne out is conveyed by the diary of the following day's events when the poet describes, for the first time, the "terrible and undignified carcases, stiff and contorted," of the dead (*Diaries*, 4 July, p. 87). The initial action at Mametz Wood would prove to be a costly failure: the Royal Welch Fusiliers alone lost 130 men and two officers.

Unlike most of the diary poems, "At Carnoy" complements the extended prose account, drawing on the natural sights and man-made sounds of a portentous day — thistles, an orange sunset, the playing of mouth-organs. More crucially, the poem conveys the impression that this precious but precarious harmony between man and nature, a nexus at the heart of Sassoon's poetic sensibility, as the invocations to nature in "Before the Battle" confirm, is under threat. Bergonzi has rightly observed: here "he traces this harmony on the very edge of its imminent dissolution" (1964, p. 95).

Chapter 9

"Goodbye to Galahad": The Somme and Its Aftermath

The Somme was another turning point. Flixécourt had restored Sassoon's essential optimism and enabled him to recharge his emotional batteries; after the carnage of the Somme offensive, he and most of his fellow soldiers found it increasingly difficult to comprehend the nature and conduct of a war that was becoming ruinously wasteful of young lives. Not only was David Thomas dead but, by the end of July, so was the man who had replaced "Tommy" in his affections, Marcus Goodall. There was little time for poetry; appalled by the post–Somme nightmare of viscid mud, putrefying corpses and the loss of dear comrades, he succumbed to a bout of trench-fever. Back in "Blighty" Sassoon's mounting anger at "Home-Front" hypocrisy issued in the first of his condensed satires and epigrams—"The Hero" is as harsh as anything Sassoon wrote—but his compassion for the victims of the war is already evident in such pieces as "The Road" and "The Death-Bed." Writing to his new friend, Lady Ottoline Morrell, Sassoon confided: "The hideous brutal cynicism of it all makes me feel the same. 'The necessary supply of heroes must be maintained at all costs' says Carson ... the irony of it. They might as well be rounds of beef, or rounds of ammunition, and decorations are chucked around like confetti at a funeral" (letter from Sassoon to Morrell, 18 November, 1916). The pacifist poet was one side of the coin; the bitter satirist the other. Back at the regimental depot at Litherland in December, Sassoon found the "year ... dying of atrophy," and nothing before him "but red dawns flaring over Ypres and Bapaume" (*Diaries*, 22 December, p. 105).

Elegy to Marcus Goodall

It was one thing to endure the hell of the front line; it was quite another to have to cope with the sudden death of loved ones. On 21 July, three weeks into the Somme campaign, Sassoon received the news of Robert Graves's "death"; one week later he dolefully recorded in his journal the all too accurate report of Marcus Goodall's demise. Shocked, emotionally drained by such doom-laden tidings, a debilitated and feverish Sassoon was sent to hospital in Amiens and thence back to England. The elegy to his companion was inserted beneath the terse diary entry for 28 July: "Still in hospital. Marcus Goodall dead of wounds" (*Diaries*, p. 99). The poem was not published in the poet's lifetime, a likely acknowledgment of its intensely private emotions. Had Sassoon decided to publish, he would, in any event, have needed to change the title, since it was his invariable practice not to mention actual people by name in his verse. Such lines as "your body thrown into a shallow pit along that wood" would obviously have distressed the family of his close companion. Moreover the apocalyptic vision of a "monster shell" that disperses all the "filth" of the "discontented slain" and then propels the victim to a meeting with a "red-faced" and presumably guilty "father god" was probably far too extreme for most people's tastes. The poem is, as Sassoon knew full well, an uneven, melodramatic effort, with the poet revealing embryonic symptoms of what Rivers would later call "war-neurosis" (Rivers, 1922, passim). Here it finds expression in the form of a nightmarish guilt—a new emotion in the poetry—that consumes the speaker: not only has he been spared this grisly end, but he dares to contemplate a rural morning in England while his friend suffers the ignominy of a ghastly, Gothic interment.

The verses have nonetheless become a quarry for other poems. Sassoon borrowed the final couplet for "To His Dead Body," which, as Hart-Davis reminds us, was written at about the same time and which refers to Robert Graves, then believed killed in action (*Diaries*, p. 99). The rhetorical question, "Was it for this…?," repeated three times in stanza one, was a device replicated by Wilfred Owen in "Futility."

A Night Attack

Sassoon also declined to publish "A Night Attack." The piece, more versified prose than poem, is not one of his better efforts. However, the personal embargo probably reflects his concern, at the time of writing, that its embryonic pacifist sentiments and the Prussian soldier's view of "damned English" might be altogether too contentious. For here Sassoon views events from a perspective at once humane and even-handed, and in so doing, offers a riposte to his own trooper's xenophobic jibe that "The bloody Bosche has got the knock."

Now enjoying a spell in tents "twelve miles from the battering guns," the soldier-poet apparently had time to recuperate and rethink. But he could not forget the sight and above all the smell of those Somme corpses; for the first time Sassoon overcomes his innate distaste for such things and describes the "rank stench" of putrefaction and the moans of wounded men in the woods. The diary entries of the time reveal the same preoccupation with "faces grey and disfigured, dark stains of blood soaking through their torn garments, all their hope and merriment snuffed out for ever and their voices fading on the winds of thought...." (*Diaries*, 13 July, 1916, p. 93).

Such harrowing sights and smells led to a reassessment of the patriotic ethic, a new view of the "Hun" from the perspective of "a Prussian with a *decent face*" (the same epithet was used to describe his own comrade in "A Night Attack") that the poet remembers lying "dead in a squalid, miserable ditch." He is indeed a "bloody Bosche" who "got the knock," but unlike his dismissive comrade, Sassoon offers an imaginative and sympathetic reconstruction of the German soldier's last, panicky moments on this earth, and reflects that he too was a loather of war who "longed for peace." The final image conveys the obscenity of a conflict that ignominiously destroys young men; here the victim, no different in essence from his English counterpart, lies face down in the slime, with his "heels to the sky" in a posture that denies him his essential dignity and grace:

> His face was in the mud; one arm flung out
> As when he crumpled up; his sturdy legs
> Were bent beneath his trunk; heels to the sky.

Died of Wounds

Less than two months earlier Sassoon had been relaxing at Flixécourt in the company of Marcus Goodall; now his friend was dead and Sassoon was, as a consequence of a temperature of 105° (*Diaries*, 23 July, p. 99), in the war hospital at Amiens and feeling physically and mentally distraught. "In extremis," Sassoon dashed off a poem that both he and Graves regarded, quite properly, as among the best he had so far produced. Clearly the experience that prompted the verses had a profound effect on an already hypersensitive poet. Later in life he would annotate the poem dispassionately enough: "I got the idea in the hospital at Amiens, where a youngster raved and died in the bed opposite mine. I think he came from High Wood at its worst" (WP, p. 41). But the *Memoirs* reveal the bleak intensity of his mood at the time: "all the horror of the Somme attacks was in that raving; all the darkness and the dreadful daylight" (p. 366).

In fact Sassoon regarded the poem as crucial to his development as a trench poet, as a chronicler of war with the potential to operate on a "higher plane of effectiveness" (SJ p. 19). In "Died of Wounds," he recalled, he "had hit on a laconic anecdotal method of writing which astonished me by the way it expressed my passionate feeling about the agonising episode described." Conscious of "the irony of my exulting in having done a fine piece of work, when I owed the opportunity for it to the death of a pathetically young officer in the ward...," Sassoon offered the judgment that while "The One-Legged Man" and "The Hero" were "merely a display of dexterous sarcasm, the graphic sincerity of 'Died of Wounds' was unanswerable" (SJ, p. 19).

Sassoon's instincts were right. The poem movingly testifies to his capacity to make emotional capital out of the direct utterance of the "pathetically youthful officer" (SJ, p. 19). Dying of his wounds, traumatized beyond endurance, the patient relives, in his last delirious moments, the futile and nightmare experience of the battle for High Wood. "Curse the Wood!" echoes Sassoon's own expression of dismay in "At Carnoy," in which disaster was merely anticipated: here terror, pain and death are senselessly inflicted on one innocent and uncomprehending victim. There is irony in the listener's initial indifference, in the mistaken belief that he is "putting it on" ("he did the business well"); more in the sardonic humor of the conclusion where "Some slight wound lay smiling on the bed." A depersonalized victim of war, at least the new occupant can thank his lucky stars that he has a "cushy" wound. Nonetheless, it is the sheer intensity of the second verse, the heart-rending cries of the dying, deranged soldier that give this poem its emotional force:

> The ward grew dark; but he was still complaining.
> And calling out for "Dickie." "Curse the wood!
> It's time to go. O Christ, and what's the good?
> We'll never take it, and it's always raining."

Graves was not far wrong when he observed: "The best stanza in this book (*The Old Huntsman*), probably in any book of war poems, is the middle one of 'Died of Wounds.' It knocks me more every time" (Graves to Sassoon, 22 April, 1917, IBI, p. 70).

To His Dead Body

For some time Sassoon had labored under the considerable misapprehension that Robert Graves had been killed in the Battle of the Somme. "To His Dead Body" was the poet's eccentric epitaph to his maverick friend, written in hospital at Amiens (like "Died of Wounds") after the arrival of news of his "death." The melancholy event was thus recorded in his diary: "and now I've heard that Robert died of wounds yesterday, in an attack on High Wood. And I've got to go on as if there were nothing wrong. So he and Tommy are together, and perhaps I'll join them soon" (21 July, 1916, p. 98).

In the poem Sassoon imagines, as in the similarly dated "A Night Attack," the bullet's progress, "when roaring gloom surged inward" and life was extinguished "like racing smoke, swift from your lolling head." Here, and not for the first time, Sassoon attempts to envisage "the moment of truth." To describe the sensation in verse is perhaps Sassoon's way of coming to terms with what he felt would be his own inevitable end. By comparison the second stanza is conventional enough until the final image, as the poet speeds his comrade on his way to a meeting with "red-faced father God."

The poem is not only a memorial to Graves the man; like "A Letter Home," it pays homage to Graves the poet. The moment of death echoes Graves's own description in "It's a Queer Time":

> It's hard to know if you're alive or dead
> When steel and fire go roaring through your head.
> [*Over the Brazier*, 1916]

Moreover, the bizarre reference to an apparently embarrassed and "red-faced" divinity, purloined from his unpublished elegy to Marcus Goodall, gives the piece an insouciant Gravesian touch.

Christ and the Soldier

Sassoon did not recover in the New Zealand hospital at Amiens and on 1 August, still incapacitated by trench fever and shaken by his Somme ordeal, he was on his way back to England. The following six months gave him further opportunities to reflect upon the significance of the conflict, to document and evaluate his own experiences. One creative result of this was that the poetry of early 1916, primarily a response to frontline "experiences" was gradually superseded by satiric poems targeted at "the Home Front" that he had unwittingly returned to. In part the consequence of his absence from the battlefield, this change of direction was primarily attributable to his growing awareness of civilian ignorance and insensitivity, to the pacifist promptings of the Garsington set, and to his realization that the "Great Advance" on the Somme had been a catastrophic failure. For the moment though, a few more trench poems came from the Sassoon pen.

"Christ and the Soldier" is one such response, though it was denied a place in *The Old Huntsman*. Much later, Sassoon, in a substantial note to the poem (WP, pp. 46–7), provided a detailed explanation of his original intentions. That these retrospective comments were made from an avowedly Christian standpoint explains their dismissive character. Sassoon labeled the poem "an ambitious failure," adding, "My carefully contrived attempt at a potent parable certainly wasn't worth printing" (*Ibid.*). Talking to Felicitas Corrigan in 1962, Sassoon was less scathing:

> My only religion was my vocation as a poet, and my resolve to do my duty bravely. I don't think I quite knew what I was trying to say. I suppose that behind it was the persistent anti-parson mentality — and it *was* difficult to swallow their patriotic pietism, which seemed unreal to many of us front-liners. But apparently a little of the reality came through to me in that tentative poem [Corrigan, 1973, p. 80].

"That tentative poem," written at Somerville College, Oxford (the date is 5 August, 1916), was intended as a "commentary on the mental condition of most frontline soldiers, for whom a roadside Calvary was merely a reminder of the inability of religion to cooperate with the carnage and catastrophe they experienced" (WP, pp. 46–7). But Sassoon, now too anxious to disassociate himself from this early, irreverent version of the poet, was all too willing to admit to his post–Somme inadequacies:

> This poem cannot be read as showing any clue to my own mental position, which was altogether confused, and became increasingly disillusioned and rebellious (I wrote "They" three months afterwards). Like the soldier in the poem, all I could say was "O Jesus, make it stop!" [WP, pp. 46–7].

Sassoon's apologia is understandable. The poem, a dialogue between the Christ figure of a roadside shrine, now incongruously in the firing line, and a soldier at his wits' end, is not only "anti-clerical" (Sassoon's epithet) but profoundly irreligious — though we should remember that the speaker is, to use Sassoon's words, "an ignorant private" (WP, p. 47). Nonetheless his riposte to Christ's request, echoing that of Christ to his disciples ("my son, behold these hands and feet"), is nothing if not realistic. Remarking that "Wounds like these / Would shift a bloke to Blighty just a treat!," the private's observation has a sardonic power that is all the better for being so unexpectedly sacrilegious, a piece of realism in stark contrast to the unctuous and no doubt incomprehensible reply of the Calvary figure, and the final vacuity of the Christian response. Such a contrast anticipates the yet to be written "They," a poem that Sassoon refers to in his later annotation.

Section two re-emphasizes this contrast between Christ's message of "resurrection, life and light" and the terse reaction of the soldier: "O Christ Almighty, stop this bleeding fight." Intended by the trooper as swear words, his response has a literal relevance in the context of the poem — a roadside crucifix framed by a bloody war. The final stanza concentrates on humanitarian issues, which, on the substantial evidence of "A Night Attack," are increasingly dominating his consciousness. One, reiterated here, concerns his growing awareness of war's victimization of both sides; the other his belief that an uncaring Christ cannot remain impervious to the carnage of "these hells." If his original miracles were not, on his own admission, "a fruitless gift," then new and efficacious ones are desperately needed now. Significantly the soldier's final statement focuses on his own capacity to empathize with grieving mothers on the other side, and interrogates Christ on the even-handedness of his so-called charity. He wants reassurance that Christ does not subscribe to the usual patriotic ideology, that "Lord Jesus" only watches over Allied trenches. He wants Christ to dispense mercy, as does the speaker of "A Night Attack," to both sides. Just as the bishop's "cop-out" phrase, "The ways of God are strange," provides no solution to the soldier's pertinent questions, so here Christ is himself lost for words ("dreamed in the desolate day"), as, in a series of ironic juxtapositions, the real world (first a twittering bird and then, more ominously "a Red Cross waggon") reasserts itself. The soldier can expect no solace from a "Lord Jesus" who, apparently, has "no more to say" about present exigencies. To his final desperate question, "O God ... Why ever was I born?," the only palpable reply is the incessant noise of battle.

Haunted

"Haunted" appeared only in *The Old Huntsman* and *Georgian Poetry 1916–17*, along with some unlikely bedfellows: "A Letter Home," "The Kiss," "The Dragon and the Undying," "To Victory," "They," "In the Pink" and "The Death-Bed." One can see why Rupert Hart-Davis decided not to include it in the *War Poems*; the poem avoids any direct reference to the conflict. Nonetheless it is so shot through with nightmarish experience, culminating in the "strangling clasp of death," that it seems, at the very least, a haunted, shell-shocked recollection of the battlefield and perhaps of Mametz Wood. The wood, so often a haven, replete with bird-song, has become, perhaps as a consequence of the Somme, a repository of gothic gloom and a claustrophobia that degenerates to blind panic. For the man wandering through the shadows has a face "a little whiter than the dusk," a pallor which betrays a fearful state of mind that finds objective correlatives in the surroundings where sunset is a "smear of red" and where the noise of thunder evokes such dread that the victim stands, transfixed like a man in a nightmare, "the sweat of horror on his face." Nostalgic memories of a rural past provide fleeting solace — the sounds and smells of hay-making, the night-jar's "churring note." But the swart, mazy wood refuses to release him from its clutches; it is an alien and grotesque world that chokes and claws. When a flapping creature makes him screech in terror, the sound betrays his position and he is confronted by an apparition —"zigzag, squat and bestial"— that appears to represent a soldier's worst nightmare. He endeavors to flee but falls, and is inexorably caught, aware in his death-throes of "slow fingers groping on his neck."

During his English convalescence, Sassoon composed three short pieces which he wrote down in his diary of 12 August. Regrettably they remained unpublished in his own lifetime. Though they do deal with themes rapidly becoming part of Sassoon's stock-in-trade, they were probably considered too contentious and too unpolished for an English readership that might be "gung ho" but was also discerning about poetry. For both "For England" and "The Stunt," the latter loosely based on an incident in which Sassoon had single-handedly attacked an enemy position and been awarded the Military Cross, are terse pieces which not only reveal his growing obsession with death and its antecedent processes, but also set these terrible experiences of the troops against the graceless hypocrisies of their English relatives. These bitter pieces differ in terms of subject matter from the most of the celebrated epigrams that came later; their initial focus is single-mindedly on the trenches, on the suffering and dying troops of both sides. But they are important demonstrations of Sassoon's newly discovered penchant for "candid and ironic comment" (SJ, p. 14), for a "hitherto unpredictable talent for satirical epigram," and for the structural procedure of adding "a knock-out blow in the last line" (SJ, p. 29). "For England," like "To His Dead Body," describes a death ("Something smashed his neck, he choked and swore") that is palpably not "glorious" but sudden and grotesque, and ends, ironically, with the studied family rituals of bereavement it provokes:

> A glorious end; killed in the big attack.
> His relatives who thought him such a bore,
> Grew pale with grief and dressed themselves in black.

In contrast, "The Stunt," a palinode to "For England," offers a picture of courage and fortitude achieved at the cost of numerous German casualties. Sassoon's own extraordinary heroism — he called it "Courage of the cockfighting kind" — brought him official recognition, but as this poem makes clear, exacerbated his growing remorse at having to kill so many enemy soldiers. "Gentle Jesus" might keep him safe and sound; he hardly ministered to the cause of Saxon peasants "scared" and "half-asleep" who had been the victims of his ferocious onslaught. Certainly encomiums from "Blighty" don't count for much when they are gained at the expense of so many dead. There is a personal price to be paid for such unrelenting heroism.

> How splendid. O how splendid! his relations said,
> But what the weeping Saxons said I do not know.

"Via Crucis" (the Way of the Cross), while again referring to the "Blighty" stereotype of "jolly soldier-boys," focuses on the pointless martyrdom of men reduced to the status of "abject beasts" by the blundering machine of war, and denied the meaningful and glorious resurrection of a Christ. Once again Sassoon questions the validity of a Christian message that has no relevance or meaning for bewildered soldiers whose deaths are inglorious and unremarked. Well might they ask if they "die in vain"; their only funeral pall is "a soaking sack — mud and rain."

The One-Legged Man

"The One-Legged Man" was Sassoon's first *public* exercise in this new epigrammatic mode. Convalescing in England, no matter how restful and pleasurable it might appear to be on the surface, usually brought the angry satirist of home values to the fore. Writing later, Sassoon singled out the poem as one of his first forays into "candid and ironic comment," adding that the initial notes were developed into two poems (the other one was "The Hero"), "with a strong sense of satisfaction that I was providing a thoroughly caddish antidote to the glorification of 'the supreme sacrifice' and such like prevalent phrases." In "The One-Legged Man," the tone is pervasively ironic, the structural procedure the increasingly familiar one of a "knock-out blow in the last line," usually in the form of a candidly direct statement which not only surprises but puts the rest of the poem in a new perspective. For what begins as a pastoral piece in which the old man (not initially identified as a soldier) counts his rural blessings — a familiar Kent landscape that Sassoon was now immersed in ("oasts with painted cowls") together with a "comfortable" settled domestic existence ("splendid to eat and sleep and choose a wife") — suddenly becomes, in the shocking final couplet, a poem about a crippled amputee.

> He hobbled blithely through the garden gate
> And thought: "Thank God they had to amputate."

As Bergonzi observes, Sassoon, "unlike some of his fellow soldier poets ... could not be content with using scenes of rural English life as a compensation and balance for the brutality of life at the Front: in 'The One-Legged Man' Sassoon thrusts the two together in angry and shocking juxtaposition" (p. 95). While Bergonzi's comment does not apply with equal truth to most Sassoon's war poems, it is certainly an accurate reflection of "The One-Legged Man." The anger moreover is Sassoon's, not the victim's. It is the crowning irony of the poem that the maimed victim of a senseless war should feel able to contemplate his luck, that "safe with his wound," he should, in a telling oxymoron, "hobble (d) *blithely*" (emphasis added) through the garden gate.

The Hero

Another "satirical drawing" — the very title is now invested with irony — "The Hero" again contrasts the innocently myopic world of the Home Front with the hell of overseas war. Such a polarization was becoming more pronounced as Sassoon, still recuperating from his trench fever, was being goaded to articulate fury by civilian misapprehensions about the spirit of the fighting men. Usually it is the actual circumstances of war, its bungled strategies, its impersonal, death-dealing machinery, the very nature of trench warfare, which precludes the possibility of any heroism. Here, for the only time in the war poetry, Sassoon singles out one of his own fusiliers for his cowardice, in the attempt to explode the journalistic fiction of universally courageous behavior by the "British Tommy."

In "The Hero" irony resides in the mother's proud conviction that her "glorious boy" has died a hero's death. Though such remarks by "Women of Britain" resonated up and down the land (*see* GTAT, pp. 188–9), they were, as Sassoon the platoon commander knew only too well, frequently outfaced by frontline realities, where the exigencies of trench fighting separated the men from the boys The officer's "gallant lies" were a predictable strategy for reinforcing not only the mother's pride but this absurd and misplaced notion of "happy-warriorism" in the trenches. In truth, Jack had been a "cold-footed, useless swine" who had tried to "get sent home," and reduced to a state of funk, had been unceremoniously "blown to small bits" — a distinctly unheroic way to go. The final irony is that no-one will remember or care, "Except" — and the remark is shot through with disdain — "that lonely woman with white hair." As Sassoon would later remark: "It does not refer to anyone I have known. But it is pathetically true. And of course the 'average Englishman' will hate it" (WP, p. 49). And the "average English woman," he might have added, as here, for the first time, the poet openly reveals his distaste for women, for those "outside my philosophy" (*Diaries*, 24 December, p. 106). It is a vituperative poem from which no one, not even his "Brother officer," escapes entirely unscathed. Sassoon was right to anticipate complaints, sardonically confiding to Ottoline Morrell that "An old gentleman wrote to the *Cambridge Magazine* and said my 'Hero' poem was an insult to the mothers of England, so I haven't lived in vain" (6 Dec., 1916, ULUT). Julian Dadd was right to offer the opinion that "few people would have had the pluck to write 'The Hero'..." (letter from Dadd to Sassoon, 12 February, 1917, IWMP).

Stretcher Case

In hospital, Sassoon was "overflowing with stored-up impressions and emotional reactions to the extraordinary things" he had observed and undergone. He "got off the mark at once" with some lines called "Stretcher Case" in which he used his "journey to Oxford in the Red Cross train for an objective and mildly satiric description of a wounded soldier's sensations" (SJ p. 5). The jaunty account in the Memoir does scant justice to "Stretcher Case." For it is neither objective nor satiric. Indeed, in common with a number of the convalescent poems of 1916, it reveals an understandable obsession with the process of dying, with envisaging the moment of death. Away from the Front, he could confront this fear more readily. Death, in the form of a bullet or exploding shell, had not yet been able to say "I choose him" ("The Death-Bed"), but he did not have to invent the feeling of lying, incapacitated, on a stretcher. After all he had earlier been rushed to hospital at Amiens with a temperature of 105 degrees. Now on his way to hospital in Oxford, Sassoon found himself on a train watching an unmistakably English landscape pass by:

> Nothing could be better than this, I thought, while being carried undeservedly from the ship to the train; and I could find no fault with Hampshire's quiet cornfields and unwarlike woods on the drowsy August afternoon.... Everything seemed happy and homely. I was

delivered from the idea of death and that other thing which had haunted me, the dread of being blinded [*Memoirs*, pp. 368–9].

In "Stretcher Case" England is no longer a repository of hypocritical or myopic attitudes; it is redeemed, not by its inhabitants but by its landscape, as the speaker gratefully renews his bond with the natural world. But the poem's dramatic impact derives from a sense of contrasts. In his delirium, the "stretcher case" flits between consciousness and dream, between nightmare memories of the "blasting tumult" of war and the golden countryside of England in August, between the "bewildered" conviction that he is blinded or dead and the slow, joyous realization that he is not only alive — and here the rhymed couplets part to emphasize the moment of recognition — but that he knows his own name:

> Then he remembered that his name was Brown.

If the romanticized landscape, "the blue serene," hints at the fact that this is indeed "Blighty," the crowning realization that he is not only alive but in England comes with the reassuring presence of familiar advertisements on railway station hoardings:

> Large friendly names, that change not with the year,
> Lung Tonic, Mustard, Live Pills and Beer.

The final section — and the poem was dedicated to Edward Marsh — is an example of a stanza written according to precepts of Georgian verse which valued a homely response to the English rural scene. Oddly, the poem was not one of the eight pieces from *The Old Huntsman* to be included in *Georgian Poetry 1916–1917*.

The Road

Recollected in this same English August was a nightmare scene from the past barely hinted at in the "glooms and quags" of "Stretcher Case." That it was a crucial experience in Sassoon's war, his initiation into the dereliction and carnage and smells of the Somme, is indicated by the diary entry of 4 July, 1916, the quarry from which "The Road" was constructed:

> These dead are terrible and undignified carcases, stiff and contorted. There were thirty of our own laid in two ranks by the Mametz-Carnoy road, some side by side on their backs with bloody clotted fingers mingled as if they were handshaking in the companionship of death. And the stench undefinable.

Sassoon's battalion was only too aware of this charnel-house scene, as they struggled "up through the mud to make a night attack on Quadrangle Trench" (WP, p. 51). These details are given poetic embellishment in "The Road" where Sassoon, ever alert to the possibilities of the "double entendre," disregards the labored "handshaking" simile of the diary and, in the image of "bloody-fingered from the fight," puns with the idea of men steeped both in the blood of others and their own. On this road through Purgatory to Hell, the poet is still able to focus on the human predicament, on a single, suffering individual, on "You in the bomb-scorched kilt, poor sprawling Jock," who, amid all this Hieronymus Bosch-like desolation, and flanked by waiting women "sick with fear," can think of nothing but sleep:

> Too tired for thoughts of home and love and ease,
> The road would serve you well enough for bed.

The Death Bed

"The Death Bed" reverses the narrative strategy of "Stretcher Case." There the soldier senses, confusedly, that he may be blinded or dying, but recovers to glimpse a real landscape; here the patient has a vision of rivers and boats but lapses into unconsciousness and death despite the pleas of a poet desperate to save him.

> Light many lamps and gather round his bed.
> Lend him your eyes, warm blood, and will to live.
> Speak to him; rouse him; you may save him yet.

The poem, in form an irregular ode, amalgamates two experiences, "a memory of hospital at Amiens and a canoe on the Cherwell" (WP, p. 53). As Sassoon recalled in *Siegfried's Journey*, during the month of August (when the poem was written) "Most of my afternoons were spent in a canoe ... a person who was able to paddle himself as far as Water Eaton on the war-time weed-choked Cherwell could scarcely claim to be an invalid" (SJ, p. 11). This image of water links these disparate impressions in the verse; water, held up to the dying man's lips, sets up the memory of "water — calm sliding green above the weir." Characteristically, death and destruction are countered, however ephemerally, by the restorative sights and sounds of an English summer's day. But as literal night in the hospital ward succeeds day, the unnamed patient's tenuous kinship with the natural world, based on the process of visualization, is broken. The imagery of water insistently returns, now in the sound of rain pattering on "drooping roses," in a symbolization of the slow "washing ... away" of life.

Stanza five provides a jarring reminder that the process of dying is rarely an untroubled one. Suddenly the victim is jerked into an awareness of his pain-racked body:

> He stirred, shifting his body; then the pain
> Leapt like a prowling beast, and gripped and tore
> His groping dreams with grinding claws and fangs.

9. "Goodbye to Galahad"

The tension builds as the poet pleads on his behalf and, by extension, on behalf of all young men destined to die. That "you may save him *yet*" (emphasis added) is directed not just at these hospital doctors but more generally at all those at home who, by exercising compassion and a genuine desire to help, might yet arrest an inexorable process whereby youth expires and "cruel old campaigners win safe through." But Death, powerfully personified (Sassoon had been reading Donne's Holy Sonnet, "Death, Be Not Proud"), has the last word. Though earlier "death, who'd stepped toward him" had "paused and stared," it now acts with grim finality. In a somber conclusion and with only "the thudding of the guns" as accompaniment, the young man is taken. In that the wounded soldier has died, the poet's passionate pleading has fallen on deaf ears, but he has tested our capacities for compassion to the utmost. Little wonder that Wilfred Owen called "The Death Bed" "a piece of perfect art" (*Collected Letters*, OUP, 1967, No. 543 to Tom Owen, 26 August, 1917, p. 488).

Chapter 10

"Unmasking the Ugly Face of Mars": August 1916 to April 1917

The autumn of 1916, mainly spent at Weirleigh "riding and hunting" (*Diaries*, ed. note, p. 102), was also the period when Sassoon became intimate with Lady Ottoline Morrell and the Garsington set. It was an important introduction. As Sassoon subsequently acknowledged, "During the next ten years or more I stayed a great deal at Garsington, where I could feel unembarrassed and at liberty to do as I pleased" (SJ, p. 20). For the moment, discussions there, particularly with the Morrells, reinforced Sassoon's pacifist views and his growing disillusion with events in France:

> The war was described as being waged for unworthy motives and it was the duty of a courageous minority to stand out against the public opinion which supported its continuance and prolongation.... For those at Garsington the war in France was all hearsay, while I was a scrap of living evidence to support their assumption that it was quite as bad as they had imagined [SJ, pp. 21–2].

So despite all the "agreeable distractions" (SJ, p. 22) the view from England was immensely disturbing, the more so since Sassoon's mother, whom he adored, was, despite still mourning the death of Hamo, unable to share his convictions: "I could get no relief by discussing the war with my mother, whose way of looking at it differed from mine.... The war had caused her so much suffering that she was incapable of thinking flexibly on the subject" (SJ, p. 27).

It was in this troubled late Autumn that Sassoon wrote a sequence of pithy, satiric pieces. Reflecting the distortions of mainstream opinion in "Blighty," they are characterized, like the earlier trial runs in the notebooks, by an epigrammatic brevity. None exceeds seventeen lines, though it is a cause for surprise that three are, despite their stanzaic divisions, barely disguised sonnets. Though the sonnet had been Sassoon's preferred verse form in the slim volumes of the pre-war years, Sassoon had not attempted a fourteen-line poem since "A Subaltern." He may have been pandering to Lady Ottoline Morrell's (elevated) notion of him "as a romantic young poet," a view he confessed he was anxious to live up to (SJ, p. 20); it is more likely that the discipline of short verse forms — sonnet or ballad quatrain alike — while offering a formal counterpoint to the subject matter, forced on him the need to concentrate his verbal fire.

The Tombstone-Maker

The first of these "satires of circumstance" was "The Tombstone-Maker," a poem bracketed with "The One-Legged Man," "The Hero" and "Arms and the Man" as having "a resemblance to Hardy's *Satires of Circumstance*." Frankly, the resemblance is not all that marked. Hardy usually displays a sympathy for his subjects; these portraits of tombstone makers, captains and bishops are steeped in vitriol. But Sassoon's capacity for acute observation, necessarily developed in the trenches, is very much to the fore. As he later recollected, "I had ... acquired the habit of observing things with more receptiveness and accuracy than I had ever attempted to do in my undisciplined past" (SJ, p. 16). In "The Tombstone-Maker" Sassoon's eye focuses on revealing physical detail and on the poetic possibilities, after the manner of Augustan masters, of comic juxtaposition.

> He primmed his loose red mouth and leaned his head
> Against a sorrowing angel's breast, and said:

"Primmed" is a happy invention. It suggests that the stonemason's prim manner is part of a hypocritical facade that merely pretends — a fact born out by the presence of Christian iconography — that soldiers deserve a decent burial. In reality all he is concerned about — an irony apparently lost on him — is lining his own pocket.

To the listening soldier-poet whose "knock-out" reply is reserved for the final quatrain, his stated values are as despicable as those of other "stay at homes" who seek to make literal capital out of the war. He should express sorrow for others less fortunate; instead he regards "scores of bodies" not as the hapless victims of a murderous war but as lost business potential. Cutting through his wheedling, the speaker shocks him by painting the German soldiery, as the propaganda machine did, as savages who "boil dead soldiers down for fat." That such gruesome behavior renders them unavailable to the Tombstone-Maker provokes in him the pious platitude about Christian souls that reminds us of the bishop's response in "They."

A Ballad

Another "lesson" for the war propagandists is provided by "A Ballad." That it did not appear in *The Old Huntsman* probably reflects Sassoon's gut feeling, when asked by Heinemann to make a "selection" for publication (SJ, p. 27), that he couldn't include too many of these mordant satires. It was bad enough that his friend Gosse should denounce the ones Sassoon *did* include as "savage, disconcerting silhouettes drawn roughly against a lurid background" (SJ, p. 28). The deliberate anonymity, both of the poem's title and of the officer it exposes, a "Captain in the Blanks," was probably an initial strategy aimed at rendering the piece publishable, but Sassoon knew that the whole business of self-inflicted wounds was just as contentious as the issue of frontline cowardice (adumbrated in "The Hero") and probably too delicate a topic for the censor-mongers. Even so it was so familiar to everyone at the Front that the practice was abbreviated to "SIW"— an acronym that would become the title of an Owen poem. Perhaps one inspiration, at least for the blustering tone of the poem, was provided by "Colonel Hensman" of the *Memoirs*, who "practised revolver shooting in his garden," "addressing insults to individual tree trunks," and who "declared that any man under forty who wasn't wearing the King's uniform was nothing but a damned shirker" (p. 379).

The poem, which employs the ballad quatrain but not its common measure, experiments with anapestic rhythms and internal rhyme — the technique recalls "The Ancient Mariner"— in an attempt to give the tale a rollicking immediacy and narrative directness. Introduced by the familiar question, "Have You Heard?," the ordinary, now hard-bitten soldier, recalls the officer's "accident" without rancor or malice. But the implication of the "story" is that "raw recruits" are the real victims of such hypocrisy: worse, it is the craven captain who, far from leading by example (as "Mad Jack" Sassoon invariably did), merely teaches "the way to blood and glory" to innocents destined only to become cannon-fodder.

They

If "A Ballad" dealt with potentially censurable material, "They" was far more likely to incur the opprobrium of the establishment since it dared to concentrate its fire on religious hypocrisy and its central repository, the Church of England. Just as in the hierarchy of the nation at war it was the senior officers who sped "glum heroes up the line to death," so in the pecking order of the church at home it was bishops, distributing their own weight in words, who gave sanctimonious voice to "just causes" and "heathen huns." "Distance," as Thomas Campbell knew, "lends enchantment to the view." While other poems in *The Old Huntsman* would confront Christianity in terms of personal experience, only "The Choral Union," a poem that echoes Blake's "Holy Thursday," sets the earthiness of the trooper against "holy women and plump whiskered men." But that piece, in any case outside the scope of this study, failed to attract much attention. Predictably it was "They" that helped polarize critical opinion and became the poem "most quoted by reviewers, both adverse and favourable" (SJ, p. 29).

The poem's title is very Sassoonesque; the pronoun "they" conveys the sense of division between the twin perspectives of home and away. Initially the bishop employs the word four times to accord the boys, unconsciously, the status of mere ciphers. But the focus shifts with the soldiers' reply. For them the clerics are on the other side of the divide; "they" belong to a milieu from which soldier and soldier-poet alike feel remote and which in turn marginalizes them.

In the first line the reader joins the bishop's congregation, attentive to the unctuous pulpit oratory that Sassoon was now finding so distasteful. But he resists the temptation to parody its mannerisms, conscious that the Bishop of London's actual words will reinforce the veracity of the poem. The prelate had recently expressed the "belief that those who were serving at the Front would return with their souls purged and purified by what they [had] experienced." For Sassoon such sermonizing was "Well-intentioned bunkum" (SJ, p. 30). But the words reverberated in the poet's head. Later, in bed, "the first few lines of 'They' came into [his] head as though from nowhere" (*Ibid.*).

The key to the poem's power resides in the ironic force of "they will not be the same." Intended by the bishop as a comment on the ennobling effect of war, the pronouncement acquires a different significance in the terrifyingly candid rejoinder of the boy soldiers. It is only when "they" recite a litany of personal disasters that the nature of the change is made starkly clear.

The bishop's statement, delivered in sententious and ringing phrases, mounts to a soaring climax, but the sentiments are clichés that fail to bear scrutiny: the notion of a "just cause"; the absurd but widely-held view that the enemy is "Anti-Christ"; the mendacity that this will be the "last attack." The sermon implies that the sacrificial victims have "bought" the right, as a consequence of their sacrifices, to make way for a morally superior race — a dubious, evolutionary ethic. And no one knew better than Sassoon that "bought it" in trench-speak meant getting blown to bits. No one wanted to "dare" death; every soldier was rightly terrified of its terminal embrace.

The contrast of the soldier's reply undermines the heroic assumptions of stanza one in terms of the reality of blindness, mutilation and insanity; the Bishop's patriotic pieties are instantly outfaced by reality. Surprise is again Sassoon's principal weapon. For a brief moment the boys seem to accept the prelate's message: "We're none of us the same!" But the exclamation mark hints at an intensity of feeling which impels the speaker to reel off a catalogue of change of an altogether more tangible and horrific kind. For indeed the soldiers are transformed, not into an "honourable race," but into maimed and pitiable objects. The intimate and homely use of the victim's names — George, Bill, John and Bert — contrasts with the lofty and impersonal sentiments of the bishop. For these are real people, real mates physically and mentally changed for the worse by the blundering machine of war. The details are listed in colloquial language. Even if they are not blinded, maddened, mutilated or killed, the brothels behind the lines will contribute their legacy. Sassoon pondered the use of "syphilitic," averring that it would be a first for English poetry (SJ, p. 30). But it also ends the roll-call of disasters in an unexpected way. After this, the bishop's final words are impotently unctuous. For there is no answer to the soldiers' lament.

A mere twelve lines of iambic pentameter, all save eleven words of the poem are in direct speech with only the incongruous "syphilitic" to leaven the monosyllabic inventory of pain. So understated and yet so instantly accessible, the poem could hardly fail to reach its target. It was, as Sassoon rightly divined, "the most publicly effective poem I had yet written" (SJ, p. 30). "Discharging sardonic epigrams at those on 'the Home Front' whose behavior was arousing my resentment" was the way forward for a pacifist poet increasingly opposed to establishment views about the war (SJ, p. 40).

Decorated

"Decorated" again demonstrates Sassoon's now well-honed technique of "two or three harsh, peremptory, and colloquial stanzas with a knock-out blow in the last line." It was, as the poet knew, a dangerously direct procedure and, when linked to tabooed topics, likely to antagonize the establishment. For this reason it was not submitted to Heinemann. Sassoon probably recognized, despite the concentration of effect and the element of surprise, that the poem strains to make a point that even Sassoon could scarcely accept unreservedly. But it does show how powerful were the tensions operating in the poet's post–Somme psyche. After all he had been decorated (he had been recommended for the Victoria Cross); and if he was still capable of feeling guilt-laden and murderous by turns, Sassoon could all too easily identify with the figure in his poem. Again the reader is kept in suspense until the final moment when his now familiar working-class spokesman — in this case "a grinning newsboy" — reveals the identity of the killer.

For the poem asks the reader to envisage a street-scene in which a criminal, a "beggar" who "did for five of 'em," is about to be brought to summary justice by "a jostling mob," or at the very least apprehended by the law. However, in a characteristic ironic reversal, the newsboy reveals that the center of attention is none other than "Corporal Stubbs, the Birmingham V.C!" and that the crowd is not lynching him but hero-worshipping a man whose murderous exploits have won him the ultimate decoration. A gauge of Sassoon's developing pacifism, the poem highlights the absurdity of a war ethic and the civilian response to it that makes heroes of killers. It was an irony of which Sassoon the officer was only too aware.

Arms and the Man

In the *Memoirs* Sassoon describes his late 1916 reacquaintance with the facts of military life:

> Early in November I went to London for a final Medical Board. At the Caxton Hall in Westminster I spent a few minutes gazing funereally round an empty waiting-room. Above the fireplace (there was no fire) hung a neatly framed notice for the benefit of all whom it might concern. It stated the scale of prices for artificial limbs, with instructions as to how officers could obtain them free of cost.... While I was adjusting my mind to what a journalist might have called "the grim humour" of this footnote to army life, a Girl Guide stepped in saying that Colonel Crossbones (or whatever his cognomen was) would see me now. A few formalities "put paid to" my period of freedom, and I pretended to be feeling pleased as I walked away... [pp. 379–80].

Of course this prose account was written twenty years or so after "Arms and the Man" which, in common with Sassoon's usual if not invariable practice, was prompted by recent experience. But the *Memoirs* are revealingly honest: Sassoon can only *pretend* to be feeling pleased; as the poem explains, he cherished secret hopes, now dashed, of a "leave extended." Though the poem's ostensible message is satiric and general, there are grounds for thinking that Sassoon is again exorcising his sense of guilt — not, as in "Decorated," at his fighting past, but at his pacifist present.

The mythological cognomen of "Croesus" — the influence of Graves is apparent here as on the Dickensian "Colonel Sawbones" — serves to distance the subject from the poet. Yet the name "Croesus" suggests material wealth (which Sassoon had), a wealth and status which not only made men into officers, but also, once they were dismembered by war, enabled them to have "free" arms and legs. There are layers of ambiguity here. The gift of "free" limbs could hardly be said to compensate the amputees for missing arms and legs; such things cannot be "restored." But there is another irony implicit in the Caxton Hall scenario. Why should officers who are, in any case, more able to pay for prosthetic appliances, "get them free." In confronting the elitist underpinnings of military life and, by implication, the lack of humanity shown to the ordinary trooper, Sassoon is facing up to a reality that will increasingly exercise his conscience during the later stages of the conflict, a conscience that will take him in the direction of socialism after the war.

Two Hundred Years After

A number of poems written during the poet's extended recuperation at Weirleigh, Garsington and Half Moon Street (the home of Robbie Ross), while often reverting to a mannered Georgianism, do add substance to the view that Sassoon's dilemma about the war was as far from resolution as ever. One course of action, a proven one, was to distance himself from what he now knew only too well were its worst excesses. In "Two Hundred Years After" he does this by the simple expedient of introducing a Frenchman "Trudging by Corbie Ridge" two centuries on. The details of the poem come from a pre–Somme notebook entry, made when Sassoon's vision of the war had not yet turned to nightmare. Imagining the scene "in a hundred or two hundred or two thousand years," he pictures

> these French roads ... haunted by a silent traffic of sliding lorries ... and tilting limbers all going silently about their business. Some staring peasant or stranger will see them silhouetted against the pale edge of a night sky — six mules and a double limber ... a line of cumbrous lorries nosing along some bleak main road... [*Diaries*, 2 June, 1916, p. 70].

Prompted by his notebook musings, Sassoon's ghosts of the past appear: "files of men," "a nosing lorry," "six mules" who still haunt the ancient battlefield. These shadowy nocturnal presences moving rations up to the front line under cover of darkness invade the consciousness first of a lonely walker and then of an old man who confirms their identity:

> Poor silent things, they were the English dead
> Who came to fight in France and got their fill.

The poem has been singled out for praise by Michael Thorpe on account of its "physical immediacy and simple expression of feeling," its avoidance of "mawkishness," its "Hardyan simplicity" (1966, pp. 32–33). For me "physical immediacy" is not a quality to be associated with a poem that lacks, quite deliberately, that sense of the palpable that informs "A Working Party" or, for that matter, Owen's "Dulce et Decorum Est." Nor am I convinced that its conclusion entirely evades the charge of sentimentality. What "Two Hundred Years After" does have is a quiet compassion and a Hardy-like wistfulness that contrasts with the satiric salvos of Sassoon's recent output.

More revelatory of the poet's oscillating state of mind are three short poems of November/December. Unlike the rather stately progress of "Two Hundred Years After," appropriately couched in sonnet form, these all employ the quatrain Sassoon usually reserved for his epigrammatic efforts. "A Mystic as Soldier," "Secret Music" and "The Poet as Hero" show Sassoon putting the spotlight on himself and his own sensibilities, the romantic poet forced by the exigencies of war to become a man of action. On a literary level, they reveal a poet returning to the poetic direction of a Georgian manner; on a psychological level, they expose a poet-soldier still uncertain about his continuing role in the "War for Civilization." Preoccupied with the need to reconcile his creative and destructive impulses, he must rally himself to a cause which he can only intermittently accept as just. All three pieces, while proclaiming the positive power of the muse and the therapeutic effects of music (a theme frequently explored in his twenties verse), insist that these harmonies will shortly be drowned by the discordant din of battle (*Diaries*, 16 July, p. 94).

A Mystic as Soldier / Secret Music

The title of "A Mystic as Soldier" is self-explanatory. Its brisk tetrameters, while acknowledging the presence of a fierce God at the Front, offer the view that the earlier feeling of religious optimism ("Dreaming Fair Songs for God") is now a misplaced response. On the killing fields, "where death outnumbers life," "fury" and "anger" rather than thoughts of a consolatory faith are the required emotions.

"Secret Music," another short confessional piece in which personal feelings are rendered in Georgian poeticisms, is a companion piece to "A Mystic as Soldier." While music has there departed from the speaker's consciousness, in "Secret Music" it does survive, even in the "world's end" of the trench-lines, a world where Death, here personified after the manner of "The Death Bed," is to be found in the memorable oxymoron of "carnival of glare." What precise forms the music of hope takes is not explained: it may be remembered melodies that provide "beauty" and "glory," or the music of a lost faith temporarily restored in the hell of the trenches.

The Poet as Hero

The third "confessional" poem in this group, "The Poet as Hero," did not appear in *The Old Huntsman* though it was published in the *Cambridge Magazine* (2 December, 1916). If it has less of the vague music of the other verses, it still pays conspicuous homage to a diction now almost eliminated from trench poem and satire alike. It is a key poem and one can see why Sassoon wanted an instant audience for it. Here the speaker sees no consolation in his earlier attitudes and offers an uncompromising explanation for his reversion from knight-errant poet, "Riding in armour bright, serene and strong," to bitter soldier-satirist. He vows to avenge the deaths of friends, to *smite* (not "right") their "wrongs" and to wring poetry and passion from negative feelings of "lust" and "senseless hatred":

> But now I've said good-bye to Galahad,
> And am no more the knight of dreams and show:
> For lust and senseless hatred make me glad,
> And my killed friends are with me where I go.

In a crowning irony the poet offers "absolution" through his "songs." The word returns us to the title of Sassoon's first poem. But now the forgiveness for his sins, though couched in pietistic terms, is *not* a Christian remission; instead it is a personal solution arrived at by the expedient of speaking his mind. The only worthwhile "absolution" derives from the twin purgatives of writing out and fighting out his feelings of anger and loss.

A Whispered Tale

Another December poem and recognizably a sonnet, "A Whispered Tale" was dedicated to "Julian Dadd of C Company, First Royal Welch Fusiliers, who got hit on the neck at Guichy on September 3, when his brother (who got the M.C.) was killed. His other brother was killed at Gallipoli..." (WP, p. 63). Julian's injury was debilitating enough. The bullet destroyed "one of the nerve-centres in the throat" and "paralysed the right vocal chord." It rendered him, in his own words, "a permanent vocal cripple" (letter from Dadd to Sassoon, 12 February, 1917, IWMP).

Seeing Dadd, who came to visit Sassoon at Litherland on 22 December, took the poet "out of himself" and away from the "confessional" mode of extreme subjectivism that had characterized much of his recent writing. Contact with the reality principle usually brought Sassoon's poetry back to the language of experience and the specifics of war. In his diary he wrote:

> Julian Dadd came to Liverpool [Sassoon was now at Litherland] for one night. He has lost his voice, being hit in the throat; it was queer to see him so excited, telling us about the First Battalion show at Guichy on September 3 in a strained whisper. Memory supplied his old voice [p. 104].

Another tribute, like "A Subaltern," to the "good simple soldier," "A Whispered Tale" offers a picture "of a rough-and ready nobility that rises above adversity" (Thorpe, 1966, p. 17), a sympathetic vignette of a man whose terrible experience of loss ("both your brothers killed to make you wise") and crippling injury have not destroyed his essential humanity. Gadd's answer to the "crater-lines of hell," like David Thomas's in "A Subaltern," is not to indulge in "babbling phrases" but to "whisper" "sour jokes" and just get on with things. Invested with the "wry" humor of its subject, "A Whispered Tale" shows Sassoon both observing keenly and exercising a compassionate memory to bring back "the voice I knew." Dadd was duly appreciative: "If you have heard half as much praise of the poem as I have, you will know that your "thoughts and expression have got home with a vengeance" (letter from Dadd to Sassoon, 31 May, 1917, IWMP).

The Distant Song

Bird song, which for Sassoon is a reminder of a rural England of idyllic and melodious associations, is invariably a potent restorative force. In both notebooks and *Memoirs* there are countless references to birds and in particular the spring notes of his favorite blackbird and its cousin the thrush, both quintessentially English songsters. At Craiglockhart Sassoon would entitle a poem "Thrushes." But in "The Distant Song" the bird is recognized only by its notes;

it is a remote presence—both "Beyond the German Line" and as vocal harbinger of a spring that seems far away in that war-torn landscape. But among "the splintered trees of Hidden Wood" where man has denatured the sylvan setting, a blackbird sings resolutely on—an incongruous reminder of spring in an alien setting. In his diary of 13 April, Sassoon had remarked:

> the still leafless trees, shivering sentries of the unhappy countryside.... And later on the voice of a thrush came to me from a long way off, muffled by the gusts of wind, a thrush singing behind the German lines [p. 55].

The poem, based on this earlier journal account, was itself reworked, many years later, for the concluding paragraph of *Memoirs of a Fox-Hunting Man* where Sassoon, giving the incident much greater prominence, recollected his thoughts on that Easter Sunday: "Standing in that dismal ditch he could find no consolation in the thought that Christ was risen" but noted that "Somewhere out of sight beyond the splintered tree-tops of Hidden Wood a bird had begun to sing."

As usual Sassoon identifies a significant moment and makes it the focal point of his poem. Another piece about conditions at the Front would have risked being repetitious, even though Sassoon was only just coming to terms with the filth and noise of existence in the trenches. So Sassoon stresses the inherent irony of his situation: aware of the irrepressible springing of spring, it can only be occasionally glimpsed in a world where man's malign efforts, directed against the restorative forces of Nature, threaten to dissolve that precarious balance:

> So he stood staring from his ghastly ditch,
> While Paradise was in the distant song.

The March-Past

"The March-Past" brings Sassoon back to the present, to the very different world of Litherland and its "Blighty" attitudes. The great Christian festivals—Easter in "Stand To: Good Friday Morning" and "The Distant Song" and now Christmas Day in "The March-Past"—provoke in Sassoon un–Christian sentiments. Here they are intensified by the poet's hatred of the place: "This place will kill the poetry in me," he confided to Ottoline Morrell (letter from Sassoon to Ottoline Morrell, 6 December, 1916), and his scorn for commanding officers who "speed glum heroes up the line to death" while enjoying a privileged life behind the lines or at home ("Base Details," WP, p. 71). Such old men Sassoon had witnessed, that very day, in the Formby Golf Club, with "their noses in their plates guzzling for all they're worth" (*Diaries*, 25 Dec., p. 106). Perhaps too much vitriol went into the making of this poem. Sassoon himself recognized this danger when recording in his notebook:

> This Christmas night I did a grim jeering, heart-rending sort of thing about a General taking the salute as we marched past him.... And I remembered old wine-faced Rawlinson (Commander of the Fourth Army) at Flixécourt last May, as we swung down the hill with the band playing, two hundred officers and N.C.O's of his Fourth Army; and how many of them are alive and hale on Christmas Day? About half, I expect; perhaps less. But I'll warrant old Sir Henry made a good dinner in his chateau... [p. 107].

The technique and gist message of "The March-Past," the use of pun, bathos and ironic juxtaposition, anticipate the more controlled satiric methods of "Base Details." As in that poem, a deliberate pun hides in the title. The march-past is not, as the corps commander sees it, a parade-ground exercise in military "esprit de corps" and an opportunity for personal self-aggrandizement. For the poet it is a literal march *past* life into death. Here in a sudden and surreal reversal, the corps commander is revealed for what he really is, not the "damned good sort" of officer jargon but an ineffectual "corps(e)-commander," a useless "mute." Despite his upper-class lifestyle (already undermined in the Popeian anticlimax of "He was our leader, and a judge of Port") and his "ribboned breast puffed out for all to see," he is unaware that he *is* a corpse commander and that it is Death — more menacingly personified than in the Donne sonnet Sassoon had just been reading (*Diaries*, p. 107)—leering from behind him, who really controls the "show" (the offensive). It is Death who takes the salute of men who are, after the manner of Roman gladiators acknowledging their emperor, "about to die."

Enemies

"Enemies," Sassoon's first poem of 1917, was written after a day's hunting with the Cheshire, his leave having been extended. It is a product of Sassoon's visionary imagination, of his remembered love for David Thomas, and perhaps an attempt to come to terms with his burgeoning guilt at having killed enemy soldiers. The setting, which has similarities with Owen's "Strange Meeting," is "Armageddon," an afterworld where the dead "hulking Germans," shot by Sassoon when his "brooding rage was hot," confront the speaker's dead comrade. (After Thomas's death, we recall, Sassoon had pronounced that he "would gladly stick a bayonet into a German by daylight" [*Diaries*, 1 April, 1916, p. 52].) As in Owen's poem, the confrontations take place in a kind of Dantesque Hell ("a queer sunless place") in which the "smile" of the English subaltern establishes a bond between the dead men which words have, not surprisingly, failed to achieve. Michael Thorpe is right to "wish Sassoon had attempted something more ample on this theme." Nonetheless his view that "though it is implicit in his war poetry ... that he has no strong anti–German feelings, his failure to crystallize this into a positive attitude exemplifies his limitations" (Thorpe, 1966, p. 33) is not confirmed by the evidence of this poem or of the earlier "A Night Attack" in which Sassoon empathizes with a young Prussian soldier and his cruel end. Certainly "Enemies" must have impressed Owen; it is to this poem's credit that it would provide the initial inspiration for "Strange Meeting," unarguably the finest poem to emerge from the war.

When I'm Among a Blaze of Lights

Another poetic report from the "Nation at Home," "When I'm Among a Blaze of Lights" reveals Sassoon's unease in a world of "cocktail bars" and "tawdry music." Naturally shy, even hermitic and certainly not interested in going to watering holes to chat up women "dawdling through delights," Sassoon preferred either his own company or that of his close circle of male friends. Here in Litherland and in the company of people he found reprehensible, he did the usual Sassoon thing: he distanced himself from such an environment by imagining himself elsewhere, comfortably ensconced in his own home among his treasured possessions, a setting he would lovingly describe in "Repression of War Experience." Suddenly his reverie is interrupted by the inevitable offer of "Another drink?" The gesture forces him to return to a hearty, back-slapping world where the soporific combination of alcohol and mindless conversation petrifies his romantic feelings and turns his "living heart to stone." It is, as Michael Thorpe says, "a rather prudish piece" (Thorpe, 1966, p. 27). The fastidious artist is repelled by the socializing antics of his fellow officers, but reveals, at the same time, a barely concealed capacity for misogyny and a disdain that shades into priggishness.

The Elgar Violin Concerto

One way of escaping from the monotony of camp life was through music. Writing in his notebook on 23 January, Sassoon waxed eloquent about its compensations: " (A few bars of Elgar's Violin C.) pp. nobilmente etc made me glorious with dreams tonight. Elgar always moves me deeply because his is the melody of an average Englishman (and I suppose I am more or less the same)." Commending the French composer Ravel for painting "a Spanish garden nocturne for me," the poet added:

> In all the noblest passages and the noblest strains of horns and violins I shut my eyes, seeing in the darkness a shape always the same — in spite of myself — the suffering mortal figure on a cross, but the face is my own. And again there are hosts of shadowy forms with uplifted arms — souls of men agonised and aspiring, hungry for what they seek as God in vastness [*Diaries*, 23 January, p. 124].

The poem is a close enough versification of the prose description but Sassoon is careful on two scores: one, he understandably gives the inspirational credit to Elgar rather than Ravel; two, he refrains, in what would have seemed a narcissistic gesture, from identifying himself with a suffering Christ-figure who is both martyr and savior. The inspiration is again classical music, but even music cannot reconcile the paradoxes inherent in Sassoon's world-view. The soulful strings remind the poet of the "sorrows of the world," but they also conjure up visions of a Christian sacrifice which now, in the context of the war, seems at once glorious and pointless ("A sign where faith and ruin meet"). Christ's sacrifice for man has not forestalled the tragedy of war; its only reality continues to be suffering and death. Music both heightens the poet's tragic sense and, paradoxically, strives to rise above mere mortal concerns:

> O music undeterred by death,
> And darkness closing on your flame,
> Christ whispers in your dying breath,
> And haunts you with his tragic name.

Blighters

"Blighters," on the other hand, pulls no punches and offers no "holier than thou" attitudinizing. While the company, that of a "pleasant and intelligent" fellow officer, made for an amusing evening at the Liverpool Hippodrome, the revue, Sassoon recalled, "provided me with a bit of material for satire ... I wrote the afterwards well-known lines called 'Blighters' in which I asserted that I'd like to see a tank come down the stalls at a music hall performance where — in my opinion — the jingoism of the jokes and songs appeared to 'mock the riddled corpses round Bapaume'" (SJ, p. 45).

As Sassoon's "farewell to England," he wanted to keep it short — and satiric; his recipe of "two or three harsh, peremptory stanzas" is here reduced to two terse quatrains. The targets are "blighters," a colloquialism employed both as a general indictment of anything that blights, and particularly directed at those who stay in "Blighty" and profit from the misfortunes of others. In the poem both general and specific meanings coalesce.

The structure mirrors that of "They," another epigram in which the "Nation at Home" dominates the first stanza, the "Nation Abroad" the second. But the "tour de force," literally, is provided by Sassoon's surreal vision of war in the form of a "lurching" tank which comes lumbering down the stalls of the Hippodrome. Only a dose of real terror can stir audience and reader alike out of their complacency and jingoism.

The piece is shot through with heavy irony. The "tier beyond tier" of the House superficially reminds the sardonic observer of serried and disciplined ranks of soldiers anticipating a "Show" in which many will inevitably perish. But here the verbs emphasize the vulgarity of an audience demeaned and disparaged by the epithets "grin" and "cackle." Worse, the chorus-line of "prancing" women are no better than harlots showing off their bodies in an atmosphere of dissipation and false bonhomie generated not by the heat of battle but by inebriation ("drunk with din"). So impervious are the audience to the reality of war that they respond by indulging in the sentimental claptrap of some vapid music hall number ("We're sure the Kaiser loves our dear old tanks").

The poet's reaction is predictably fierce. The absurdly sentimental view of these lumbering leviathans gives Sassoon an opportunity to develop the stock personification in a grimly comic way, to wish on this "House" a nightmare vision of the hell that is trench warfare. For Sassoon's tanks do "lurch" in a manner reminiscent of drunken "blighters or chorus-girls swaying to syncopated rag-time tunes." But now, if the poet has his way, they will "lurch towards the wealthy cacklers in the stalls," the rhythms of their progress as metronomic as those of rag-time, but remorseless, inhuman. Now it will be the turn of these blighters to experience that abject terror that is daily currency for the ordinary "tommy."

The soldier may dream of "Home Sweet Home," but the words of this song also embody a falsehood. For this microcosm reflects, if more nakedly, the values of a blighted nation whose jingoism mocks the victims of war. And by extension it *is* a national malaise, for the "House" could also signify that chamber where politicians spout just as obscenely about the glamorous heroics of the conflict, and whose denizens are accorded an equally fierce punishment in "Fight to a Finish." Finally it is left to the soldier-poet and not the chorus to remind his readers of the carnage of "riddled corpses." "Bapaume," the site of a bloody offensive, may rhyme with "home," but the name, remote and desolating, sounds a death-knell by way of conclusion.

Life-Belts (Southampton to Havre)

"Life Belts" was a sonnet for which Sassoon never sought publication, his last production before returning to "the unmitigated hell of the 'Spring Offensive'" (*Diaries*, 7 February, p. 130). Later in the war Sassoon would essay another composition on a similar theme when, returning to France for the last time, he would describe the doom-laden progress of the troopships from Alexandria to Marseilles. The 15 February notebook had described the train journey from Waterloo with "relatives and friends blinking and swallowing sobs" (*Diaries*, p. 132); the poem charts the soldiers' continuing progress across the channel where "comfortless war breaks into each blind brain." The poet attempts to empathize with their feelings, but instead manages to project his own prejudice against women when describing men who, half-recovered from their war experiences, "must grope again / For some girl-face." The "life-belts" of the title are their hopes for an unlikely, and to Sassoon, distinctly unpromising, future:

>...like life-belts in a wreck
> They clutch at gentle plans — pathetic schemes
> For peace next year.

It is left to the poet to reflect, bitterly, on a fate that will inevitably turn their "pathetic" dreams to nightmares.

Conscripts

In "Conscripts," Sassoon forsakes the short epigrammatic sally, which had become his stock-in-trade during convalescence in England, for a longer reflective piece — five stanzas of six lines with rhymed couplets at the end of each verse — in which the irony, for once, is directed at himself. Shortly to return to France and the trenches (his trip from Southampton to Le Havre on 15 February occasioned the diary poem "Life-Belts"), "Conscripts" takes as subject Sassoon's drilling of young men at Litherland, an activity which he had recorded in his diary of 27 December, 1916: "Clumsy recruits ... *On* garrrd! Long-point at the stomach etc. Red-and-black-striped-jersey instructors with well-poised bodies and wasp-waists, moving easily among the bunchy, awkward privates — pathetic crowd of willy-nilly patriots and (?) heroes!" (*Diaries*, 27 December, p. 110). The question-mark provides an important clue to the poem's summational stance: initially scornful of recruits' "attractive attitudes" that have no place on the parade-ground, the speaker gradually reveals how unwillingly he accepts his role of squad bully, and finally answers his own journal query about "heroes" by asserting that in the final analysis not only did the least attractive of these "squaddies" reveal "stubborn-hearted virtues," but, "in extremis," came through with flying colors — "stood and played the hero to the end."

The poem is, "inter alia," a manifestation of Sassoon's attempt to express his personal feelings in a way acceptable to his readership. True, it begins as a public poem on an innocuous theme, the drilling of raw recruits (*c.f.* Henry Reed's Second World War poem, "Naming of Parts"), a piece that could be published in *The Spectator* without causing offense. Indeed, writing to Lady Ottoline Morrell, Sassoon alerted her to its impending appearance in print, adding, "So I am really becoming highly respectable" (letter from Sassoon to Morrell, 6 December, 1916, ULUT).

But the middle section reveals the suppressed emotions of the parade-ground; the enforced role of "raucous" martinet contrasts not only with Sassoon's romantic and libertarian spirit — "how I longed to set them free" — but with homoerotic longings barely concealed by the employment of such arch personifications as "Young Fancy — how I loved him all the while," the parapraxis of "joy was slack" and the innuendo of the drill command to "Press on your butts!" Indeed the final "confession" hints at a sexual activity which, while it may be more desired than actualized, is not altogether erased by the deliberately flippant tone of:

> And many a sickly, slender lord who'd filled
> My soul long since with lutanies of sin,
> Went home, because they couldn't stand the din.

The passage provoked an extraordinary reaction from Sassoon's friend Edmund Gosse. To Morrell the poet revealed: "Gosse wrote and rebuked me for my 'libel on the House of Lords' in the *Spectator* one. I can't imagine how he read such a thing into the harmless lines" (letter from Sassoon to Morrell, 16 March, 1917, ULUT).

The transition from lust to war is significant, both in the context of these "harmless lines" and in terms of Sassoon's progress as a war poet. Honest enough to confront his feelings, however obliquely in the poem, Sassoon characteristically assuages his sense of personal guilt about his sexuality by declaring his faith in the common soldier's virtues. The poem's gnomic conclusion offers an encomium to "kind, common men"; it is the "awkward squad" of the opening line rather than "sickly slender" aristocrats who will not only stubbornly endure, but who will be metamorphosed, finally, into be-ribboned heroes. It is the *poet*, both as a clandestine lover of men of his own class and as public parade-ground bully, who needs to reproach himself; he has feelings for some of these conscripts but will still be prepared to ship "them all to France" and possible death. Ironically and disturbingly, it is those he "despised" on the parade-ground, those he can "count as friend" "hardly a man of them" because of their ordinariness, who will emerge as heroes. Now free of any erotic or elitist prejudice imposed on them by the voyeuristic poet, they will not only survive the war but will march "resplendent home with crowns and stars."

If the conclusion, sentimental and jingoistic by turns, hardly rings true — after all, Sassoon was strenuously denying the heroic stance and saying "goodbye to Galahad" in other poems of the period — it is not difficult to see how such a conclusion allowed the poet an opportunity to exorcise his own feelings of shame and guilt. Adrian Caesar finds the poem unsatisfactory in other ways, arguing that "the juxtaposition of the 'common ones' who are virtuous with 'lords' who are 'sickly' and implicitly 'sinful,' serves to celebrate an idea of 'manliness' which is inextricably bound up with military values." What Caesar sees as "the false oppositions of aesthete and soldier" are, in his estimation, "resolved by denigrating the former to the enhancement of the latter" (Caesar, 1993, p. 82). While this is undoubtedly true, what the poet is primarily concerned to offer is a sardonic comment on his *own* predilections. Increasingly Sassoon would sublimate both his homoerotic feelings and his class-consciousness for the greater good of a shared sacrifice with his men. In this sense, "Conscripts" is a watershed poem, an attempt to confront issues of both private and public identity that would preoccupy him more and more.

Base Details

"Base Details" sees Sassoon returning to his now proven epigrammatic manner. The first poem of the so-called "Spring Offensive" of 1917, it was part of the diary entry for 4 March. The earliest of the verses to be included in *Counter-Attack*, it is, like "The March Past" and the yet to be written "The General," "directed against types rather than attitudes"; in its "simplicity and singleness of effect" it resembles, as Johnston remarks, "the clever, hard-hitting political cartoon" (Johnston, 1964, p. 105).

The poem reveals Sassoon's now consummate mastery of the mode, from its effective, punning title, its tersely alliterative epithets of "puffy petulant face" and "guzzling and gulping," to its keen ear for the idioms and cadences of officer-speak. The equivocal title, a reference both to the officers at the Base ("details" were men in military parlance) and to the base or craven characteristics of staff officers, shows Sassoon unwilling to give the game away in the title, as he had so nearly done in "The One-Legged Man." The poem, through its own descriptive "details," reinforces its own satiric assumptions; indeed, much of its robust vigor derives from the speaker's mocking identification with these "Scarlet Majors at the Base." The phrase, a likely echo of Robbie Ross's "screaming scarlet majors" (SJ, p. 29), constitutes another pun, a reference both to their red uniform flashes and to a complexion reflecting their port-soaked, choleric dispositions. At Litherland Sassoon had already developed a healthy dislike for such people; in his notebook entry for Christmas Day he had referred to "old men with their noses in their plates guzzling for all they're worth" (*Diaries*, p. 106). Now in Rouen and waiting to go "up the line" these feelings were ignited again:

> A Brigadier-General came and sat down a few feet away. He had the puffy, petulant face of a man with a liver who spends most of the year sitting in London clubs. He began guzzling hors d'oeuvres as though his life depended on the solidity of his meal [*Diaries*, 27 February, p. 139].

The upper-class but ultimately schoolboyish speech of "Poor young chap" and "this last scrap" emphasizes once again the disparity between these old guzzlers, bloated with good living, and the "glum heroes" whom they "speed" (the word is evocative, granted the rate at which young conscripts were dying) "up the line." But Sassoon, as usual, reserves his "knock-out blow" for the last round. Only when "the war is done and youth stone dead" will these self-satisfied and deluded old men "toddle" home (their gait as senile as their speech) and, in a final, bathetic gesture, die in their own beds. As Sassoon's diary had put it: "You will guzzle yourself to the grave and gas about the Great War, long after I am dead with all my promise unfulfilled" (*Diaries*, 4 March, p. 140). In the poem Sassoon wisely avoids such a subjective response. The ironic contrasts in the verse are there to tell their own tale: on the one hand, self-inflicted gluttony and ignorance, on the other the unavoidable prospect of death or mutilation in the trenches.

In the Church of St. Ouen

On the same day, 4 March, Sassoon wrote "In the Church of St. Ouen." After all the anger that had been generated by watching "these bald-headed incompetent belly-fillers" (*Diaries*, p. 140), he felt the need to distance himself from such negative emotions. In "Base Details" a sense of ironic detachment is generated by the contrasts *within* the verse; here the poet invests an entire sonnet with positive and subjective emotions — his yearning for the numinous, his search for a state of grace which the trenches cannot satisfy. The church at St. Ouen certainly did. Writing to Felicitas Corrigan nearly fifty years later, he still remembered the experience: "But St. Ouen completely got me — I liked it far better than the Cathedral (Rouen) which didn't make me feel holy at all" (Corrigan, 1973, p. 84).

By then the septuagenarian Sassoon was the most devout of Roman Catholics. But as this poem makes clear, the young officer already longed for an epiphany; the "purple passage" of the notebook (Sassoon's own description of a piece sent to Ottoline Morrell), shows he came close to one:

> He had wandered into this astonishing Roman Catholic temple to stare at the coloured windows. And now, in the gathering gloom, glory faded slowly from those gateways of heaven, those jewelled frescoes of tracery and brightness. There were smouldering flames in the great rose above the organ — hell-fires stoked for heretics.... In the house of God he had found, not God, but beauty.... He was going away from all this, going away to the naked horror of the War, that he already knew so well [*Diaries*, p. 138].

The poem captures this sense of spiritual beauty, a beauty that will shortly be obliterated by the intrusive "music" of battle:

> Hearing rich music at the close of day,
> The Spring Offensive (Easter is its date)
> Calls me. And that's the music I await.

But if the voice of the devotional poet is anticipated in this poem, it is a voice that still searches rather than finds, even in the Église de St. Ouen:

> My spirit longs for prayer,
> And, lost to God, I seek him everywhere.

It seems curious that Sassoon did not publish this poem during a lifetime that ended with the resolution of his spiritual quest. Perhaps his abiding conviction was that the sonnet was too "purple," too self-indulgent for public consumption.

Return

No such authorial doubts surround "Return," which was "written on the train at night" as Sassoon returned to catch the "music" of the Spring Offensive. The music in the poem was "the boom of guns along the hill"; the "return" is both to the Front and to the haunting voices of those already killed in battle. Sassoon disliked the poem, regarding it as "An example of entirely artificial emotionalism. The dead are underground all right, but they don't care whether I come back or not. This is the sort of poetry I'm always trying to avoid writing" (*Diaries*, 29 March, p. 143).

As usual Sassoon's instincts were right. The device does have a respectable provenance — Sassoon may, for instance, have read Hardy's "Spectres That Grieve"— but here the procedure lacks conviction and veracity. Too reliant on studied poeticisms, the whisper's prophecy of approaching death ("Have patience and your bones shall share our bed") is followed by the assertion that for the present they will live on in his memory, "quickened in my blood." That at least was an honest assessment of the poet's state of mind.

Foot Inspection

The activity in "Foot Inspection," a poem included in the notebook for 3 April, is mundane enough: men, tired after a long route march, have taken off their boots to ease the pain of blistered and swollen feet and to allow their officer to inspect them. The officer is in a caring and attentive frame of mind as he first peers through the chinks in the barn at this intimate scene, then joins his charges, conscious of their weary, weather-beaten faces and stiff limbs. Like a lover he regards them with "pity and stabbing tenderness"— the oxymoron recalls the "good fury" of "The Kiss"— as his eyes meet theirs. The tenderness stabs: he is pained by the sorrow of a love that must remain unspoken and yet exceeds that conventionally expected of an officer for his men.

The main focus of his concern is Morgan, for whom he reserves a special place in his affections (and to whom he would later dedicate "Journey's End"). Dramatic irony resides in the fact that the poet-officer confesses to himself that he would be willing to die for this soldier if such an act of selflessness might release Morgan from future embroilments. A Christ-like gesture aimed (it follows a foot-inspection that recalls Christ's washing of his apostles' feet) at a particular "disciple," it is also an expression — and the use of "die" carries sexual nuances — of Sassoon's homoerotic yearnings:

> How glad I'd be to die, if dying could set him free
> From battles.

Characteristically Sassoon deliberately lowers the tone in the public gesture of the conclusion. A joke relieves the tension, the everyday world of practicalities reasserts itself in the banal details of "grimy socks," "cigarettes" and what the officer hopes is the trooper's perceived image of him as a "decent bloke." His personal feelings must needs remain private and undisclosed.

The Optimist

In "The Optimist" Sassoon reverts to his proven satiric manner, the target once again the "base details" of his earlier epigram. The formula of "two or three harsh, peremptory and colloquial stanzas" with a knock-out blow in the last line is now one of the hallmarks of his sardonic verse; furthermore he has learnt to employ an ironic title that does not telegraph the poem's ultimate coup de grâce. Deftly Sassoon builds up a picture of a behind-the-line "optimist" by allowing him to indulge his own anti–German flag-waving — from the safety of H.Q. — in the clichés of "brass hats" and politicians:

> We'd "got the Germans absolutely beat,"
> And he'd "come back to watch them getting hell."

Only in the final stanza does the poet expose the reasons for the man's "optimism" — he has been "wounded in the head" and is no longer "quite the ticket." By implication neither are the politicians and generals who mouth these chauvinistic platitudes; at least this absurd "optimist" is a genuine victim of war. That he is unaware of the mental effects of his head wound should make him a figure of pathos. But his irrational warmongering is not only dangerous; it is, in Sassoon's eyes, positively diabolic. It is not for nothing that, when asked if he has been wounded in the head, he should reply with an inane smile that his condition is "A souvenir of Devil's Wood!"

The Rear-Guard

Sassoon knew that "The Rear-Guard," unlike some of his recent efforts ("The Return" for example), was "a strong poem." Written from his hospital bed at Denmark Hill, it was the only "trench piece" to stem from Sassoon's brief but searing spring experience of the Hindenburg line. Sassoon had never before witnessed death and mutilation on the scale he here encountered as the survivors mingled with the corpses of yet another failed offensive. In his diary of 14 April, two days before he was shot in the shoulder, Sassoon both recorded the ghastly scene and presaged his own demise:

> And everywhere one sees the British Tommy in various states of dismemberment — most of them are shot through the head — so not so

> fearful as the shell-twisted Germans. Written at 9.30 sitting in the Hindenburg underground tunnel on Sunday night, fully expecting to get killed on Monday morning [p. 155].

This entry is the key to a poem that not only recalls in harrowing detail the physical decomposition of war's victims but invests a routine activity with a huge human significance. For "groping along the tunnel," part of the rabbit-warren of the front line that Sassoon had inspected for the first time on 13 April, he encounters a recumbent soldier. Himself sleepless, he irritably asks him the whereabouts of "headquarters" and, receiving no reply, swears and kicks the sleeper. As he flashes his light, recognition dawns; the man cannot respond because he is unanswerably dead, yet another pathetic, decomposing victim of war:

> Savage, he kicked a soft unanswering heap,
> And flashed his beam across the livid face
> Terribly glaring up, whose eyes yet wore
> Agony dying hard ten days before;
> And fists of fingers clutched a blackening wound.

The poem derives its authority from a number of sources. Its attention to detail, to the pathetic detritus of war, "tins, boxes, bottles," "a mirror smashed"— presumably like its owner — reveals a quality that would characterize Owen's poetry. The remarkable imagery of "fists of fingers" may well have been suggested by the poet's festering hand condition which had recently required medical treatment (*Diaries*, 12 April, p. 153). The situation, so recently encountered, is nightmarishly revisited. The descent into this Dantesque Inferno of underground shafts is here convincingly sustained, as its rotting bodies mingle with a humanity reduced to "dazed muttering creatures underground." It is a world from which the speaker only escapes in the final stanza where "with sweat of horror in his hair," he unloads his sense of hell "behind him step by step" as he returns to a "twilight air" that is, paradoxically, more dangerous because more exposed than the subterranean world of the trenches. But even this is, by implication, preferable to the hell he has just experienced. If the observer's relief is palpable, so too is his compassion for the ordinary victim of war, here rendered the more convincing because preceded by an act of apparent callousness.

Sassoon knew the poem was an effective piece of description, commenting later that though it was written "ten days after I was wounded" and when Gosse "thought I was suffering from severe shock," it was "a strong poem" (WP, p. 76). To Ottoline Morrell he had been less guarded, enthusing from his hospital bed: "I have done the best 'horrible poem' I shall ever do since I came here" (letter from Sassoon to Morrell, April 1917, ULUT). What Sassoon does not acknowledge here is the fact that he often wrote most compellingly when under emotional stress — as future poems such as "Dear Roberto" would testify — and when the memory of actual events was freshly etched in his mind. Sassoon's diary, a quarry for the poem's setting, characteristically makes no mention of a "strange meeting," only recording:

> I went to bed at 5am, after patrolling our 900-yard front —*alone!*— in a corridor of the underground communication trench of the Hindenberg Line — a wonderful place [*Diaries*, p. 154, 14 April].

Wilfred Owen clearly found the poem a seminal one. There are a number of resonances from it in "Strange Meeting": the comparison of the trenches to Hell, the meeting with a dead soldier, the Dantesque or Virgilian vision of lost souls, even the imagery of prodding "encumbered sleepers" and the opening escape into a "profound dull tunnel." All these features suggest that Owen knew and admired Sassoon's poem. What Owen adds is a visionary statement in which the dead man comes alive and becomes both the poet's "alter ego," destroyed by war's dehumanizing force, and a German soldier pointlessly killed. In presaging a continuing era of modern violence, Owen's verses become a prophetic statement in the same way as Yeats's "The Second Coming" or Eliot's *The Waste Land*— poems soon to be written.

To the Warmongers

Also written while convalescing at Denmark Hill Hospital and first jotted down in his notebook on 23 April, "To the Warmongers" was another of those poems whose angry and uncomfortable denunciation of the war and its horrors rendered it unsuitable for publication in *Counter-Attack*. Its form is an uncharacteristic one and may derive from his reading of Hardy's "A Death-Day Recalled" or Graves's "The Assault Heroic"; its jaunty trimeters act as a counterpoint to a ghastly catalogue of "horrors from the abyss" where young faces are "sucked down" into gaseous mud, their limbs twisted "awry" in "brutish pain." Intended as a stark message to "the warmongers" who still insist that heroism and Christian values prevail in their "triumph half-divine / And the glory of the dead," it also reveals Sassoon's turbulent emotions at the time. His renewed sense of guilt, a guilt earlier adumbrated in "Enemies," stems from his own apparent inviolability. Part of the process of bloodletting, he has somehow escaped final retribution. He is left accursed and inconsolable as he recalls the last moments of his doomed comrades. The speaker's wounds are emotional, not physical, but they are wounds that cannot be healed:

> But a curse is on my head
> That shall not be unsaid,
> And the wounds in my heart are red,
> For I have watched them die.

Wounded

Also written at Denmark Hill Hospital, "Wounded" is a very different poem, so mannered that Sassoon quite properly kept it unpublished in the diary. All the old clichés come flooding back as he tries, without much conviction, to capture the sensation of a newfound peace. Slipping in and out of consciousness, he imagines sylvan scenes ("a forest murmurous with green") and woodland flowers that become tangible presences in bedside roses and narcissi. The nightmares have receded; a few days of sanctuary in hospital have washed away for himself and his fellow patients the "squalor and misery and strain of ten days ago" [*Diaries*, 24 April, p. 160].

The General

Sassoon's contempt for the military authorities (rather than warmongering civilians) resurfaces in "The General." That the poet's second volume *Counter-Attack* made Heinemann distinctly uneasy and was nearly suppressed before publication may be in part due to a poem which, more than most intended for the collection, "violated the rule against criticism of the conduct of the war" (Johnston, 1964, p. 106).

Close in spirit to "Base Details" and "The March-Past," "The General" is Sassoon's shortest published war poem. Silkin regards it as "a slighter poem with the same concerns" as "Base Details" but it is "slighter" only in terms of its abbreviated form — seven lines of brisk tetrameters (Silkin, 1987, p. 160). It owes its considerable power not just to the usual Sassoon "coup de grâce" — and none of his epigrams has a more telling reversal in the final line — but to the convincingly authentic dialogue and the shifts of tone and rhythm which characterize the piece. The initial jaunty "Good morning, good morning!" of the General and the desperate bonhomie of the soldiers' view that "He's a cheery old card" frames a moment of sheer disillusion in which the verse slows to a bitter curse at what the General, aided and abetted by his "incompetent swine," has actually achieved. That Harry and Jack can momentarily suspend these feelings is a measure of their fortitude and trust, a trust horribly betrayed by a conclusion which still manages to shock the reader by its matter-of-fact finality:

> But he did for them both by his plan of attack.

The battle of Arras offers up yet another example of incompetence, a wrong-headed strategy in which the general's "plan of attack" accounts not for an unseen enemy but for the long-suffering and tolerant British "Tommy."

The Hawthorn Tree

Intended as a song (to an old tune), "The Hawthorn Tree" is about as close to pastoral lyric as anything Sassoon managed to compose in 1917. It manages to capture something of the direct unpretentiousness of a Hardy "reverie" or Wordsworth lyric. That it appears in the *Collected Poems* next to the misogynistic "Glory of Women" and "Their Frailty" is a reminder that, thirty years on, Sassoon believed these strategically placed verses would provide a palinode to what Thorpe calls the "bitterly accusing" poems "with their unqualified scorn for the selfishness of women's love" (Thorpe, 1966, p. 33). By taking his cue from Hardy, Sassoon permits the woman in "The Hawthorn Tree" to express her feelings; the accusatory "you" of "Glory of Women" and the distancing "she" of "Their Frailty" are here replaced by a mother's empathetic awareness of her son's longing for home. The poem's opening understatement, "Not much to me is yonder lane," betrays an intensity of feeling the mother is unable to put into words. Even "a shower of rain" serves to remind her of unstated emotions that can only be expressed by tears if her son dies. Like the Wordsworth of the "Intimations" ode, who could reflect that "the meanest flower that blows" produced "thoughts that do often lie too deep for tears," the May blossom which they both know and love becomes a visual reminder of the unspoken bond between mother and son, an objective correlative for a renewal that she knows may well be doomed.

Death in the Garden / A War Widow / A Quiet Walk / In an Underground Dressing-Station

True to form or at least to his self-appointed role of poet, Sassoon continued to write during May and June, acutely aware of the irony inherent in his position. Now convalescing in "a very pleasant country house (Lord and Lady Brassey's), where perfect good taste prevails, and nobody sleeps in the clothes he wore last week and this" (*Diaries*, 13 May, p. 163), Sassoon was deliberately attempting to repress all thoughts of the war, "shaking off the furies that pursued me ... an Orestes freed from the tyranny of doom. The war is a vague trouble that one reads about in the morning paper." The English spring was performing its usual therapies, the reviews of *The Old Huntsman*, published on 8 May, were encouraging. In this mood he wrote not only "The Hawthorn-Tree" but in the same couple of days, "Death in the Garden" and "A War Widow."

By the following week, when he wrote "A Quiet Walk" and "In an Underground Dressing-Station," his tranquil mood had disappeared. But even in an escapist frame of mind, he could not forget his comrades in arms. "Death in the Garden," like "The Last Meeting," embodies a dawn vision of a loved one. But the omens are presageful: the dawn is "grey," his ghost is "lonely" and "astray." As the wind stirs, he vanishes with a sudden finality that convinces the poet that he has, at that very moment, expired in battle:

> I knew that he was killed when I awoke.
> At zero-hour they shot him in the head
> Far off in France, before the morning broke.

"A War Widow," on the other hand, demonstrates not Sassoon's love of man but his antipathy towards women. Still recuperating at Chapelwood Manor, the home of Lord and Lady Brassey, Sassoon was continuing to enjoy the role of "country wanderer," roaming the "narrow lanes, light-hearted as a lambkin, emotionless as a wise gander" (*Diaries*, 16 May, p. 167). But if he was becoming uncomfortably aware how slight an impact his war verse appeared to have made on the aristocratic Brassey family, he was more disappointed that his poetry, now published in a single volume, had failed to exert discernible influence on a wider and less privileged readership. He felt a sudden sense of his own insignificance — a "name ... not worth preserving ... his 'place' ... only a little book of songs he had made." Writing in his diary Sassoon recorded "A Conversation" in which, he wrote, not without irony, of "a Great Lady" whose aristocratic and elitist attitudes smacked of "an alien intelligence that would not suffer the rebellious creed that was his" (*Diaries*, 15 May, p. 166).

Subsequently, at Chapelwood, Sassoon encountered "a fashionable young woman whose husband was campaigning in the Cameroons.... A fine pair of pearls dangled from her ears and her dark blue eyes goggled emptily.... 'Life is so wonderful — so great — and yet we waste it all in this dreadful War!' she exclaimed" (*Memoirs*, p. 466).

Sassoon wrote all this down much later. At the time, the incident, unrecorded in the notebooks, became the main inspiration for "A War Widow," a trial-run for Sassoon's other poems about women and the war, a verse caricature based on this fashionable but apparently vacuous young thing:

> "Life is *so* wonderful, so vast! — and yet
> We waste it in this senseless war," she said,
> Staring at me with goggling eye-balls set
> Like large star-sapphires in her empty head.

Whatever the distractions, the horrors of the Somme and the more recent memories of Arras would not go away. Even Chapelwood Manor provided one disconcerting reminder when Sassoon, receptive to the good vibrations of "hawthorn-drifts" and "sunlit clouds," encounters a smelly, prostrate body which sent "old, ugly horrors crowding back." "A Quiet Walk," which charts this experience, offers a reminder to the poet that not only do harrowing memories of the war resist repression but that they will resurface at the most inopportune moments. "In An Underground Dressing-Station," a poem revised on the following day though begun back in April at the Front, is Sassoon's acknowledgment of this fact, of his continuing need to confront these demons. The theme, that of a soldier dying in agony, recalls "Died of Wounds"; the terse, condensed manner, that of the recently completed "The General." It is as though Sassoon, in the "no holds barred" search for an unvarnished veracity, is prepared to give us the bloody details, even if it means using a parenthetical prose-like aside: "(He'd got / A bullet in his ankle and he'd been shot / Horribly through the guts)." Granted that, the doctor's final entreaty, kindly intended though it is, seems beside the point:

> "You *must* keep still, my lad." But he was dying.

Supreme Sacrifice

Sassoon wrote one more poem at Chapelwood Manor in which he returned to the theme of "War Widows" and the 1916 piece, "The Hero." "Supreme Sacrifice" again demonstrates the poet's antipathy towards women, and in particular those whose misplaced optimism and "spiritual brightness" enables them to rationalize the brutality and senselessness of "a hopeless show." The specific target was Lady Brassey; the specific lode mined by Sassoon, his own "A Conversation" in which he had recorded her discrepant views:

> She listened to him, with her grey hair and tired white face and later spoke animatedly about how "death is nothing ... And those who are killed in the war — they help us from 'up there,' *they are all helping us to win*" [*Diaries*, 15 May, p. 165].

Sassoon's response to this idea in the poem mingles the forthright and sardonic, but he keeps his own counsel:

> I thought "The world's a silly sort of place
> When people think its pleasant to be dead."
> I thought, "How cheery the brave troops would be
> If Sergeant-Majors taught Theosophy!"

By a strange irony Sassoon was soon hoisted by his own petard. At Craiglockhart he would complain to Robbie Ross of being "hampered by the constant presence of an iron-haired Theosophist in my room all the time" (*Diaries*, 25 September, p. 187).

Chapter 11

"When Will It Stop?"
May 1917 to January 1918

Sassoon's visible distress at the Front-Line carnage had already resulted in the first of his great trench poems. He knew that "The Rear-Guard," written in hospital at Denmark Hill but based on a Hindenburg line experience, was special. Later Sassoon would write to Meiklejohn that "the best poem in it (*Counter-Attack*) is 'The Rear-Guard.'" "Blighty" hypocrisy, as usual, had also triggered a satiric reaction ("To the Warmongers" and "The General" are the best of these) and a rash of conflicting impulses that seemed irreconcilable. Writing to Graves he confided:

> I can't make up my mind which course to adopt (There can only be two). If I decide that I must keep up my reputation as a hero, I must go back as soon as possible.... The alternative is to scheme and plot and wriggle for a reasonable job at home.... In other words I must either go back tout de suite, or (tacitly refuse to go back at all and tell everyone what I'm doing) [letter from Sassoon to Graves, 23 April, 1917].

What Sassoon did decide to do, both as a consequence of his discussions with the Morrells and Bertrand Russell and his growing preoccupation with the suffering of his men, was to "scheme and plot" and, by making a formal and very public protest, "tell everyone" what he was doing and hope thereby to influence events. Ottoline Morrell remembered his angst-ridden mood at the time: "He hated it. How could he possibly train others to go out there knowing what they would have to go through. 'They will all be killed or maimed.' He has suddenly become more aware of all its horrors, and feels caught in a trap, passionately longing to make some protest against it" (Morrell, 1975, p. 181).

Sassoon's ringing statement of defiance, sent to his Commanding Officer, and to a number of important literary figures and subsequently read out in parliament, accused the politicians of "callous complacence," of needlessly prolonging a war now entering a new phase of "aggression and conquest." Suffering was the recurrent motif in the "Protest"; it was the "suffering of the troops" which was being prolonged "for ends" which Sassoon believed to be "evil and unjust" (*Diaries*, 15 June, p. 173).

In August Sassoon, now a huge political liability, was sent — in a tactical maneuver stage-managed by Graves — to a hospital for shell-shocked officers in Scotland. In the meantime Sassoon had written two of his finest and least typical war poems, the combative "To Any Dead Officer" and the confessional "Repression of War Experience." At Craiglockhart, where Sassoon spent the next five months, he not only composed a batch of mordant satires but poems such as "Prelude: The Troops" and "Counter-Attack," poems which sought to re-live the harrowing events of the trenches. Technically these poems may owe a debt to Sassoon's discussions with Owen, and the need, impressed on him by his analyst W. H. R. Rivers, to unburden himself of his repressions. Moreover, the desire to return to his martyred men, which had never entirely disappeared, now returned with renewed intensity, doubtless fostered by Rivers's attempts to channel his "pacifism" in more practical directions, to persuade him that his concern for his men could most usefully be satisfied by looking after them at the Front. A number of anguished short poems, neither trench poems nor satires, focus on this dilemma.

To Any Dead Officer

In a letter to Bartholomew dated 4 July, 1917, Sassoon wrote of "To Any Dead Officer":

> "I solemnly affirm that it is the best war-poem I've done, and Robert Graves says so too. So there! But it is so d — — d pathetic that I can (not) bear to hawk it round to Massingham and Co. (and probably get it sent back again)..." Anxious for it to appear in print, he added, "I think it is the sort of thing that people *ought* to read, because it is so different to the countless elegies that have been done. You will observe that it is written in the slang of the subalterns, and I am sure it is all right" [Keynes, 1962, p. 37].

The idea of creating a poem based on a dialogue with a dead fellow-officer hardly constituted a new direction for Sassoon in 1917. More than a year before, in "The Last Meeting," he had documented a visionary encounter with the ghost of David Thomas, and had written "To His Dead Body" to the supposedly dead Robert Graves. What *was* new and what excited the poet was what he later called its "slangy telephonic" technique. By adopting this breezy, conversational manner and by giving the poem an impersonal title he was able to focus on his friend's essential ordinariness: a decent soldier who "stuck to" his "dirty job and did it fine."

Bathetic rhymes ("done in"/"save your skin") contribute both to this unpretentiousness and to the poem's colloquial vigor; the familiar "you" (repeated thirteen times) gives a sense of intimacy to the relationship. But the "telephonic" technique renders the final "solution" with particular poignancy, for the voice at the other end of the line, whether enjoying "everlasting day" or something less heavenly, can now offer no response; his garrulous trench banter and talking "shop" are like the chattering subject of "A Subaltern"—things of the past. He is, in a telling pun, "beyond the wire," literally in "No-Man's Land," and out of contact. Set against the callous political cant of "we've got stacks of men"—so many expendable assets—is the reality of *any* individual's death—here a parched, lonely and agonizing expiration.

When Sassoon wrote "To Any Dead Officer," he was in a state of considerable agitation. He had just "put on paper" his "short statement" about a conflict transformed from one of "defence and liberation" into one of "aggression and conquest," a protest which makes pointed reference to "the political errors and insincerities for which the fighting men are being sacrificed" (*Diaries*, 15 June, p. 173). Here this indignation is given public expression in verse, with the final stanza mimicking "our Politicians," their hackneyed platitudes and sadistic reveling in a carnage likely to thrive on their force feeding for "at least two years" more.

Putting his views "on paper" in prose that brooked no argument had been a salutary experience. It was also a creative "trigger"; it gave Sassoon the material for the poem and brought back, he recollected much later:

> a comprehensive memory of war experience in its intense and essential humanity. It seemed that my companions of the Somme and Arras battles were around me; helmeted faces returned and receded in vision; joking voices were overheard in fragments of dug-out and billet talk. These were the dead, to whom life had been desirable and whose sacrifice must be justified.... Perhaps the dead were backing me up, I thought; for I was a believer in the power of spiritual presences.... By the time I went to bed I had written a slangy, telephonic poem of forty lines [SJ, pp. 53–4].

In his analysis of the poem Jon Silkin argues that Sassoon's attitude to his "dead officer" is "not wholly sympathetic," that the opening stanza "unfolds an exaggerated mockery which is turned partly upon the man, but mainly upon the sanctimoniousness that surrounds those ideas concerning a 'compensatory' afterlife" (Silkin, 1983, p. 162). True, Sassoon *is* deriding conventional concepts of a Christian heaven or hell ("everlasting day"/"night") but even in life the human victim is treated—and Sassoon's later prose reference to "essential humanity" reinforces this view—with a wry compassion. This is hardly surprising since the poem's portrait was modeled on Lieutenant Orme, a close friend killed in action on 27 May, 1917. Perhaps the soldier lacks heroic stature if judged by patriotic paragraphs—he hates "tours of trenches" and longs for home—but he is representatively human and humane; he *is* "Any Dead Officer who left School for the

Army in 1914" (Full title in Cambridge reprint). There is no irony in the poet's imaginative "rebuilding"; here is a man sympathetically remembered for making the best of a bad job, who "joked at shells" and who even "in extremis" could offer "some cheery old remark."

The only apparent "switching of sympathy and alienation in fact occurs in the final stanza where the telephone caller, in a not atypical "volte face," suddenly adopts the language of the politicians and thereby appears to embrace their jingoistic platitudes. After all, the victim is only one among "stacks of men," just another "dead officer." Far more important is the upholding of a conspicuous heroism (getting killed "in a decent show," and the perceived need to crush Germany "under the Heel of England").

But such a reading misses the point of Sassoon's satire. For this is a conclusion that mingles intense personal grief—note the intrusive and confessional "I'm blind with tears / staring into the dark"—with a coruscating and bitter sarcasm aimed at the clichés, at once chauvinist and perverse, of power politics.

Apart from its novel use of a hot line to heaven, the poem's sardonic manner is typically Sassoonesque. "It's hell," "No earthly chance" and "bloody Roll of Honour" all show the poem's characteristic capacity to forge simple but deadly puns from the plain-speak of the trenches. Only when empathizing with those "dying slow" does Sassoon allow his profound sense of compassion to manifest itself. But the punch, as usual, is delivered in the satiric conclusion: with its sudden ellipses (an expressive technique Sassoon was developing), its shifts of perspective from private sorrow to public cant, from lingering death to jingoistic platitude, from the penultimate stanza's haunting mood of compassion for human suffering to a concluding volley of fierce anger directed at armchair strategists. *Any reader* imagining that the speaker has become a mouthpiece for the warmongers is ignoring the bitter invective of the final lines. The mourning friend really *is* "staring into the dark," into an abyss created by politicians and from whose depths no victim has any "earthly chance" of "crawling back."

Repression of War Experience

"Repression of War Experience" is a watershed poem, as significant, in terms of its exploitation of a key moment in his psychic development, as anything Sassoon wrote during the war. That he realized that the poem was both an example of "repression" and an attempt to come to terms with its operations is clear from a title which not only employs a term drawn from Freudian psychoanalysis but also pays homage to Rivers's professional interest in "anxiety-neurosis" and subsequently the subject of his December lecture to the Royal Society entitled "The Repression of War Experience." It is unlikely that Sassoon waited six months before giving the poem this title. Soon after composing it, Sassoon would be at Craiglockhart War Hospital, in regular contact with Rivers and undergoing treatment to relieve his "anti-war complex" (the psychiatrist's own term) and other distressing symptoms apparently brought on by "repression" of his trench experiences. In a letter dated 26 July, the first reference to his doctor, Sassoon refers to "Rivers, the chap who looks after me ... I am very glad to have the chance of talking to such a fine man" (*Diaries*, 26 July, 1917, p. 183). Less than a year later, Rivers, no longer trying to dissuade Sassoon from his pacifist views, had assumed in the poet's eyes a God-like eminence. "I must never forget Rivers. He is the only man who can save me if I break down again. If I am able to keep going it will be through him" (*Diaries*, 9 May, p. 246).

All this was in the future. For the moment, and the pastoral setting of the poem makes this clear, Sassoon was resting at his mother's home at Weirleigh. There he was recuperating both from the effects of "a snipers bullet through the shoulder" (*Diaries*, 16 April, p. 155) and from psychical trauma in the form of an "anxiety neurosis," occasioned not only by memories of Front Line atrocities but also by his 15 June decision to confront the establishment by publicly denouncing its war policies. It is worth reminding ourselves of its opening salvo:

> I am making this statement as an act of wilful defiance of military authority, because I believe that the War is being deliberately prolonged by those who have the power to end it. I am a soldier, concerned that I am acting on behalf of soldiers. I believe that this War, upon which I entered as a war of defence and liberation, has now become a war of aggression and conquest [*Diaries*, 15 June, p. 173].

Now, at the moment of composing the poem, he was awaiting official reactions, in the certain knowledge that they would be powerfully antipathetic and that his artistic reputation, his military career, perhaps even his life, could be in jeopardy. In a follow-up letter to his commanding officer, Sassoon gloomily confessed, "I am fully aware of what I am letting myself in for" (*Diaries*, 4 July, p. 177). Wounded, "shell-shocked," Sassoon had now taken on the authorities in a head-on gesture whose wisdom even his friends Graves and Ross seriously doubted. It can be safely concluded that his state of mind at the time of writing "Repression of War Experience" was turbulent, troubled, shot through with conflicting emotions. As Rivers would later remind him, it was a condition probably exacerbated by his officer "training in repression" and his consequent inability to "dwell upon ... painful experience ... in such a way as to relieve its horrible and terrifying character" (Rivers, 1920, p. 219). The poem, in form an irregular and unrhymed ode, is significant not just because it charts, both consciously and unconsciously, a key episode in Sassoon's war. It deals with the whole notion of "repression," albeit before he had discussed the process with Rivers, in a richly ambivalent way. Though it is the only poem, apart from "To Any Dead Officer," written during the heart-searching period that culminated in his statement of "wilful defiance," it contains no overt reference to the protest; if it was one of those thoughts on which, in the words of the poem, he had "gagged all day" and which now threatened to "come back to scare him," it was single-mindedly eliminated from the poem. To sublimate these emotions, to give poetic embodiment to them (though "To Any Dead Officer" had tried) was simply too painful an experience to contemplate during the lengthy and necessarily intense process of creation.

Not that Sassoon seems to have been entirely unaware of the Freudian theory of "repression" and its attendant dangers. He might not have read Freud in depth but the fact that he uses the term suggests that he could hardly have been ignorant of the basic principles of Freudian "repression" and his celebrated metaphor of a "door-keeper" standing "on the threshold" between the "anteroom" of the unconscious and the "reception room" of the conscious, a "personage" who examines the various mental excitations, censors them and denies them admittance to the "reception-room when he disapproves of them." As Freud explains, these thoughts "are 'incapable of becoming conscious'; we call them, *repressed*" (Freud, 1973, p. 250).

Not everything in Sassoon's poem is "repressed." Sassoon does allow, across the threshold into consciousness and into the public domain of the poem, some ghoulish memories that he has "gagged all day"; he is attempting to confront that problem that beset all convalescing soldiers: how to cope with these memories that you would rather repress out of consciousness at the consequent risk of their terrible re-surfacing in dream and nightmare. And not only in dream. The state of evening reverie was equally vulnerable. As Rivers explained: "If unpleasant thoughts are voluntarily repressed during the day, it is natural that they should rise into activity when the control of the waking state is removed by sleep or is weakened in the state which *precedes and follows sleep and occupies its intervals*" (Rivers, 1920, p. 199; emphasis added). That his "treatment" by Rivers, aimed at the "removal of repression," would in the future help him cope much better with an "anxiety neurosis" to which he was consistently prone, is evidenced by the Craiglockhart poems themselves. Some of these would reveal a Sassoon able again to re-live his "war experience" through their cathartic expression in verse. For the present — and the "evidence" is in the poem — facing up directly to the worst circumstances was more difficult. Only at the conclusion of this poem, with his deflecting strategies undermined by the insistent noise of gunfire, is Sassoon able to repudiate the distancing devices of poetic language and, in a rough-hewn and demotic unleashing of pent-up emotion, openly declare: "I'm going stark, staring mad because of the guns."

Read in this way, "Repression of War Experience" is a dialogue between the "I" and "you" of the divided self, in which the "I" of the present, apparently relaxed moment is constantly pressured by another self that is traumatized by invasive memories of an ineradicable past. Such "disassociation" or "splitting of consciousness" was, in Rivers's estimation, often exacerbated by "some shock or illness" (Rivers, 1920, p. 195). In such a state, being alone with one's thoughts, albeit at home, was not necessarily a tranquilizing experience. For the therapies which the poem describes: talking to himself; performing mechanical little rituals such as lighting candles or his reassuring pipe; contemplating the weather, or watching a fluttering moth, are less than convincing strategies for suppressing the looming specters of war. What the poet must do, for his apparent peace of mind, is to control the way in which these memories encroach on his consciousness and enter the world of the poem. They may be glimpsed through the "door-keeper's" portals but they are blurred and indistinct, premonitions rather than hard-edged images. The "ugly thoughts" of the poem remain thoughts, disembodied and abstract; significantly, only when they are metamorphosed into images of "old men with ugly souls" does Sassoon allow reality — and it is a reality unconnected with the trenches — to intrude. Even the dead, at least the rotting corpses of men killed in battle, are manifestly erased from the poem's memory; they are replaced by old men, ghostly presences of "horrible shapes in shrouds." Only at the end can anger, an emotion repressed for twenty-eight of the poem's thirty-eight lines, be no longer ignored. Finally, maddeningly, the actual sounds of war invade his consciousness, provoking an uncensored irruption of feeling.

Such an understated, indeed largely unstated view of war's horror might be seen as a vitiation of the poem's effectiveness as well as — according to the Rivers theory of "repression" — damaging to the psyche of the anxiety-ridden soldier-poet. But poetry traditionally employs the oblique mechanisms of figurative language, and much of the uneasy ambivalence of "Repression of War Experience" derives not only from Sassoon's refusal to confront the "experience" unequivocally but also from his richly connotative and uncharacteristic use of metaphorical tropes.

It is worth considering how this links with psychoanalytical theory. For Freud, repressed thoughts issued in dreams, via the processes of condensation and displacement, as images of a visual and usually symbolic cast. Rivers, summarizing Freud, expresses it thus: "... the manifest content becomes the expression of the wish through a process of distortion, whereby the real meaning of the dream is disguised for the dreamer" (Rivers, 1923, p. 4). Admittedly "Repression of War Experiences" is a poem and not a dream. Nonetheless it is a highly associative poem, in which the use of ellipsis suggests a creative reverie in which the processes of symbolization and metaphoric displacement can flourish. Such metaphoric displacement is evident in the resonating images of the poem: candles, pipe, books, rain, roses and, above all, the solitary moth. All are familiar presences, variously associated with domesticity, leisure, an English summer evening. They are there, physical, observed objects incorporated in the poem, to assist the process of personal recuperation, reassuring things that help the soldier-poet forget the horror of the trenches. But it is late evening, a vulnerable time of day, and all these images generate associations that the poet would like to repress; it is only because these latent and metaphoric meanings are *initially* unacknowledged by the poet that they survive in the text. Each time the poet introduces an image, it is to find that it brings with it unwanted overtones that he has sought to smother, that he has "gagged all day." Thus the prosaic lighting of candles acquires associations of votive offerings to the dead, then, in the moth's likely incineration, the scorching, maiming effects of war that confront the would-be hero ("And scorch their wings with glory, liquid flame"). The comforting pipe is suddenly not so comforting. Lighting it reminds him uneasily of its function in the trenches. Here, as there, he tries to calm himself by the reassuring observation, "Look! What a steady hand." But the fact that he has to count fifteen before he is "as right as rain" is sure proof that he is anything but calm; whether pipe or gun, the trembling way it is grasped betrays his fragile state of mind.

    The cliché "right as rain" fails to reassure; instead the process of free association leads the day-dreamer to wish for a real downpour and "bucketfuls of water"; he is desperate for a purifying agent to "sluice the dark" and wash away the recurrent sense of horror. Even the roses are charged with symbolic force as the pathetic fallacy, an echo perhaps of Keats's "droop-headed flowers all" and the consequent invitation to "glut thy sorrow on a morning rose," invests them with the poet's own guilt-laden and mournful emotions. More disturbingly, the symbolism of "hang" and "dripping heads" is redolent of the carnage of the battlefield; these images remorselessly return him to areas of experience he is trying to forget. He searches desperately for yet another source of solace. Books ... a constant source of consolation in the trenches and here reassuringly lining the walls, books are, he reflects, "a jolly company." But the innocuous personification refuses to suggest a comforting jollity. Instead the word "company" reminds him of a military unit; the orderly ranks of tomes "standing so quiet and patient," of soldiers awaiting orders. The desperate injunction, "O *do* read something," is yet another strategy for repressing these resurgent memories — after all, books encapsulate the "wisdom of the world." But again unsought associations proliferate: as his eyes roam the bookshelves, the leather spines recall soldiers dressed to die in "*dim* brown" (emphasis added), and then, like the more colorful books, turned "black and white and green, to every kind of colour" in death and putrefaction. The poet averts his imaginative gaze by staring prisoner-like at the blank ceiling, only for the moth to reappear. Initially, we recall, the poet attempted to reject its symbolic implications with "No, no, not that — Its bad to think of war." Now its presence, "one big dizzy moth that bumps and flutters," painfully reminds him of his own confused state of mind. Like the moth he is liable to self-destruct, fatally attracted to the very things that may destroy him.

    Even the garden beyond, a sanctuary for moths and men alike, provides no consolation. The very air is "breathless," at once holding itself in dreadful anticipation of some catastrophe, and devoid of life; the spectral trees conjure up images not of the heroic dead of earlier poems such as "The Last Meeting," but of ghoulish apparitions, ghosts of old men who, far from dying courageously in battle, have "worn their bodies out with nasty sins." That this particular "nasty thought" was very much on Sassoon's mind at the time is indicated by a notebook entry written four days after his "statement" in which he had asked: "Is there anything inwardly noble in savage sex instincts?" before embarking on a denunciation of "the elderly male population ... old men like ghouls, insatiable in their desire for slaughter, impenetrable in their ignorance" (*Diaries*, 19 June, p. 176). Like the diary entry, the imagery in the poem conflates twin aversions: one, a hatred of old men; two, a disgust at the gross physicality of heterosexual intercourse. That these men are presumably copulating with young women while young men die vainly for a lost cause is doubly abhorrent.

At this juncture, the poem appears to provide evidence of another level of "repression," of which the poet's "door-keeper" was probably unaware, that of sexual repression. Freud is instructive here, since he uncompromisingly links repression to sexual drives, maintaining that "the symptoms serve the purpose of erotic gratification for the subject; they are a substitute for satisfactions which he does not obtain in reality" (Freud, p. 250). Sassoon, we are reminded, was not yet a patient of Dr. Rivers, and though he would talk with him about his dreams, it is unlikely that he discussed his sexuality with an analyst more concerned with repressions engendered by "war experience" than by sexual proclivities. But the fact remains that Sassoon was a homosexual, though on the evidence of the diaries and letters he was chary of airing the fact. One aspect of his war experience, an intensely fructifying one, was his daily contact and kinship with other young men. Of course one didn't have to be "just so" in order to develop loving relationships; the pressure-cooker atmosphere of the front line ensured that. Moreover, most officers would already not only have encountered a whole tradition of homoerotic literature, but would have experienced non-physical "crushes" at public school; J. R. Ackerley observed that while he "never met a recognizable or self-confessed adult homosexual" during the war, "the Army with its male relationships was simply an extension of my public school" (*My Father and Myself*, quoted in Fussell, 1975, p. 273). Homoerotic feeling *was* acceptable in the trenches; homosexuality was not. As a consequence, Sassoon was obliged to sublimate his homosexuality: in platonic friendships, in sentimentalized hero-worship, by writing pastoral elegies to dead comrades, or, as in this poem, by adopting a puritanical, even misogynistic stance. Not that these responses in any way invalidate the truth and intensity of his own emotions. These erotic feelings were, I believe, as much a source of tension to him as the now publicly documented conflict between Sassoon the pacifist and Sassoon the warrior.

Such emotions reside in the subtext of "Repression of War Experience." They are "gagged" out of existence more successfully than the memories of war, but they occasionally slip into sight, shadowy evidences from the palimpsest of the poem. Such parapraxes were, as Rivers knew from his reading of Freud, often revelatory of the psyche's inner workings. "Slips of the tongue," he explained, "are the expression of tendencies lying below the ordinary level of waking consciousness ... the expression of some unconscious or subconscious train of thought (which) intrudes into a sentence with which it has no obvious connection" (Rivers,

1920, p. 232). So while these "ugly thoughts" refuse precise, conscious identification, they do slip in — in potentially subversive ways. Thus his pipe, which is subsequently "let out," has, on this reading, potentially erotic associations; the procedure of "count fifteen / And you're as right as rain" is a relief mechanism not entirely devoid of sexual connotations. The poet dares not "lose control" of these feelings; if he does, they will "drive [him] out to jabber among the trees"; he will be regarded as "mad," perhaps recognized as sexually deviant and ostracized in consequence. The garden, the poet observes, in a phrase that says more than it intends, "waits for something that delays." But however "dizzy" and dislocated the thinker's present state of mind, now is not the time for revelations about his sexuality. Indeed, by a process of transference, his own sense of self-disgust issues in the denunciation of the "nasty sins" of old men, "wearing out their bodies" in heterosexual congress, an activity which is nonetheless part of a "natural" sequence of erotic events that may be denied the speaker.

So what conclusions should we stress in relation to "Repression of War Experience"? Writing poetry is, in psychoanalytic terms, a sublimatory activity, a re-channeling of basic drives so as to make them socially acceptable and potentially useful. I have argued that in the poem Sassoon is sublimating, however obliquely and erratically, his repressed sexual instincts. Rivers is again instructive here. Talking about neurosis, he offered the opinion that "new symptoms often arise in hospital or at home which are not the immediate and necessary consequence of war experience, but are due to repression of painful memories and thoughts ... arising out of reflection concerning this experience" (Rivers, 1920, p. 186). In other words, war anxiety might trigger the release of other deep-seated and quite unrelated repressions. That such suppressed feelings do surface in this poem is almost certainly the case.

But Sassoon's primary repressions centered on memories of the trenches; they were the direct consequence of a war recently experienced, nightmarishly recalled, and now, in his statement, apparently rejected. In *Instinct and the Unconscious*, Rivers would identify three kinds of "war-neurosis." The first, he suggested, produced anesthetizing physical manifestations such as blindness, paralysis or mutism; a second form led to extreme lassitude, enervation and disorders of sleep; a third resulted in "mental instability and restlessness with alternations of depression and excitement ... similar to those of manic-depressive insanity" (1920, p. 232). It does not take much to realize that Sassoon, though displaying some symptoms of the second kind of neurosis (from 2 June to mid–July he seems to have written only two poems), was mainly a victim of the third variety. That much at least is clear from a remarkable poem that reveals the processes of "repression" and, at the same time, attempts to come to terms with them by exorcising these horrors through the act of giving them poetic embodiment.

If Sassoon does not altogether succeed in exorcising these battlefield ghosts, he also fails to repress them effectively, since they crop up in the unlikely guise of homely symbols and metaphors. What Rivers *would* succeed in doing was to help Sassoon to give expression to his deepest memories and fears. One unlikely by-product of this release, is the Craiglockhart poems "Glory of Women" and "Their Frailty," pieces which give vent to the poet's inherent distaste for women and especially their role as rivals for men's affections. Much more important, his stay at "Dottyville" under Rivers allowed Sassoon to release his pent-up feelings in two ways: one, in powerful poems — "Prelude: The Troops" and "Counter-Attack" for example — in which he dares to relive, in graphic detail, his ghastliest moments of the war; two, Sassoon was persuaded that a positive and socially acceptable outlet for his erotic feelings and a way of dealing with his pacifism that could be of practical benefit was to lead his men — literally from the front. Eventually the Riversian exorcism probably helped Sassoon to come to terms with his homosexuality and its attendant complex of attitudes. Initially, it helped him to understand the mental mechanisms of "repression" and to deal with a now declared pacifism that must have intensified his desire to escape from all those memories of a trenchscape "where all is ruin, and nothing blossoms but the sky."

Sassoon's stay at Craiglockhart was not entirely happy. But that it did help him deal with these "war experiences" is evidenced by a body of work which not only faces up to the terrible effects of "shell-shock," or recalls, in such expressions as "butchered frantic gestures of the dead," the remorseless scenes of carnage at the Front, but returns to an imagined event more often repressed than any other by all combatants, the actual "experience" of dying, of "choking, of "drowning," of "bleeding to death." Though Sassoon was not able, any more than his surviving comrades in arms were, to ameliorate his abiding sense of horror and outrage, he would, thanks to the renewed therapy of poetry and the good offices of "my reasoning Rivers," manage to exorcise some of these ghosts in due course.

Lamentations

Two more poems, "Lamentations" and "The Effect," were also composed during the eventful summer of 1917. Both draw on remembered incidents from the Arras campaign and show Sassoon, starved of recent material for poetry, still anxious to maintain his pacifist perspective on the war. "Lamentations" reveals a poet quite unable to recall any redeeming feature in a conflict where men are dehumanized by the "bleeding war." In the guard room a young soldier howls and beats his chest like a madman. There is a telling irony in the sergeant's puzzlement that this raving is "*all because* [emphasis added] his brother had gone west." The poet's view is characteristically compassionate. It is precisely because of such personal tragedies, Sassoon concludes, that men are reduced to gibbering idiots (the extended eighth line with its rush of noisy verbs makes the point very effectively). Beside themselves with grief, they are quite unable to think of king and country. Sassoon had been re-reading his February diary where he had made the same observation in reflective prose:

> For the soldier is no longer a noble figure; he is merely a writhing insect among this ghastly folly of destruction. His kingly reason is fooled and debauched by the dire pangs that his body must endure [*Diaries*, 22 February, p. 133].

"Lamentations," like "The Hero" twelve months earlier, demonstrates that even the common soldier can be debauched by the harrowing experiences he "must endure." It was a stance Sassoon was understandably unwilling to adopt too often; he prefers to laud the homespun virtues of the trooper. But there is every excuse for these "lamentations; such rampant grief demands an outlet, however over the top. There is rarely any nobility in death and often none in suffering.

The Effect

The irony directed at the sergeant in "Lamentations" is gentle enough. He has witnessed so many human tragedies that any demonstrable excess of feeling seems beside the point. But Sassoon was always prepared to pile on the invective when it came to civilian attitudes. One can imagine his fury on reading an account by a "war correspondent" in the yellow press: "The effect of our bombardment was terrific. One man told me he had never seen so many dead before." This observation, presented first as epigraph to "The Effect," repeated in the opening line of verses one and two and then elaborated in the final stanza, produces an incremental effect that characterizes many ballads, a form that Sassoon was increasingly attracted to. Such a statement, repeated like a slogan, provides an ironic counterpoint to the ghastly facts of "death" with which the poet/soldier refutes this empty boast. Unlike the correspondent safe behind the lines, the reader is forced to contemplate death on the Hindenburg line. Initially "sprawled in *yellow* daylight" (the transferred epithets in the poem are striking), the corpses are re-animated in stanza two, but only as a consequence of the passing soldier's jittery state of mind. Their deaths are final and irreversible. Sassoon concludes with an even more gruesome description of a comrade's death-throes:

> Flapping along the fire-step like a fish,
> After the blazing crump had knocked him flat ...

Whether it is the insane grief of the brother in "Lamentations" or the paroxysms of the dying soldier in "The Effect," the Sassoon "effect" is to explode the myth of death as either a desirable end for enemies or a heroic resolution for patriotic soldiers. The effect of trench warfare, whether on body or mind, is appalling in terms of sheer human waste. Lest we have missed this "effect," the ironic finale reveals a sardonic speaker playing the same fatuous numbers game as the correspondent. Resorting to street-trader slang, he offers as many "nice fresh corpses, two a penny ... as ever you wish."

A Wooden Cross (To S.G.H.)

In mid-August, one of Sassoon's best friends was killed. Writing to Lady Ottoline Morrell, who had done so much to sustain Sassoon through the trials and tribulations of his protest, he confessed to having "been knocked flat once again, by the best sporting friend I ever had getting killed on August 14 — in France. He was indeed my greatest friend before the war — a Winchester boy named Gordon Harbord, whom I met in 1908 and saw constantly afterwards. When the *un*intellectual people go it is much the worst — one feels they've so much to lose" [*Diaries*, 5 Sept., 1917, p. 184].

As was frequently Sassoon's practice, he wrote an elegy to his fellow fox-hunting enthusiast and included it in his diary (as part of the 5 September entry). Too private for public consumption, it remains, like his piece to Marcus Goodall, another dear comrade killed just over a year before, a moving testament to the poet's inconsolable sense of loss. What makes it worse is that he remains, "Doomed to outlive these tragedies of pain," with "scores of banished eyes" as constant reminders of his "companions" and "peers." The only consolation is provided — the stanza might have been culled straight from *Georgian Poetry*— by memories of hunting together in pre-war Sussex:

> Till, blotting out today, I half believe
> That I shall find you home again on leave,
> As I last saw you, riding down the lane,
> And lost in lowering dusk and drizzling rain,

But the nostalgic tone (Sassoon had just been writing "a cub-hunting poem for him" when he heard of Harbord's death) (*Diaries*, 5 September, p. 184) gives way to a bitter sense of the purposelessness of a death which has "earned a glorious wooden cross." The final blast, the sentiments of the "protest" writ large, is that the war is "a sham, a stinking lie," and that "glory" is nothing more than "a crowd of corpses freed from pangs of hell."

Dreamers

Apparently the second poem to be written at Craiglockhart, "Dreamers" signals no new directions for Sassoon's poetry. Indeed the sonnet reverts to a rather tired formula, that of contrasting the world of heroic illusion with that of unvarnished truth. The deliberately grandiose language of the opening verse, a self-conscious harking back to the poetic moment of "Absolution," presents a stereotype of soldiers who "stand in the great hour of destiny," anxious to win "Some flaming, fatal climax for their lives," and who, "in extremis," dream only "of firelit homes, clean beds and wives." Stanza two presents a predictably different picture of these soldiers, now confined in squalid trenches, "gnawed by rats ...

lashed with rain," and dreaming not about a lost world of cosy domesticity, but a world of male diversions:

> Bank-holidays, and picture shows, and spats,
> And going to the office in the train.

Sassoon was, on the evidence of the editorial to the *Hydra* of 1 September, beginning to recover: "Many of us who came to the hydra slightly ill are now getting dangerously well. In this excellent concentration camp we are fast recovering from the shock of coming to England." For a poet whose muse throve on excitement, he was perhaps too relaxed. A reversion to a hackneyed subject and the assertion of active masculine values suggests the absence of a genuine *creative* impulse.

Editorial Impressions

Not always a sufficiently stern critic of his own work, Sassoon did, on his own admission, strike out a number of poems which he had shown to Roderick Meiklejohn, "mostly failures which I have since destroyed" (letter to Ross, 17 Sept., *Diaries*, 1917, p. 186). On the other hand he told Robbie Ross: "I have done some good ones since Roderick was here," amounting to "about 300 lines of verse." "Editorial Impressions" was clearly one of the "good" ones. Sassoon dispatched it to the *Cambridge Magazine* where it was published on 22 September, 1917. Like "The Effect," it targets those "Gentlemen of the Press" who still insisted on cosmeticizing or dramatizing by turns what they reported from the Front for the dubious benefit of their civilian readers. Talking loftily in a bar of "the amazing spirit of the troops" and of "flying chaps" … "Soaring and diving like some bird of prey," the reporter encounters the voice of experience in the person of a mere "lad" who has been "severely wounded in the back." The probable roles have been reversed. The voice of innocence should be the young "lad," that of experience the hard-nosed reporter. But it is the disabled trooper who quietly listens to these "big impressions" and then makes a pointed reply. For it is real experience of battle that has bred in the soldier a healthy cynicism for such journalistic antics, even if his sarcastic retort *is* lost on his listener:

> The soldier sipped his wine.
> 'Ah, yes, but it's the Press that leads the way!'

It is a remark more truthful than the soldier's sarcasm allows. For though the press will never "lead the way" into battle, they *are* still dictating opinion and influencing those responsible for the conduct of the war.

Wirers

One of the consequential but unheralded activities of trench warfare was wiring. Sassoon often refers in his diary to wiring parties — required both to cut enemy barbed wire and repair their own — but though it was a hazardous enterprise, its very mundaneness made it difficult to write about in verse. Nonetheless, as frontline activity, wire-cutting was sufficiently important for Sassoon to equip himself with two reliable pairs of cutters from the Army and Navy store in Victoria. About to lead an all-night wire-cutting party he reflected: "I found myself fingering with pardonable pride my two pairs of wire-cutters ... it is possible that I did over-estimate their usefulness, but their presence did seem providential" (*Memoirs*, p. 326).

In "Wirers," the patrol is *mending* the coils of barbed wire but the men remain helplessly exposed by the Bosche flares, as Young Hughes, "badly hit" during the sortie into No Man's Land, can testify.

The poem, composed in the relatively placid atmosphere of "Dottyville," captures through its use of present participles — "unravelling, twisting, hammering" — some of the atmosphere of fearful, frenzied activity, though the last line offers a typically bathetic if not entirely convincing conclusion:

> .... no doubt he'll die today.
> But *we* can say the front-line wire's been safely mended.

More interesting is the poem's experimental metrics and rhyme-scheme. Forsaking alternate rhymes for what, in the repeated "going out" of the opening couplet, approximates to Owen's innovative device of para-rhythm, and breaking up the regular strophes in the search for an expressive form, Sassoon's poem seems to demonstrate the impact of his burgeoning friendship with Owen. As he later acknowledged, this process was a symbiotic one: "It was indeed one of those situations where imperceptible effects are obtained by people mingling their minds at a favourable moment" (SJ, p. 60).

Does It Matter?

Sassoon's next Craiglockhart poems show the poet returning to proven methods. "Does It Matter?," one of his best-known and most successful epigrams, was triggered off by his incarceration in "Dottyville." Though it was proving restorative, especially when Rivers was available (he had been ill), Craiglockhart could generate, as he confided to Graves, a "truly awful atmosphere." It was "a place of wash-outs and shattered heroes. Result: go to bed every night tired and irritable, and write querulous peace-poems" (*Diaries*, 4 October, p. 189).

By "querulous peace-poems" one assumes Sassoon meant pieces that, by exposing the commensurate ghastliness of war and civilian attitudes towards it, demonstrated his own "anti-war complex." "Does It Matter?," one of more than twenty poems written at Craiglockhart, in part fits his own description, though its straightforward language and ballad-like directness (the device of incremental repetition recalls the procedures of oral verse) hardly merit the epithet "querulous." Once again Sassoon contrasts the "two nations": the "Nation Overseas" epitomized by the maimed, blinded and shell-shocked victims of war — Sassoon had recently written to Ross about a "friend ... one arm amputated and will probably lose the other" (25 September, p. 187); the "Nation at Home" by the well-intentioned humbuggery of "people" in "Blighty" who, like the correspondent of "Editorial Impressions," patronizingly play down these silent human disasters on the basis of "We don't worry so why should you?":

> Does it matter?—losing your sight?...
> There's such splendid work for the blind;
> And people will always be kind...

What gives the poem its raw power is the terse, half-line vignettes of these disfigured, displaced war veterans, juxtaposed incongruously to the trivial social rituals of gracious living, veterans forced to endure not only their own mutilation but the pointless platitudes of "do-gooding" women. While the silent victims are allowed *no* say, their world of amputation, darkness and shell-shock is mute but eloquent testimony to the fact that these horrors really *do* matter to the ever-growing ranks of "shattered heroes." Craiglockhart provided, both for Sassoon and Owen, constant reminders of war's maiming and mutilating capacity. Like Owen, Sassoon was increasingly anxious to expose and analyze the effects of the war on its survivors. Owen's "Disabled," "A Terre" and "Mental Cases" would all examine the plight of the wounded, the maimed and the mentally disabled in the same way as Sassoon's "Does It Matter?," "Survivors," or, on a purely personal level, "The Repression of War Experience."

How to Die

In "How to Die," Sassoon returns to his obsession with the sensations of dying. Though elsewhere — "The Death-Bed" does so memorably — Sassoon describes its grim, hallucinatory manifestations, here the poet concentrates on the exalted mental state of the dying hero as he expires against a romantic backcloth of grandiose atmospheric effects, accompanied by a palpable sense of the numinous:

> He lifts his fingers toward the skies
> Where holy brightness breaks in flame;
> Radiance reflected in his eyes,
> And on his lips a whispered name.

Such a picture, reinforced by the numerous contemporary illustrations of soldiers expiring with eyes cast heavenwards, was, as the poet well knew, at complete odds with the facts. But Sassoon subtly undermines such an affirmatory vision, not by denying its credibility, but by apparently aligning himself with those who denigrate "people" disposed to tell the truth about war:

> You'd think, to hear some people talk,
> That lads go west with sobs and curses...

By offering only an *ironic* insight into the reality — that soldiers go swearing to their muddy graves — Sassoon permits the misguided public to cleave to their hymn-like vision of "Christian soldiers" who will not only give up their lives for the greater glory of heavenly salvation, but will do so decorously and "With due regard for decent taste."

The Fathers

Like "Base Details" and "The General," "The Fathers" provides, in Silkin's neat summational phrase, a "brilliant juxtaposition of brutal facts with an elderly insensibility and bewildered ignorance" (1987, p. 160). There is no doubting the continuing force of Sassoon's antipathy towards an older generation who make patriotic noises from their cosy homes and complacent clubs, while exhorting the flower of England's youth to go to war and get killed, and often, in Sassoon's estimation — though not on the evidence of this poem — to indulge their "ugly sins" on the young widows left behind. Worse, they subscribe to the stock civilian belief that not only is war " fun," but that all "Huns" — a term never used in anger by Sassoon — are cowards only waiting to "bolt across the Rhine." Characteristically the epigram gathers momentum once the "goggle-eyed" old boys begin to exchange their jittery platitudes. Sassoon's ear for "club-speak" is unerring — he had heard plenty of it at Rouen and Formby, not to mention his London club — and the bathetic rhymes (lad/Baghdad, fun/gun) underpin a line of chat that has all the sophistication of a child's rhyme. The poet's verdict on them is damning. They "toddle" out, assuredly "impotent" in more ways than one; victims, unlike their sons, not of some murderous war machine, but of booze and senility.

Attack

One of two trench-line poems written during October, Sassoon's note to the poem pinpoints its origin: "From a note in my diary while observing the Hindenburg Line attack" (WP, p. 95). Of all the passages of the war, this one, now six months behind him, seems to have been most indelibly imprinted on the poet's frazzled consciousness. As his diary of 14 April had recorded: "The dead bodies ... are beyond description especially after the rain.... Our shelling of the line — and subsequent bombing etc.— has left a number of mangled Germans; they will haunt me till I die" (*Diaries*, 14 April, 1917, p. 154).

The poem is unusual on several counts. Its thirteen-line form is an oddity. So too is the atypical reference to toppling tanks, apparently taken from his diary account of 13 April: "one of our tanks stuck in the mud getting over the trench — very wide." But the poem's central focus is on that most desperate of all battle procedures: "going over the top," that moment when, in a memorable line, "time ticks blank and busy on their wrists." Though Graves had written about the "moment of truth" in "It's a Queer Time," it was not an experience that Sassoon had explored imaginatively in verse. Perhaps his reading of Barbusse's novel, with its frenzied descriptions of infantry attacks, persuaded Sassoon to try. The "furtive eyes" and "grappling fists" that clutch at life, flounder, like hope itself, in the clogging mud and prompt the final, despairing cry, at once blasphemous oath and plea to an insensate God: "O Jesus, make it stop!"

Survivors

"Survivors" is the only Craiglockhart poem to be prompted, not by Sassoon's "anti-war complex" or his memories of the trenches, but by life among the inmates of "Dottyville." He wrote about his hospitalization freely enough in letters and journal, but being "a healthy young officer, dumped down among nurses and nervous wrecks," was not an easy situation to render into poetry (*Memoirs*, p. 523). His early impression, conveyed to Ottoline Morrell in a letter of 30 July, refers disparagingly to "160 more or less dotty officers. A great many of them are degenerate-looking. A few are genuine cases of shell-shock etc" (*Diaries*, p. 183). By October he had, on the evidence of "Survivors," got to know some of them rather better, a charitable progress that similarly operates in the poem.

"Survivors" opens with the usual civilian platitudes about recovery and "longing to go out again"— the tone recalls "Does It Matter"— but the poem gradually lays bare such mendacities as a catalogue of walking disasters is itemized. The final couplet degenerates into broken rhythms:

> Men who went out to battle, grim and glad;
> Children with eyes that hate you, broken and mad.

At least they were *men* before the conflict "shatter'd all their pride," and turned them into shell-shocked wrecks whose "dreams ... drip with murder." For it is the war that has transformed purposeful soldiers into infantile madmen. It was not a situation calculated to assuage Sassoon's state of mind, especially since their neurasthenia reminded even a relatively "healthy young officer" of his own obsessions. He might endeavor to distance himself from their "disconnected talk," but he could not avoid the same "haunted nights," the same "subjection to the ghosts of friends who died." And unlike the other "survivors," such a "subjection" meant he was becoming ever more anxious to return "to battle grim and glad," ready to suffer with his Front-Line comrades.

Sick Leave

Riddled with guilt, Sassoon was now obsessively "wrestling with the problem of how to reconcile his pacifist convictions with the feeling that he was betraying his comrades by not returning" to France (Thorpe, 1966, p. 29). Being marooned in "Dottyville" along with these "boys with old, scared faces" exacerbated his growing sense of remorse, a feeling more in evidence in the poem's original title, "Death's Brotherhood." Of the three poems which focus on this preoccupation, "Sick Leave" (the others are "Autumn" and "Banishment") is the most successful. While Sassoon's use of a thirteen-line stanza may look like an arbitrary decision, it is justified perhaps by the way it conveys a sense of suspense and incompleteness, of something unresolved (the same could be said of "Attack," another thirteen-line poem). The poem finishes with an unanswered pair of questions that were currently haunting the poet.

> "When are you going out to them again?
> Are they not still your brothers through our blood?"

For he is not just "betraying his comrades" by staying in "Blighty": he is coming to the realization that not only can his quest for personal love ("they whisper to my heart") be assuaged by a war-bonded companionship, but that he prefers the blood brotherhood of the front line to the "bitter safety" of Craiglockhart. The poem turns on this potent oxymoron, a figurative encapsulation of the tension he is having to live with.

Fight to a Finish

One of the charges most frequently leveled against Sassoon is that his satires are too black and white, that among his serious limitations as a poet is a refusal "to recognise that bald refutation and assertive description are not always adequate, especially if one is at the same time to persuade sensuously and experientially" (Silkin, 1987, p. 166). While I think this judgment seriously underestimates Sassoon's capacity for ironic detachment, it is a charge that poems such as "Fight to a Finish" cannot easily rebut. Another satiric attack on "yellow pressmen," the poem has obvious affinities with "Editorial Impressions" and the prose epigraph to "The Effect." But the strategy, whereby "Grim Fusiliers" are turned on craven journalists who have enjoyed a "cushy" time at home, recalls the bitter reversal of "Blighters," where German tanks are invited by the angry poet to "come down the stalls" and dispense some frontline realism. Charging the "yellow pressmen" with fixed bayonets, those boys who have in a bitterly ironic aside "refrained from dying," have at last an equivalently "cushy job." In a military-style mopping up operation the soldier/poet joins his "trusty bombers" (both bombardiers and fusiliers avenge themselves in this poem) to "clear those Junkers out of Parliament." The name is an apt one. Junkers were land-owning aristocrats, like so many politicians, but they were not English but German. The implication is obvious. Members of Parliament are no better than their Prussian counterparts; worse, they may be colluding with them in prolonging an unjust war.

The poem reveals Sassoon at his most vituperative. The scenario, an entirely fantastic one, is testimony to Sassoon's fluctuating moods, as he veers from anxious comrade to angry satirist. As his letter of 28 October to Ottoline Morrell admits (the poem had been published the previous day in the *Cambridge Magazine* and was referred to by the poet "as fairly effective in its way"), Sassoon was "not depressed — only strung up for supreme efforts" (*Diaries*, p. 193). The epithet "strung up" is instructive. Sassoon was clearly in a highly emotional state. This was a poem that he *needed* to write, an opportunity to give vent to emotions of anger, frustration and even revenge. Little wonder that Rivers thought the poem "very dangerous" (*Diaries*, p. 194), not only because of its potential public impact but as a reflection of his patient's obsessional state of mind.

Over the top it might be, and fuel for those critics who see Sassoon as too often motivated by negative emotions. But perversely, "Fight to a Finish" does, more than any other poem, genuflect to the idea of people power: it suggests, however misplaced its methods, that proletarian power needs to be directed against the established mechanisms of the state. In that sense, the poem oddly prefigures Sassoon's flirtation with socialism in the twenties.

The Investiture

"The Investiture" poses an oddly uninviting view of Heaven where the conferral of war medals is conducted by a deity whom Sassoon has long since ceased to view in conventionally Christian terms. The poem opens with the stock notion of a God welcoming heroes to "Elysium's meadow-land," rather after the fashion of "To His Dead Body." But Sassoon's dead friend, probably the fox-hunting Gordon Harbord of the earlier elegy, is out of place in such a sanitized world; still wearing a "blood-soaked bandage" he is homesick for the youthful pleasures he has left behind. The poet can only reply that if he "were there" — and the specter of a death-wish is barely suppressed — he would enliven the staid celestial proceedings with the kind of boyish pranks they indulged in on earth. Yet even such innocent pastimes as snowballing, hunting or walking fox-hound puppies are pastimes now subtlety changed by the ineradicable experience of war: now they *would* confront Death with skulls for snowballs; hunt not in English copses but in the killing woods of the Somme.

Regrettably, neither the role of "Fox-Hunting Man" nor "Infantry Officer" is open to the occupant of Elysium; in a romantic farewell, the loved one is left to "roam forlorn along the streets of gold."

Thrushes

There are literally hundreds of references to birds in Sassoon's prose writings, preponderantly allusions to his favorite blackbirds and thrushes. Part of the soundscape of a departed England, heard but rarely seen, thrushes now have a poem to themselves, an appropriately innocuous subject for the *Hydra,* the literary journal at Craiglockhart.

The literary progenitor, as for "Autumn," another "Dottyville" poem, is Shelley. However, Sassoon refrains from apostrophizing his thrush after the manner of "To a Skylark" and instead invests the poem with a panoply of poeticisms and sound textures. "Scornful of man" (Shelley's bird is "scornful of the ground") and his earth-bound toiling, Sassoon's thrush is all air and song. By contrast, man's contact with the cosmos serves only to remind him of his own sorrows. He is "a haunted woodland whispering," "baffled" by circumstances that he cannot control and aware of an anguished world in need of salvation, but apparently deserted by a God who shows no inclination to offer any compassionate proof of his existence. Man is a creature everywhere surrounded by a desolation of his own making:

> Who hears the cry of God in everything,
> And storms the gate of nothingness for proof.

Glory of Women

"Glory of Women" and "Their Frailty" were published together in Sassoon's favorite weekly journal, the *Cambridge Magazine,* on 8 December, 1917. "Glory of Women" is the better of the two poems, as Sassoon realized when writing to Robbie Ross: "I sent Massingham a *very good* sonnet, but he hasn't replied. It is called 'Glory of Women' — and gives them beans" (*Diaries,* 3 October, 1917, p. 188). Of all the war poems it most trenchantly expresses Sassoon's disdain for women and what he saw as the female temperament. At its worst a kind of misogyny fueled by his conviction that women had no place in his world of fox-hunting, cricket, race-riding and now soldiering, it was at root a product of a homosexuality which he could no more openly admit than could soldiers "wounded in a (un)mentionable place." Such a line, by referring to the sexual taboos of the day, obliquely points the reader in the direction of Sassoon's own repressed feelings. By 1917 "Women of Britain" were hardly endearing themselves to the troops with their jingoistic letters to newspapers, of which "A Mother's Answer to 'A Common Soldier,'" published to enthusiastic notices in the ultra-conservative *The Morning Post*, was simply the best known (GTAT, pp. 188–90).

The poem, a companion-piece to "Supreme Sacrifice" and "The Hero" as well as to "Their Frailty," is more satirically charged than these earlier efforts. It draws its considerable power from its concision, some double-edged alliteration ("blind with blood"), an insistently repeated and accusatory "You," and a final image of a *German* mother that manages, by the proven procedure of the "knockout blow," to take the reader by surprise:

> O German mother dreaming by the fire,
> While you are knitting socks to send your son
> His face is trodden deeper in the mud.

Such optimism is cruelly misplaced but at least it has, as Sassoon well knew, an understandable *human* dimension. Sassoon is less prepared to condone women's predilection for "decorations" and "heroes," an extension of their eroticized love of glamour and outward show ("By tales of dirt and danger fondly thrilled") and a determination to believe — what Sassoon was increasingly inclined to *disbelieve* — that British was best. Such a deliberate patriotism as "laurelled," employed without irony in "To My Brother" (1915), here acquires a sardonic edge. While the sonnet's conclusion shows his compassion for all the male victims of war, regardless of the side on which they fight, it uncharitably stresses the pointlessness of the female war effort, whether it be making shells or "knitting socks" to send a son who will never wear them.

Their Frailty

Like so many of the Craiglockhart poems, "Glory of Women" focuses its attack on "Blighty" values. Sassoon, simply by *being* in Scotland, was part of that home-front conspiracy. But at least he *knew* what was really going on; he suffered from none of those "false appreciations" of war which he regarded as "the especial prerogative of women" (Silkin, 1987, p. 161). Many of these female misconceptions were, in Sassoon's jaundiced view, a result of a possessive and obsessive love which rendered "mothers and wives and sweethearts" temperamentally incapable of seeing the larger perspective, or of developing an over-arching concern for all young soldiers. Worse, they still urge a conventionally benevolent god "to send" their darling son "home again." It is "Their Frailty" that "they don't care

/ So long as He's all right." But the message is less effectively conveyed than in "Glory of Women," perhaps because of Sassoon's own situation. Sassoon knew, as a consequence of the death of brother Hamo, how intensely mothers grieved. It is the "wives and sweethearts," rivals for the affections of "Husband and sons and lovers," that the poet is making his primary target.

Atrocities

"Atrocities" was altogether stronger meat, one of a growing number of poems Sassoon knew sailed too close to the mark for immediate exposure. According to Farmer it was written at Craiglocklart and originally called "A Murder Case." This early version, crossed out, carried the words: "This was too much for Heinemann," written above the text in pencil. A shorter and toned-down version was "published in the first American edition of *Picture Show* ... the longer version is unpublished" (Farmer, 1969, p. 19).

This is hardly a cause for surprise. Even the revised, twelve-line satire is ablaze with white heat, as strong a piece of invective as anything Sassoon wrote. While the new title "Atrocities" no longer accuses the poem's aggressor of murder, and by implication all such acts of callous butchery, it is, in its more generalized way, just as accusatory. For the subject is the vexed one of killing off prisoners, forbidden by the Geneva Convention but nonetheless, as Graves testified in *Goodbye to All That*, unofficially condoned. Another of Sassoon's barroom bullies, in "drunken-boasting mood," talks of how he dispatched prisoners by imprisoning them in dug-outs and then throwing grenades in after them.

> ... 'Camerad!' they cry;
> Then squeal like stoats when bombs begin to fly.

The man's sadism is sickening enough. Worse then, that the listener is aware of his capacity for cowardice and trickery. Another of Sassoon's blustering bar-flies, he "wangled" his way back to "Blighty" as soon as things "looked unwholesome."

Break of Day

Thorpe calls "Break of Day" "a tenuous reverie ... which for a few moments before the attack tranquillises the soldier with peaceful memories of 'riding on a dusty Sussex lane / In quiet September,'" adding that "Sassoon seems unsure whether to intend the dream as a blessing or a mockery sent by 'God's blank heart grown kind'" (1966, p. 28). The answer is almost certainly both: thoughts of rural England do calm the troubled breast but they also underscore the ghastliness of imminent death or mutilation in an alien landscape. The contrast between "the untroubled past" and fearful present is by now something of a cliché in Sassoon's war verse, but in "Break of Day" the comparison is sustained by analogies drawn from fox-hunting. Such memories of an "earth ... telling its old peaceful tale" are produced by associative odors and sounds: in "The Dream" the smell of cow dung will rekindle memories of sweaty feet and the unmentionable odor of putrefaction; in "Break of Day" the reminiscent smells of autumn emanate from the dank environment of the underground dug-out. The autumnal mood and "chilly air" recall the dawn drawing of "the Big Wood"; the "lonely note of the horn" evokes powerful memories of the hunt. Like the Keats of "Ode to a Nightingale," the poet's reverie allows the soldier a temporary escape from the nightmare present where, "dry-mouthed" and thinking only of "the damned attack," he contemplates his own "immolation."

But the memory, Keats's "deceiving elf," can only work so far. Sooner or later, in his case sooner, the soldier will again wake up to the horrid reality. The wood they are going to "draw" is a human battleground where *men* are hunted to death and where pursuers and pursued are both equally at risk; the sound that brings him back to his "sole-self" is the signal to begin the fateful attack.

"Hark! there's the horn: they're drawing the Big Wood."

In the sub-conscious recesses of his mind, the war has always been there; it might have been temporarily metamorphosed into the setting of "Big Wood," a "crashing woodland chorus" or the "volleying Crack" of the huntsman's "thong," but unfortunately it has never gone away. Like the fox-cub exposed among the bracken of the "Long Spinney," the soldier is about to be driven out into the open and hunted down.

Banishment

The unresolved tension in Sassoon's psyche is closer to resolution in "Banishment," a Craiglockhart poem written against the growing realization that though the war is worse than ever, the poet must return to face the music with his comrades-in-arms. The carefully chosen title reveals his determination to return — at Craiglockhart he is *banished* from his rightful kingdom — to the world of the trenches. Such sentiments are reflected in a letter to Robert Graves of 19 October (*Diaries*, p. 192). Cotterill has told him that conditions at the Front are now "more bloody than anything he has yet seen," but Sassoon insists "they will have to give me a written guarantee that I shall be sent back at once," adding "My position here is nearly unbearable, and the feeling of isolation makes me feel rotten" (p. 191).

A conventionally wrought Petrarchan sonnet, this poem offers an apologia to his fellow soldiers for rebelling against the war; regardless of his anti-war convictions, his real place is with them. The poem is only rescued from the banalities of its overwrought poetic diction (both language and message show the poet reverting to 1916 models) by its impassioned declaration of a "love" which has misguidedly caused him to become "mutinous"—the choice of word is interesting in that it suggests the misguided nature of his "protest"—and to rail against the senseless carnage. But he now recognizes that this same "love" must drive him back to the Front, "back to grope with them through hell." Still "riven by grappling guns," these tormented souls will forgive him if he returns to the "pit"; only by such an act, Sassoon is persuaded, can his real love for his men be demonstrated and recognized. It is no final solution, for to return is to collude with his men in the deaths of others, but at least there is comradeship in sacrifice.

Autumn

Nonetheless the pervasive sense of guilt will not go away. Nature, in the form of "October's bellowing anger," reinforces the poet's conviction that the "harvest" of battle is "fruitless." Yet the "bronzed battalions of the stricken wood" remind him inexorably of his exposed and needy men. For once, nature, in the form of a desolating Scottish wind that scatters the blood-red leaves, cannot console. Autumn is here no Keatsian "season of mists and mellow fruitfulness" but a tempestuous equinoctial season infused with dramatic life after the manner of Shelley's "Ode to the West Wind." The Romantic poet's "pestilence-stricken multitudes" become, in Sassoon's pastiche, "battalions of the stricken wood"; Shelley's forest "lyre," the trees' "lament." But Sassoon's lines carry none of the optimism of Shelley's concluding "If winter comes, can spring be far behind?" For the speaker, the dead leaves of autumn are all too reminiscent of lives "scattered in flocks of ruin." The accusatory finale is very much a reflection of Sassoon's growing obsession with in his own culpability:

> O martyred youth and manhood overthrown,
> The burden of your wrongs is on my head.

Prelude: The Troops

"Prelude: The Troops" was a poem that Sassoon rated sufficiently highly to use as the opening salvo to *Counter-Attack*. Reading Barbusse—the epigraph to the volume is taken from *Le Feu*—and talking to Owen had rekindled Sassoon's compassionate spark; as Quinn observes: "In the post-protest poems ... there is a muting of rancour and a stronger feeling of sympathy and solidarity with the men for whom Sassoon's protest was conceived" (1993, p. 200). In particular his discussions with Rivers at "Dottyville," where he initially dismissed the bulk of the inmates as "degenerate-looking" (*Diaries*, p. 183), had convinced him that the only positive way forward was to praise his "brave companions" and, if possible, rejoin them at the Front.

In "Prelude," the men initially appear "like the survivors of the deluge in *Le Feu* ... paralyzed by the enormity of their common misfortune" (Johnstone, 1964, p. 96). But Sassoon also focuses on the unfailing capacity of the troops to find ways of coping even in a land "Where all / Is ruin." Barbusse's French soldiers are provoked by the circumstance of war into a grim mirth bordering on madness; on the other hand the English "Tommy"—and here Sassoon employs a metaphor drawn from the barbed-wire of No Man's Land—can stubbornly

> ... grin through storms of death and find a gap
> In the clawed, cruel tangles of his defence.

Nonetheless the troops are required, with all the finality of a death-sentence, to "march from safety" (the inversion is close to Owen's "Nations trek from progress" in "Strange Meeting") and into a landscape where, memorably, "nothing blossoms but the sky," and where "grass green thickets" are left behind for:

> Sad, smoking, flat horizons, reeking woods,
> And foundered trench-lines volleying doom for doom.

The visionary conclusion recalls "Two Hundred Years After" with its imagery of ghostly battalions of the dead. Even Death, again personified, will remain grieving on the battlefield while "the unreturning army" passes through "some mooned Valhalla," its eerie moonscape at once unearthly and a reminder of the pockmarked, cratered surface of No Man's Land. Despite some rhetorical over-writing in stanza three and the occasional lapse into cliché ("bird-sung joy"), the poem paints a memorable picture of ordinary young men waiting for a death that *will* come despite their efforts to "endure." That their "hardihood" remains "unvanquished" is remarkable but no cause for consolation. Suffering may ennoble but it does *not* save:

> The unreturning army that was youth;
> The legions who have suffered and are dust.

Counter-Attack

Of all Sassoon's bulletins from the battleground, "Counter-Attack" is arguably the most completely realized, a fact acknowledged implicitly in the poet's decision to use its title for the 1918 volume of war verses and reflected in its appearance in a multitude of anthologies. Johnston accords it the highest accolade, observing of the harrowing opening description:

> Few other lines in World War One poetry can equal this passage—
> with Sassoon's characteristic ironic fillip at the end—in sheer graphic

> intensity. To the horrors of simple carnage are added the frantic, intermingled, struggling grotesqueries of violent death: the final degradation of the human body which made war such an intolerable outrage to the poets who first confronted its effects [1964, p. 97].

Originally drafted in July 1916 (the beginning of the Somme offensive), it reflects Sassoon's unbridled horror at the Mametz slaughter and in particular the appearance of the dead. This kind of shocking *detail* is tribute to Sassoon's meticulous diaries; when the poet relies on his memory, the minutiae of the conflict are rarely recalled in the same way. In his diary of 4 July, 1916 (he even includes the time — 12:30) he had written:

> These dead are terrible and undignified carcasses, stiff and contorted ... side by side on their backs with bloody clotted fingers mingled as if they were handshaking in the companionship of death. And the stench undefinable. And rags and shreds of blood-stained cloth, bloody boots riddled and torn [p. 87].

The opening stanza of "Counter-Attack" even contrives to heighten this prose description of mutilation and decay. Some of the dead, now gruesome objects, have been deprived of all dignity. Their bodies, still horribly human, are "rotten" piles of "greeny clumsy legs," "bulged, clotted hands," or "naked sodden buttocks, mats of hair." Others, frozen into immobility at the very moment of their violent ends, "sprawled and grovelled along the saps" or "wallowed like trodden sand-bags." In the midst of this holocaust, an ironic note is incongruously sounded: "And then the rain began, — the jolly old rain!" As if both the quick and the dead have not endured enough, here, as the last straw, comes the drenching, deadening rain.

But the living have yet more to endure. Stanza two describes the bombardment by enemy "five-nines" and captures the growing sense of panic experienced by one soldier. In the confusion, a counter-attack is ordered: by an officer "*blundering*" — the pun is effective — "down the trench."

> "O Christ, they're coming at us!" Bullets spat,
> And he remembered his rifle ... rapid fire ...
> And started blazing wildly ... then a bang

The soldier, exposed to withering enemy fire, becomes yet another statistic in the catalogue of corpses. The poem peters out, exhausted, as the soldier bleeds to death in a pool of sucking mud:

> Lost in a blurred confusion of yells and groans....
> Down, and down, and down, he sank and drowned,
> Bleeding to death. The counter-attack had failed.

In sheer graphic intensity, the poem is fit to rank with Owen's "Dulce et Decorum Est." Nothing of Sassoon's more effectively conveys a nightmare vision of the dead, in putrefaction, and a sense of the blind panic engendered in one

"Tommy" by a murderous combination of utter fatigue, "galloping fear" and finally the brute incompetence of a "blundering" officer. There is no sentimentality in the poem, but the Zolaesque realism of the opening description finally shades into compassion and a capacity to empathize with these lost victims of the war.

Twelve Months After

In "Conscripts" Sassoon had adopted the familiar role of parade-ground martinet — not a role he savored except as a poetic device whereby he could reveal his affection for his charges. The Craiglockhart poem "Twelve Months After" sees the speaker reacquainting himself with his Number Seven Platoon of the previous year, his memory jogged by an old list or photograph. In fact Sassoon may well have been reading his December 1916 diary. There, critical of Litherland ("a dreary drab flat place"), of the "hopeless, never-shifting burden" of the war and of the recruits ("mostly a poor lot — ill trained truss-wearers"), he also reflected: "Last Christmas was at Montagne. Richardson, Edmund Dadd, Davies, Jackson, Pritchard, Thomas, Baynes *have been killed since then*" (p. 105; emphasis added).

The poem offers a less dismissive picture of his charges, perhaps because he has his named friends of *two* years earlier in mind. Realists to a man, they mumblingly reject his morale-raising "The war'll be over soon." While they are a well-drilled unit, responsive to his commands, the officer knows them as distinctively brave individuals. He even knows the real age of Davies, an old soldier who had probably lied in order to enlist:

> Jordan, who's out to win a D.C.M. some night
> And Hughes that's keen on wiring; and Davies ('79),
> Who must always be firing at the Bosche front line.

The gap between the stanzas on the page is deliberately wide. The words of the popular marching song, "Old soldiers never die; they simply fide a-why!" ring as false as the poet's own opening statement. For in the intervening year, these "old soldiers" — young in years but old in experience — have all been killed. "All present and correct" and proudly "erect" on the drill square, Gibson and Morgan, Jordan and Hughes, even the archetypal "old soldier" Davies, are no longer "present" or "erect"; the drawn-out hexameters of the conclusion offer a terrible reminder that the Somme has made a mockery of the ditty:

> That's what they used to say before the push began;
> That's where they are today, knocked over to a man.

Chapter 12

"Waiting for the End, Boys": January 1918 to March 1919

Sassoon's letters to Lady Ottoline Morrell give the clearest indication of his resolve to rejoin *his* soldiers. On 11 February he wrote: "I feel I ought to be back with my Welshmen having a rotten time. I wish I could go there. The people in England (and Scotland) make me feel a longing to escape from them." A month later he observed: "I don't think there is any doubt about my going back to the war — as I've taken to war nightmares again, which means I've got the idea very strongly in my mind" (letter from Sassoon to Morrell, 13 November, 1917, ULUT). He did eventually return to the Front — in the trenches for a mere five days in the following July — but in the meantime his war was conducted away from the Western Front, first at Limerick and then in Palestine. A winter spent in Southern Ireland during the hunting season proved a bracing tonic. He rode with the hounds whenever he could escape from the business of training recruits, and produced a number of reminiscent poems that are predominantly elegiac in tone. The highs and lows of his existence were duly reported to Ottoline Morrell. During one week and after spending four days "hearing tedious and irrelevant details about anti-gas methods," he "got away for a jolly ride in the country and had a hunt with the Muskery hounds" (letter from Sassoon to Ottoline Morrell, 27 January, 1918, ULUT). But he was well aware, as he wrote in his notebook, that it was "a drugged peace, that *will* not think, dares not think. I am home again in the ranks of youth — the company of death" (*Diaries*, 12 January, p. 203).

On 21 January, Sassoon learned he was being posted to the Middle East instead of France: there followed a period in Palestine during which he wrote few poems, his vituperation focused mainly on the philistinism of his fellow officers, his optimism on the "grandeur" of a country "gradually pouring into me like water into an empty well" (letter to Morrell, 2 March, 1918, ULUT). When he finally got to the Western Front, *Counter-Attack* had just been published (27 June) to considerable acclaim, with the first edition rapidly selling out. But on 13 July, a "bloody bullet" almost accounted for Sassoon and sent him back to "Blighty" for the last time. Twice laid low by trench-fever and now wounded for a second time, for Sassoon the eventful war was finally over. Reduced in hospital to a state of "sleeplessexasperuicide," during which he penned a remarkable verse-letter to Robert Graves, he characterically allowed his bile to rise in a final sequence of "Home-Front" satires composed in the months before the Armistice. The tragic annihilation, coupled with the mental and physical maceration of so many "loyal and brave" soldiers, would rankle for ever; only in "Everyone Sang" would Sassoon, for a brief moment, offer up a hymn of hope to the future of mankind.

In Barracks

By the time Sassoon came to write another training camp poem, he had already left the dreaded Litherland, where his body stood about for hours on parade, for Limerick; there he found "something closely resembling peace of mind" (*Memoirs*, p. 564). One of the results of this tranquil spell in Ireland was "In Barracks," verses included as the diary entry for 9 January (*Diaries*, p. 202). The first 1918 poem to be included in *Counter-Attack*, it has none of the hectoring tone of the Craiglockhart sequence, none of the suppressed anger of "Twelve Months After"; instead there is the pleasurable sensation of "watching the boys drill and do P.T., or lecturing lance-corporals in barrack-room of an afternoon. Their young eyes always meeting mine — frank and happy" (*Diaries*, p. 203). Such a mood informs the poem; there is hardly a suggestion of the horrors that may await the new infantry recruits. Only in the final imperative, to banish from their "dreamless ears" the bugle's "*dying* notes" (emphasis added), does Sassoon hint at things to come. The conclusion may well have been inspired by Graves's "The Last Post," which had, in its turn, triggered off a soulful aside to Ottoline Morrell in an earlier letter:

> Out in the dark square last night when I was seeing the barrack-day wound up, and the bugler stood and blew the last post, the truth and beauty of his poem came home to me. That last post is a very moving thing with silence and darkness closing over it [letter from Sassoon to Morrell, late 1916, ULUT].

The sense of the parade-ground instructor as voyeur is much more pervasive as he watches the "Young Fusiliers, strong-legged and bold" in stanza one; they become the "lusty Fusiliers" of stanza two where the transferred epithet barely conceals the observer's own erotic desires.

A Moment of Waking / Journey's End

The day before, on 8 January, Sassoon had written two short and very different pieces. Both are probably unfinished. "A Moment of Waking," which experiments clumsily with a variable line and anapestic rhythms, describes a nightmare in which he imagines he is dying; "Journey's End," dedicated to WMM, is "a rather feeble sonnet" for which Sassoon failed "to evolve the last six lines" (SJ, p. 75) and that eventually found its way without the last two lines into *Siegfried's Journey*. It was, Sassoon recollected, "written ... after a conversation with a bemedalled and congenial brother officer who took a gloomy view of his prospects of coming through alive" (SJ, p. 74). The poem, unexceptional save for the moving simile of war's "years, like gutted villages in France / Done with," promises his friend salvation and companionship.

Together

A sonnet, "Together" forms part of the diary entry for 30 January. Sassoon placed it at the conclusion of *Counter-Attack*, thus ending the volume less stridently than he began it with this memorial to Gordon Harbord. The poem exists in two versions. An earlier draft written in ink and dated "Aug–Dec 1917" in Sassoon's own hand was composed during his Craiglockhart period after the poet had been "knocked flat" by hearing of his death (*Diaries*, 5 September, 1917, p. 284; see also Farmer, 1969, p. 23). But the version in *Counter-Attack* is quite different and seems to have been revised at Fedamore, Limerick, after a long day's hunting had revived memories of his friend. It is this version, dated precisely by Hart-Davis as "30 January 1918," which appears in the published *War Poems*.

The prose journal for that day describes the activities of the hunt in some detail: typically, the poem, like the Craiglockhart version, focuses on the human figure in the landscape. Caught up in the excitement of the chase, the speaker will be concentrating on keeping up with the hounds, but when the frantic activity of the chase is over, he will dwell lovingly on the memory of his fox-hunting friend. On the way home he will be there, an unseen but palpable presence; after galloping together "along the glistening lanes," the ghostly companion will part imaginative company and "say goodnight" "at the stable door" before the poet settles in front of the evening fire.

Memory

Written two days later, the cancellation of a day's hunting — "Twenty three miles for nothing. Very sad" (*Diaries*, 1 February, p. 209) — may have contributed to the rather different tone of "Memory." The gently reminiscent mood of "Together" has gone; instead the opening verse proliferates with images of youthful exuberance, with the poet "gay and feckless as a colt," and the natural world — in the transferred epithet of "carolling meadows"— a reflection of his heady lust for life and his kinship with the burgeoning spirit of spring. But the experience of war has changed everything; this state of innocence and freedom has now gone forever, replaced by an awareness of death that has burnt away his innocent dreams and provokes the tumult of emotions expressed in the lines:

> For death has made me wise and bitter and strong;
> And I am rich in all that I have lost.

Now the objective correlatives of his feelings are nightingales, darkness and silence, emblems of a "vanished summer." While the expression "But now my heart is heavy-laden" recalls Housman's "with rue my heart is laden," the mood is one of Keatsian melancholy; the overwhelming desire is to "glut" his "sorrow on a morning rose" and luxuriate in the sense of loss. Innocence has been replaced by experience; just as summer has vanished, so too have the faces of friends which can now be recalled only by the exercise of memory.

Remorse

Though Sassoon had, on the evidence of his Limerick diaries, successfully returned to his role of "fox-hunting man," the entry for 5 February reveals an artist ever anxious to remember and record the brutal facts of war. Perhaps the fact that the hunt had "killed" that day (*Diaries*, 4 February, p. 209) was all the stimulus Sassoon's memory needed. In any event "Remorse" is based on a series of associative leaps. The speaker returns, compulsively, to the blind, blundering world of the trenches where, muddied, soaked and assailed by the noise of bursting shells, he wonders, "Could anything be worse than this?" The question jogs his memory. The answer is "Yes." Full of remorse, he recollects a nightmarish scenario with German soldiers being bayoneted to death. In "The Kiss," the fusilier was merely instructed in the use of the bayonet. Here in a situation that is all too real, even the soldier can empathize with plight of enemy soldiers:

> Green-faced, they dodged and darted: there was one
> Livid with terror, clutching at his knees ...
> Our chaps were sticking 'em like pigs.... "Oh hell!"

The "O hell" returns Sassoon's soldier to the present, to the realization that here in "Blighty" he must bottle up these nightmare memories and the sense of guilt that goes with them. Like the old men of "The Fathers" or the mothers of "Glory of Women," the speaker's father believes in a propaganda machine that still tells of "dying heroes" and "deathless deeds." The horrid reality of "sticking 'em like pigs" is a circumstance his soldier son dare not reveal to him.

Dead Musicians

In Sassoon's poetry and prose there is a pervasive sense of music's associative and restorative capacity, whether it be the melody of bird-song, the lyric impulse of poetry, or the grander harmonies of classical music. But only in two poems, the earlier "Elgar Violin Concerto" and "Secret Music," a 1916 poem, and now "Dead Musicians," is great music asked to work its spell on the poet of war. That it can no longer provoke profound emotions is a reflection of Sassoon's new priorities. "Dead Musicians" are, as the equivocal title indicates, simply that. Even Bach, Beethoven and Mozart are not only literally dead but evoke no emotions comparable in intensity to those the poet now feels for "friends who died." Paradoxically, all those great "fugues and symphonies" which once *did* build "cathedrals" in his "heart" and gave the poet, as in the Elgar poem, a pervasive sense of the numinous, now lack real significance. Even the language the poet employs to describe this earlier exaltation is deliberately inflated, not without a parodic edge.

Now it is the slangy speech and the contemporary rhythms of the fox-trot and of ragtime which evoke the most poignant feelings; it is these popular songs which the listener plays to "charm" back into imaginative existence the "ghosts" of lost comrades. But such ghostly presences offer only an ephemeral source of solace. The mourning poet realizes that such upbeat music is a mixed blessing: the songs *do* remind him of comrades, but also of the harsh reality that they are no longer of this world. When the music stops, he is, like the listener in Keats's nightingale ode, forced to return to the real world, to accept that he is alone with his memories, and that nothing can alleviate the sense of loss. Round his head he guiltily wears — like the mariner his albatross — "a wreath of banished lives"; to play the joyous music of ragtime on the gramophone is to be reminded of dead loved ones. The only solution is only to turn off the machine.

> They've got such jolly things to tell,
> Home from hell. With a Blighty wound so neat ...
>
> And, so the song breaks off; and I'm alone.
> They're dead.... For God's sake stop that gramophone!

Invocation

"Invocation," another elegiac poem from the Limerick period, lacks the personal focus of "Together." Its reliance on a mannered euphuistic diction, employed without ironic overtones, and the reiterated desire to "escape" the trenches for the "clear cock-crow airs" more than hint at a reversion to an earlier poetic manner. The poem reverberates with familiar sounding epithets — "whispering trees," for example, has already been used in "The Last Meeting" and "Before the Battle" to evoke a nostalgic atmosphere in which the poet can commune with nature. But unlike its companion piece, "Together," which is redeemed by its fox-hunting memories, "Invocation" remains on the plane suggested by its title, a pantheistic expression of homoerotic feeling couched in a spuriously ornamented language, an "invocation" to his "song's desire" to "come down from heaven's bright hill," to "bring me in your eyes ... stillness from the pools of Paradise." Were it not for the evocative opening image of "drumming shafts of stifling death," one could imagine the lyric as an antebellum exercise in romantic pastoral.

Suicide in the Trenches

By 12 February, 1918, Sassoon was on his way to Cherbourg, the name of his boat ("The Antrim") the only reminder of Ireland. Ten days later, when "Suicide in the Trenches" appeared in the *Cambridge Magazine*, Sassoon was already in Italy en route for Alexandria. The poem, probably the last piece to be composed at Limerick, uses a simple ballad stanza, three tetrameter quatrains, that both in its formal concerns and its reference to "lads" shows the impact of his reading of Housman. Like "Lamentations," its subject is the dehumanizing effect of a war that can transform happiness to degradation or even worse, suicidal despair. The jaunty rhythms and nursery-rhyme opening provide a counterpoint to the deadly serious subject matter: how, asks the poet, can "a simple soldier boy" be driven to the insane expedient of putting "a bullet through his brain." In the spare monosyllables of stanza two Sassoon captures the immediacy and impersonality of the tragic ballad.

> In winter trenches, cowed and glum,
> With crumps and lice and lack of rum,
> He put a bullet through his brain.
> No one spoke of him again.

A pity then, that in the hectoring tone of the last stanza, in the haranguing of the "smug-faced crowds," the poet's coolly objective stance should be replaced by a too obtrusive anger.

Concert Party

Once on his way back to the war, Sassoon was disappointed not to rejoin his regiment immediately at the Western Front; instead he was sent to Palestine (Gaza) via Taranto, Alexandria and Kantara. In general Sassoon abhorred the behind-the-lines company of his fellow officers; in Kantara Base Camp even the birds were a solace, "a tiny glimpse of 'real life' in this arid waste of officer mentality" (*Diaries*, 2 March, p. 219). He was, on his own admission, bored by the inactivity, confiding to himself: "This place is the absolute visible expression of time wasted at the war" (*Diaries*, 4 March, p. 219). "Concert Party," one of two poems of this period, was Sassoon's only creative response to Kantara, a poem heavily dependent on the imagery of the diary entry for 17 April:

> Night of stars; half moon overheard; two men with grey soft hats; three women in short silk skirts; jangling ragtime piano, a few footlights shining upwards, just reaching the faces of these puppets — these players; and overall the serene canopy of night in Egypt. They sing their songs ... all around — a mass of men — dim, moonlit hour [p. 235].

"Concert Party" is a tone poem, atmospheric and evocative, full of shadowy color and sound, as Sassoon's exercises in this mode invariably are. But the poet is distanced, a watcher of what he regards as the fripperies of "some actor bloke" and "warbling ladies in white." More somberly and more predictably, his thoughts are with the "*shadowy* mass of soldiers" (emphasis added) who, "drunk" on these Blighty "memories," will all too soon be back at the Front. Even now, they have a potentially tragic dimension as

> Silent, they drift away, over the glimmering sand.

The poem only hints at such fantastic feelings. Later, in the *Memoirs*, Sassoon would remember: "It was as though these civilians were playing to an audience of the dead and the living — men and ghosts who had crowded in like moths to a lamp" (*Memoirs*, p. 605).

Night on the Convoy

"Night on the Convoy," written on the voyage from Alexandria to France, versifies observations in the diary of 4 May:

> I watch the *men* lying about the decks in the sunlight, staring at the glittering glorious blue sea and the huge boats ploughing along in line — six of us, and nine or ten destroyers ... I like to see them (the men) leaning against each other with their arms round one another — it is pathetic and beautiful and human (but that is only a sexual emotion in me — to like them in those attitudes) [*Diaries*, 4 May, p. 242].

Such erotic longings are largely displaced from the poem, though the picture of decks "spread with lads in sprawling strength" reveals a poet in voyeuristic mood. But the "anguish" of "going home" as victims, an emotion which informs the diary entry ("part of the huge dun-coloured mass of victims that passes across the shambles of war into the gloom of death"), is present in the poem as a threat which returns, at the end of each stanza, to haunt the speaker's consciousness, and then swells, diapason-like, in the poem's conclusion. Even the troop-ship seems sensitive to these fears:

> We are going home. The troop-ship in a thrill
> Of fiery-chamber'd anguish, throbs and rolls.
> We are going home ... victims ... three thousand souls.

"Concert-Party" barely hinted at such feelings. Two months on and in the process of being inexorably transported back to the Western Front, Sassoon could anticipate another battle of Arras where "dumb with pain," he had "stumbled among the dead." There is scant consolation in such thoughts. All the soldier-poet can do is to be there again with his suffering men, aware that history has an unfortunate habit of repeating itself.

Reward

Like "Invocation," "Reward" is in essence a love-lyric, but here the ostensible "love," expressed mainly in tetrameters, is directed not at a beloved dead comrade (a recurrent theme of so many poems) but at *all* the men under him; it is a responsible love, one that "guards the door" but will, if required, go with them to the grave. Such a "responsible" love was a way of channeling his homoerotic feelings in acceptable directions; a sublimatory procedure given additional philosophical backing by his recent reading of Georges Duhamel's *La Vie des martyrs* in translation (he had begun reading it on 21 May), and from which he had recently quoted from in his diary: "To make up one's mind to die is to take a certain resolution, in the hope of becoming quieter, calmer and less unhappy. The man who makes up his mind to die severs a good many ties, and indeed actually dies to some extent" (Duhamel, 1918, p. 145, quoted in *Diaries*, 24 May, p. 257). Such passages clearly reinforced Sassoon's mood of fatalism; he had been recently preoccupied, as the diaries attest, with a death wish. Three days earlier, on 2 June, he had written to his close friend Roderick Meiklejohn in the following terms: "(As you know, I do *all* I can to make their lot as happy as possible and they are wonderfully cheery). One feels all this sunshine is the opening scene of a tragedy." This sense of foreboding, present in both letter and poem, proved prophetic; on 13 July Sassoon was shot in the head and escaped death by millimeters.

Interestingly, while the poet's sexual feelings are repressed, they are, once again, not entirely erased from the poem. "From their eyes the gift I gain / Of grace that can subdue my pain" is a kind of code-speak; eyes and eye-contact encrypt homoerotic responses, a male-gaze of mutual attraction. By substituting "his" (for the poem's "*their* eyes"), one can place the poem in a context of recrudescent male love that accords with events of the same day where he watches Jim Linthwaite: "Something drew me to him when I saw him first ... and I've loved him ever since (it is just as well he's not in my present Company)." He adds,

"But there was a great deal of sex floating about in this particular effort" (*Diaries*, 5 June, p. 262). Such feelings are there, albeit sublimated and given a respectable context in the poem's conclusion:

> O brothers in my striving, it were best
> That I should share your rest.

I Stood with the Dead

In 1961, the *Sunday Telegraph* review of Sassoon's *Collected Poems* offered the judgment that the poet was one of those technically proficient but minor versifiers, able only "in extremis" to produce memorable verse: "Then," opined the reviewer, "the hitherto stagnant depths of the natures are suddenly churned up." Sassoon delighted in quoting a description which went on to allow that the churning up process could be seen at work in "I Stood with the Dead." His mordant response was: "Written in June 1918! Appeared in *The Nation*, 13 July, the day I was shot in the head" (Corrigan, 1973, p. 24).

Though Sassoon could not have known it at the time, the poem's initial appearance in *The Nation* provoked official ire on a scale probably unmatched by any of his other war verses. Still smarting from Sassoon's "Protest" a year earlier, and desperate to seize on any "evidence" of discrediting instability, military intelligence in the form of Brigadier-General George Cockerill wrote to the editor of the left-wing organ: "If Lieutenant Sassoon is now writing verse such as appeared [in the journal], it would appear that his mind is still in chaos and that he is not fit to be trusted with men's lives" (Sassoon File, Public Record Office). Cockerill also asked Massingham when the poem had been submitted, in the hope that the editor would link it to the period of the protest, thus providing further evidence of Sassoon's mental instability at the time. Feigning forgetfulness, Massingham did not reveal the poem's recent provenance.

Couched partly in solemn anapestics, and making skillful use of repetition, the opening stanza "I Stood with the Dead" takes Sassoon back to the vengeful 1916 mood of "The Kiss" and "The Poet as Hero." The warning glare of the red morning sun provides an objective correlative to the blood-boltered vision of the poet. Surrounded by nightmarish corpses (the word "dead" is repeated five times), he vows to avenge both the massed victims of war, allowed no dignity in their "crumpled disgrace," and the individualized loves he has lost in the carnage of battle. But pity, as so often in Sassoon, supplants anger, as he recalls the face of a "lad" — the term carries homoerotic associations — his face drenched by the pitiless rain, his eyes blurred in death. Both the general and the particular have been memorialized in recent poems; here they coalesce in the same verses. The punning conclusion offers no relief: it conveys a touching bathos as the distraught and bereft officer orders his men to fall in for their pay. Sadly, there can be no response. They have already fallen in death and paid the ultimate price with their own lives.

Trench Duty

Placed next to "I Stood with the Dead" in Hart-Davis's edition of *The War Poems*, "Trench Duty" and the poems that immediately follow ("Joy-Bells," "Song Books of the War," "The Triumph") were all published in *Counter-Attack* (June 1918), and so properly belong to a somewhat earlier period of the war. "Trench Duty," a sonnet, shows how capable Sassoon is of concentrating his effects — mainly sounds and sensations that are sometimes combined as in "splashing mirk"— in a trench-scape where the starry night is complemented by "candle-chinked" light and the "flickering horror" of the guns. But despite "starlight overhead," which *should* require extreme caution, one man has been shot and killed. Such an outcome prompts the speaker to ask: "Why did he do it?" Whether the question refers to the sniper or his victim is not made clear. Nor the reasoning behind the action. Whatever the reasons, the fact remains that a soldier has died and the speaker is still "wide-awake." So much for lucky stars. These actual stars have nothing to recommend them. "Blank stars," they have been both agency and witness as another soldier loses his life.

Joy-Bells

Eighteen months have elapsed since Sassoon last targeted the Anglican church, but "Joy-Bells," sandwiched between "They" (1916) and "Vicarious Christ" (1919), sees Sassoon renewing his mordant attack on bishops. More bitterly satiric poems, "They" and "Vicarious Christ" owe their freshness and immediacy to recent encounters with clerics that had left their mark on Sassoon; "Joy Bells" has only the sound of church bells to remind the poet, in a daring and not entirely successful metaphor, of brazen "fierce-browed prelates." Whether the poem was inspired by an actual incident is difficult to ascertain, though *Memoirs* does allude to a 1917 address by the Archbishop of Canterbury in which he proposed Sunday working to assist the war effort (*Memoirs*, p. 455).

"Joy-Bells" is a cleverly constructed piece: it opens with an innocuous plea to "ring you sweet bells," but follows with an ironic exhortation to melt down these same bells whose "tones are tuned for peace" into military weaponry, to convert their soothing chimes into the whine of shells. Such bellicosity has a human equivalent, whereby a spiritual emblem of Christian charity is metamorphosed into a martial and belligerent symbol. By this token the bishop, like the bell, is converted into a "fierce-browed prelate," conniving in destruction and dispensing jingoism, rather than preaching the virtues of peace and universal brotherhood. Just as the "motor-bus" has shouldered new responsibilities in wartime, so the poet sardonically affirms, "let our bells and bishops do the same."

Colin

The last elegy of Sassoon's war was written as a consequence of the death of Lt. C. N. Dobell of the Royal Welch Fusiliers, one of the few friends to have been in action with the poet from the inception of the Somme campaign. Reading the news in *The Times* on 12 June was, for Sassoon, a desolating experience: "Little Colin who was with me at Mametz Wood. And I took him out hunting with the Limerick Hounds last February, his first real day's hunting. 'It can't be true, it can't be true,' I thought. But it's there in print" (*Diaries*, 12 June, p. 266).

The loss occasioned two poems: one a private piece simply entitled, "Colin"; the other, written six days later, the moving Housman-like ballad, "I Stood with the Dead." "Colin," perhaps because it *is* so subjective, is less openly homoerotic, though the companion is described in terms redolent of male love as one of the "lads whose words and eyes I can't forget." Its tone is more resigned than that of the diary note, less elevated in style than the earlier elegies to David Thomas, Marcus Goodall and Gordon Harbord. That the death provoked Sassoon, characteristically, to fierce anger, is evidenced by its companion poem; in "Colin," aware of the calm temperament of his subject, the dominant emotion is one of quiet acceptance:

> Colin's dead to-day; he's gone away;
> Cheery little Colin, keen to hunt;
> Firm and cool and quiet in a stunt.
> Is there any more to say?

Song-Books of the War

Such personal grieving is subsumed in "Song-Books of the War," where Sassoon focuses on the more general fear, that history has a nasty habit of repeating itself. The sprightly tetrameters provide a counterpoint to the poem's central concern, namely that in fifty years, lessons learned from the "shambles that men built / And smashed, to cleanse the world of guilt" will have been forgotten. In 1964, "adventurous lads" will behave in exactly the same way as those of 1914. Excited by snatches of the old marching songs, they will misguidedly yearn for the "dazzling times" supposedly enjoyed by the troops and look forward to new opportunities for heroism.

For once the speaker—"some ancient man with silver locks"—is invested with a dignity and sense of proportion rarely accorded old age in Sassoon's poetry. But we should remember that he *is* in the best position to remember; he is a battle-scarred veteran who will never forget, as Sassoon will never forget (and he lived another 49 years) that

> War was a fiend who stopped our clocks
> Although we met him grim and gay.

The image is powerfully ambiguous. Whether its victims are literally dead or merely condemned to a period of arrested development, the war has proved a senseless and expensive failure, a disaster for which the generals — and here Haig, for the only time in the war verse, is singled out for opprobrium — must take full responsibility. However, the generation gap that World War One has done so much to widen, will remain. Granddad, despite his firsthand experience as a young soldier of a young man's war, is dismissed by a new generation of "lads" who not only regard him as "past it" but who are only too anxious to let history repeat itself.

The Triumph

After the business-like tetrameters of "Song-Books," the languorous anapests of "The Triumph" signal a very different topic and treatment. Its eight lines chart a progress from the conventional inspiration of nature ("a bird's lone cry in the glen"), an inspiration lost in the terrible flickering gloom of the fight, where cruelty and despair are the dominant emotions, to a final beatific vision of soldiers returning from the fray, elation clearly visible in their triumphant faces.

The poem was published in *Counter-Attack* but omitted from the *Collected Poems*. It is apparently slight, a studied exercise in romantic pastoral. But it does reveal, through its poetic codes, a homoerotic yearning that will bear fuller scrutiny. The sounds from the world of nature, the sounds the poet identifies with, are a "whisper" and a "lone cry." The word "whisper"— and it is a recurrent epithet in Sassoon's poetry — suggests something secret, a confidence to be divulged only to initiates; the "lone cry" intimates that this erotic yearning is a plaintive and often isolating condition even though it can, given the opportunity, find passionate expression:

> On dawn-lit hills and horizons girdled with flame
> I sought for the triumph that troubles the faces of men.

In such an idyllic world, nature, both human and non-human, merges in romantic images of beauty and fulfillment. War, on the other hand, reduces the lover to an unfulfilled role where he is, by turns, assailed both by sadistic emotions ("cruel and fierce with despair") and feelings of abjection, even of masochism

("I was naked and bound: I was stricken"). Positive feelings of love, albeit of a necessarily idealized kind, flood back, however, when the speaker looks into the "faces of men," comrades who have returned from the abyss to be with him.

Battalion Relief

"Battalion Relief" was presumably composed — ironically in view of its powerful subject matter of presageful omens — just before Sassoon was "sniped" (on 13 July). It is a marching piece with the accompanying officer keeping a paternal eye on his company and cocking a tolerant ear to the banter of the recruits, a poem that, in a characteristic procedure, blends personal observation and reflection with the colloquial chat of the troopers. The contrasts are conventional enough: the fertility of patterned, sun-drenched crops set against the imminent and dark destruction of the front line, the battle-weary commander's realistic musings juxtaposed to the recruit's surprised "Christ, ain't it lively, Sergeant? Is't a battle?" But an early note of menace is sounded in the parenthetical aside ("Harvest soon / Up in the Line"). Unfortunately it *will* be harvest time, not only for these fields of corn, but also for the lives of these marching men. The title of the poem is double-edged. These soldiers are indeed going to relieve the troops "Up in the Line"; unfortunately the new battalion will experience the reverse of relief once it arrives there.

The speaker muses despondently on this situation as the Front looms ahead; he becomes more aware of his men's real predicament, "sweating and blindly burdened" as they file off, likely victims of death's embrace in those "two dark miles" that separate them from the trenches. In ironic contrast comes the naive response of the recruit who apparently already appears to regard his sergeant-major as an oracular father-figure:

> ... Oh Sergeant-Major, don't get shot!
> And tell me, have we won this war or not?

The Dug-Out

When Sassoon composed "The Dug-Out," it was still unclear, even in July 1918, what the answer to the recruit's naive question might be. Such a question was hardly on his mind as he wrote the poem. In *Siegfried's Journey*, the poet reflected on the poem's gestation: "While at Lancaster Gate I wrote eight vigil-haunted lines, 'The Dug-Out,' which are probably more memorable than anything I could have achieved in confederacy with a Propaganda Ministry" (SJ, p. 71). Sassoon's memory seems to have let him down — originally the piece was longer — but as he remarked to Ottoline Morrell at the time, he "intended cutting out the last four lines" which "weaken the effort, though they are part of the picture — the glimmering country outside the door" (letter from Sassoon to Morrell, 27 August, 1918, ULUT).

"The Dug-Out" was one of the last poems to stem directly from the lived experience of the trenches, a poignant moment now recollected in the supposedly tranquil setting of the American Military Hospital (his similarly dated "Dear Roberto" makes only fitful reference to the front line). Sassoon was not the only person to recognize its merits. Thorpe, who quotes the entire piece in his critical study, argues that the poet achieves a creative tension between "subjective and compassionate feeling":

> He avoids the sentimental treatment the subject invites (a lament for the doom of the clean, corn-haired youth in the full flower of manhood, etc.); he focuses attention instead on the symbolic ugliness of the youth's posture, which is reinforced by the body's alienation from the candle. Sleep is a cruel mockery of death: not just the youth's, or of all those who have died, but of the poet's own that may be imminent. When he shakes the youth by the shoulder, it is the instinctive reaction of one who shares his vulnerable humanity [Thorpe, 1966, p. 34].

The poem is intensely realized in imaginative and emotional terms. Both evocative observation and sensitive confession, it combines the compassion of an Owen — an emotion Sassoon was keen to emulate in his verse — with a personal, vigil-haunted recollection. Written two months after the diary note, with its reference to "Handsome Jowett asleep on the floor, with his smooth, sensual face and large limbs (as usual, he looks as if dead)" (*Diaries*, 19 May, p. 252), the poem clearly draws on the notebook impression. But what Sassoon achieves is something the notebook entry does not attempt; it daringly juxtaposes the sleeping comrade's unromantic attitude ("legs ungainly huddled"; "sullen, cold, exhausted face") to the watcher's loving concern; that it still "hurts [his] heart to watch you" is a confession of the intensity of his feelings at that revelatory moment. Moreover these are emotions so profound that he is compelled to act in an apparently irrational, even insensitive way: he "shakes his companion by the shoulder" to wake him. Only in the last line do we realize why. The watcher is "haunted," as he has been throughout this bloody conflict, by the loss of loved ones. Even to be reminded of death, or of the already dead by the recumbent form of a loved one, is more than he can endure.

Just before Sassoon went "up the line" for the last time, another poetic milestone was reached with the publication, much delayed, of *Counter-Attack* on 7 June. All the material had long since been with Heinemann, but as early as January Sassoon had felt that the publisher was "*trying* to put me off ... afraid that a new book would spoil the sale of *The Old Huntsman*" which was "selling quite well." He added, "And he is nervous about some of the poems" (letter from Sassoon to Morrell, 27 January, 1918, ULUT). At all events the second volume of war poems was now finally out, its garish blood-red and orange-yellow cover perhaps intended as a symbolic reflection of its contents. The first edition sold out within weeks, a tribute both to Sassoon's growing reputation and to shifting public opinion about the conflict. Sassoon wrote to Morrell from Lancaster Gate that all 1500 copies had gone, adding, "it is a commercial idea but I confess I am rather pleased about it" (letter from Sassoon to Morrell, July, 1918, ULUT).

Sassoon's frontline tour with his battalion had been short-lived, though his frequently expressed desire to die in action with his comrades and expunge his feelings of guilt had come perilously close to realization. As he fatalistically observed in "Dear Roberto," the first poem to be written from his hospital bed, he had "timed his death in action to the minute." Death did not "choose him" as it had the young trooper in "The Death-Bed," but its breath had never been so close. To Lady Ottoline Morrell he explained:

> At exactly 3.40 a.m. on July 13 I had an accident (July 13 last year I rejoined my unit at Litherland). I was coming in from a patrol and a bullet struck me on the side of the head with an awful bang and here I am at the base! I had only been in the line 5 days and I simply hated leaving my poor soldiers up there ... without me to look after them.... Those few days were very wonderful. But they nearly smashed my box of poems that time — "another half-inch would have sent me dead or dotty" — the doctor said [letter from Sassoon to Morrell, 15 July, 1918, ULUT].

Within a whisker of being killed, he did not entirely escape being "dotty" for part of his stay at the Red-Cross Hospital. His private verse letter to Robert Graves, dispatched on 24 July, revealed a feverish poet plagued by emotions that fluctuated wildly between self-belief and self-doubt, between horror at the prospect of returning to the frontline on one hand, and anguish at loss of contact with his men on the other. Such chaotic feelings produced one of the most arresting poetic documents of Sassoon's war.

Once restored in body, Sassoon reverted to his usual "Blighty" practice of writing escapist lyrics (at Lennell in Scotland he would try his hand at "a few nature pieces and quiet things") (letter from Sassoon to Meiklejohn, 15 September), or targeting establishment insensitivity. The autumn and winter of 1918 produced a series of terse epigrams aimed at "Great Men" and Germanophobic generals, at "home-front" majors ("A Last Word") and bellicose "Bishop Byegumbs." Before the Armistice, there would be a thinly-veiled attack on the monarch in "Devotion to Duty." But Sassoon could never forget his "poor soldiers," or indeed the equally "loyal and brave German opposition"; in "Reconciliation" the positive note still reverberates for all these ordinary soldiers still slogging it out at the Front.

When peace finally broke out, Sassoon's Mercutio-like sensibility displayed very mixed emotions. The "mob patriotism" of the London crowds compelled him to denounce a "loathsome ending" to a "loathsome tragedy" (*Diaries*, 11 November, p. 282); and the parade of be-ribboned big-wigs sparked off the bitterly ironic "Return of the Heroes." But "Everyone Sang," which Sassoon dubbed his "Innisfree" and a piece that arrived spontaneously, showed that Sassoon could, in his more optimistic moments, envisage a brave new world where "the singing will never be done." The following years produced a few poems on the Great War, but his own participation, to all intents and purposes, ended on that fateful July morning. Indeed, by September 1918, Sassoon, though cognizant of the fact that unless "I can get the sort of job I want, I shall have to go back to the war...," regarded such an outcome as "a pity — as I have begun to believe that I could develop my poetic talent a good deal by careful study." Convalescing at Lennel in Berwickshire, he received a letter from Winston Churchill threatening to find him an "unsavoury, dangerous and exhausting job" (letter from Sassoon to Meiklejohn, 15 September, ULUT). Such a job did not materialize. In late September his burgeoning interest in socialism attracted an offer (not taken up) to stand as Hampstead Labour candidate; in the following March, the *London Gazette* announced that "Lt. (Acting Captain) S.L. Sassoon M.C. ... is placed on the retired list on account of ill-health caused by wounds 12 March and is granted the rank of Captain." Both public and private wars were over.

Letter to Robert Graves (Dear Roberto)

"Dear Roberto" is, along with "To Any Dead Officer," "The Rear-Guard," "Repression of War Experience" and "Counter-Attack," one of the key poetic documents of Sassoon's war.

Conditions for artistic composition of any kind were not propitious. Incarcerated in hospital and suffering from insomnia and a nervous exhaustion that rendered him near suicidal ("sleepless exasperuicide"), Sassoon's mind had, on his own admission, "worked itself into a tantrum of self-disparagement" (*Memoirs*, p. 654). As his letter of 4 August to Vivian de Sola Pinto also confirms, not only had he contracted yet another "dose of fever which left me rather futile," he was also besieged by nightmarish memories of "people being blown to bits" and affronted by "outbursts of national vulgarity" (*Diaries*, p. 277). He also confessed to Ottoline Morrell that he had been traumatized by "a most pathetic letter from my servant in France which has rather unsettled me. He says he never saw a company so upset at losing an officer!" (letter from Sassoon to Morrell, July, ULUT).

In view of all these distractions, it is surprising that Sassoon was able to write his verse letter to Graves at all. Nonetheless it is a crucial document, the poet's farewell to the war and the last poem he wrote to be based on recent experience of the battlefront. The accidental bullet that ended his active involvement triggered off a piece that would not otherwise have been written. More important, it is a piece that opens up a whole Pandora's Box of conflicting emotions, emotions that had been tearing Sassoon apart for some time and which were now intensified by his head wound and consequent traumatic separation from his men.

From a formal perspective the poem is equally unusual; its expressionistic procedures no less than its erratic content convey a sense of "nerves gone phut and failed." The opening immediately betrays an exasperation with the fact that the poet's demise, both predicted and desired in his "deathly" verses ("I Stood with the Dead" was published on 13 July) had failed to materialize. In a number of earlier 1918 poems, Sassoon had longed for emotional reunions with his blood brothers at the Front; here the romantic tone has been superseded by one that is self-disparaging and sardonic:

> ... the quivering songster failed to die
> Because the bloody Bullet missed its mark.

The candid tone continues in stanza two where Sassoon feels by turns remorseful and relieved as a sardonic prayer is offered up to the civilian agencies that have returned him safely if hardly unscathed to the prospective embrace of the Motherland ("O Gate of Lancaster, O Blightyland the Blessed").

But nemesis, if not in the form of a lethal bullet, then at least in the shape of a "dragon" of a nurse, is at hand. By refusing Sassoon the consolatory presence of his literary friends (who had previously arrived "en masse"), she exacerbates the tendency of the poet's brain to go "a-hop." The telescoped names in the text — "MarshMoonStreetMeiklejohnArdoursandenduranSitwellitis" — reflect not only the overwhelming if wished-for presence of the Half Moon Street set but, like the frenzy of "Jabber — Gesture — Jabber — Gesture," the state of mind of a speaker whose nerves have gone to pieces. In fact, Sassoon had implored Roderick Meiklejohn to come and see him, admitting:

> I am feeling rather a wreck — a touch of fever, and have been simmering like a kettle since Sunday, and horribly repressed [that word again] in consequence. But I hope I'll be well enough to see you on Saturday, if you can come in. Your face haunts me. You are so faithful [letter from Sassoon to Meiklejohn, "Wed-night," ULUT].

Some sense of order returns in stanza four of this decidedly irregular ode. The source of calm is Rivers, Sassoon's doctor and father-figure from Craiglockhart. Writing to Ottoline Morrell, Sassoon alluded to the visit: "Have seen no one today except Rivers ... had some difficulty getting in, although he is supposed to be allowed in any time of the day or night. That female dragon is most unpopular" (letter from Sassoon to Morrell, "Saturday night"). As at Craiglockhart, Rivers was able to reassure Sassoon, to remind him of his achievement as poet and officer — one can feel his self-belief returning in the "gallant and glorious lyrical soldier" — and to convince him again that the way forward, in the parlance of a rugby-player keen for a scrap, was "Back to the Front / For a scrimmaging stunt."

But Sassoon's "wobbly-witted" brain seems unable to focus on one thing for any length of time. It is as though all the conflicting emotions of the war are clamoring for attention in his brain. Though he may be a gallant soldier, he suddenly recalls how adverse weather conditions at the Front invariably cool the ardor of the would-be hero. Then he remembers that he is writing to Robert Graves and slips in a barbed comment about his propensity for borrowing money from Sassoon. The poet's half-Jewish origins and the traditional association of Jews with usury — a connection Sassoon is at pains to repress in both notebooks and poems — prompts a lacerating rhetorical question which he fires at his friend: "Why keep a Jewish friend unless you bleed him?"

This ruthless exposure of self continues, as Sassoon veers from self-congratulation ("he's the topic of the town") to a sense of his impotence in the face of nothing more fearsome than Mrs. Fisher, the "dragon" of a matron. Though he is delighted to receive Jolly Otterleen's "golden daisies" (the name is a conflation of Rosaleen, Graves's sister, a nurse at the hospital, and Ottoline), he is mortified that the matron refuses to let his friend see "the wonderful and wild and wobbly-witted sarcastic soldier-poet with a plaster on his crown." The poetic response matches the actuality. To Ottoline Morrell he revealed: "I begged to be allowed to see you for a few minutes but the woman pursed up her mouth. I fear your accent betrayed you and they suspected ... hmm.... Propaganda.... But such flowers — ordinary country flowers. Not a sign of Bond Street about them" (letter from Sassoon to Morrell, "Thursday," ULUT).

But as the next verse makes clear, the invalid, now calm enough to be able to sleep "from two to four," is then "excited" by the arrival of news from his own 25th Battalion in the form of a letter from its commanding officer, a letter which commends his own company for "doing better and better." Reiterating the theme of so many other post-protest poems, Sassoon wants to be there to share their moment of triumph, to receive — what is more important to him than anything else and which he had expressed unequivocally in "The Triumph"— the admiration and love of his men.

The words of the popular song ("You made me love you: I didn't want to do it") reassure him. Despite his concerns about the war and his sexuality, he *has* won the affection of his men ("I made them love me"). And these men, we should recall, are ordinary soldiers, not known for loving their officers, men who did not initially "want to do it." As a mark of his own affection, the poet has sent them a "glorious gramophone" and the appropriate record of "God send you back to 'em." That the homecoming will be, in a remarkable image, "over the green eviscerating sea," indicates just how pessimistic he suddenly realizes he feels about such a reunion.

Such a vision — and the poem is full of associative leaps after the manner of "Repression of War Experience"— returns him to the nightmare reality of trench warfare and to the realization that he is not only ill (he had an intermittent temperature of 102 at Lancaster Gate), but that in his despairing moments he is as scared as anyone else of confronting those "five-nines" once more, and longs to become a part of peaceful, rural England, surrounded by his talismanic books and composing pastoral verses about "Daffodils and Geese." The punning oath which follows — "O Jesu make it cease" — a procedure reminiscent of the early war poetry, forces on him the realization that if the war were over, he would not have to make these agonizing decisions about going back, or be haunted by these recurrent specters. But such temporizing is pointless: the verse sounds a desperate note that is reflected in the harsh internal rhymes of "take me/make me/break me," as the masochistic poet pleads to Rivers to exercise his paternalistic authority and insist on his return to a Front that *will* assuredly break him before delivering the "coup de grâce." In a final, manic gesture, the wounded hero further confuses his already scrambled senses, but he is at least safe in the knowledge that the public's final accolade will focus on his undying and dying love for his men:

> O Rivers please take me. And make me
> Go back to the war till it break me.
> Some day my brain will go BANG,
> And they'll say what lovely faces were
> The soldier-lads he sang
>
> Does this break your heart? What do I care?
>   Sassons

The flip conclusion, a typical Sassoonesque piece of bathos, shows the poet ultimately reverting to a devil-may-care attitude that, in the light of the tormented paragraphs of the rest of the poem, carries no conviction whatsoever. "Dear Roberto" is a remarkable poem, both as personal confession and creative experiment, probably unrealized at the time, in expressive form. The marked changes of mood, the eruptions of anger and self-loathing, mirror not only Sassoon's erratic state of mind but the unusual fact, as the July letters confirm, that it was composed over a period of days if not weeks, during an extended period of illness and stress. The fractured syntax, coinages and telescopings, the poem's wildly variable line and stanza lengths, the use of the dash to suggest a disordered consciousness — all these show Sassoon jettisoning his principles for formal verse-making.

A merciless piece of self-exposure, the piece was assuredly *not* intended for public consumption. That Robert Graves should print it, a decade on, in *Goodbye to All That*, sounded the death-knell for their faltering friendship; that Sassoon should place an immediate embargo on its appearance in print was emphatic proof that he regarded Graves's action as unprincipled and opportunistic. That Graves did excise nine lines, including the confused and confessional final stanza, omitted the Jewish reference and the name "Otterleen," and substituted the affectionate nick-name "Sassons" for "Dotty Captain," demonstrates some concern for Sassoon's feelings. Graves's failure to consult his friend before publishing the verse-letter did not. That the poem mysteriously appeared in a pirated edition a few months later further undermined one of the most creative friendships of the Great War.

Great Men

As Sassoon lay, morose and ill in hospital, he was reminded at every turn, of "the callous vulgarity of the majority here." One event in particular, which he observed from his hospital window, so infuriated him that he responded by jotting down an irritated note in his diary. He had, he declared, been witness to "an outburst of national vulgarity yesterday — Thanksgiving for the war or something. A 'Shrine' in the park (gift of Waring and Gillow 'erected at a cost of several hundred pounds') — one of our insults to the dead" (*Diaries*, 4 August, pp. 277–8).

All Sassoon's ire surfaces in "Great Men," an ironically entitled piece which heaps scorn on the familiar targets, now quite literally in his sights, of brass hats and politicians. His satiric impulse had been strangely quiescent during the previous six months; now the sight of so-called "Great Men" tacitly approving "a monstrous tyranny" in the shape of a tasteless ceremony provokes a bitter denunciation of official attitudes. The reference to "what these wars are worth," juxtaposed to the "wars they *wage*" (emphasis added) of the previous line, is double-edged: these "marshals" and "ministers" know the real cost in human lives but insist on emphasizing instead the cost of erecting meaningless monuments. The poem's rhetorical exhortation is apposite. Why aren't these "mouthings" — a precisely pejorative epithet — reserved for those who really *count*, those who gave everything and who now lie unremembered in simple cemeteries with only "wooden crosses" to mark their sacrifice. The bathetic conclusion sounds the right note: humility and sincerity constitute the proper response, not the elitist self-congratulations of so-called "great ones."

Trade Boycott

Like "Great Men," the September "Trade Boycott" was sent to his favorite *Cambridge Magazine*. If Sassoon were to "warn" his public effectively — and this cautionary role of the trench poet was later endorsed by Owen — then he needed an instant readership. The weekly *Cambridge* supplied such a need. "Trade Boycott" shows Sassoon again reverting to his proven epigrammatic manner; the diary entries have mysteriously dried up, but he has got his second wind as far as satire is concerned. Subtle changes are detectable in his epigrammatic method. Perhaps as a consequence of Owen's freer versification, perhaps because of the experiments of "Dear Roberto," Sassoon is becoming less fixated on regular strophes. In "Great Men" the brisk trimeters are interlarded with slow, ruminative five-stressed lines: here the regular syllabics of the opening stanza are suddenly brought up short by the curt language and dramatic internal rhymes of "He's a list in his fist."

Yet another attack, albeit less furious than some, on the old men of the war, the mindless belligerence and chauvinism of General Currycombe (the Dickensian name hints at a "hot" temper) is rendered even more ineffectual by the fact that he "toddles round"— an epithet that recalls the personalities of "The Fathers" and "Base Details." Moreover the general is on "half pay," a retired officer quite out of touch with the reality that right-minded folk, the poet among them, do *not* hate the Germans. That the general has not asked the poet to sign his silly boycott of German merchants implies moreover, that he is a coward at heart— all "Bull-dog" bluster and no real substance:

> But the signatures are few;
> And he hasn't asked for mine.

Reconciliation

The notion of reconciliation with the "loyal and brave" soldiery of Germany rather than hatred for them, adumbrated in "Trade Boycott," becomes the central theme of "Reconciliation." It is a distance away from the warrior-like concept of forgiveness proposed in the 1916 poem "Absolution"; indeed the compassion evident in these verses alone gives the lie to critical pronouncements that deny the existence of tenderness in Sassoon's war verse. The "Blighty" character is yet another mother who, rather than continuing to mourn the loss of her son, has nourished negative emotions of "hatred harsh and blind." The poet's message is unequivocal: rather than rekindle feelings of outraged pride at her "hero's grave," she should endeavor to cultivate an inclusive sympathy, to learn anew the meaning of forgiveness. When visiting the literal Golgotha where the victims of both sides have fallen or been interred (often, alas, the same spot), she may discover, among the fellow mourners, "the mothers of the men who killed your son." The very idea has a shocking impact on listener and reader alike. Nonetheless it rings true. Though some mothers are there to mourn their own loved ones, perhaps others *are* returning to grieve selflessly for everyone who gave their lives. What is imperative is the need for all bereft mothers to unite in a common bond of compassion and reconciliation.

Memorial Tablet

Written, like "Reconciliation," in November 1918, "Memorial Tablet" expands on an idea there alluded to, that of pointless memorials to the "glorious dead." It was a message Sassoon would restate a number of times after the war, as such monuments proliferated throughout Northern Europe. But here the location is not the Brussels of the New Menin Gate or the Hyde Park of "Great Men," but the unsung environment of an English village, a sacrosanct setting previously immune to Sassoon's satiric barbs. Regrettably the gulf of class and generation is glaringly explicit even in the rural shires; the "returning" trooper — returning, alas, only in spirit — spills the beans about his "squire," relic of another age and caste, who "nagged and bullied till I went to fight." That he did fight and did endure a typical soldier's death, mute and helpless as he was smashed into a pit of "bottomless mud" by an exploding shell, is but one more statistic in the ghastly annals of war. Sassoon, however, grants the trooper an audience he would never otherwise have; he allows him to return from Hell (he has already endured one hell in the viscid slime of Passchendaele) to tell a harrowing tale that the roll of honor in his parish church does not: how he suffered "two bleeding years" of "anguish" (the pun is characteristic) in trench conditions the squire never dreamed of. Sadly classism, a growing concern of the poet's, and hypocrisy still rule the rural roost in the squire's domain. Not only is his retainer dead, his name "low down upon the list" among the "other ranks" stands as a memorial to a non-existent "glory." The "gilded name" on the church tablet does not impress the country lad turned soldier turned ghostly voyeur; the answer to his sardonic question, "What greater glory could a man desire?" has already been given, the expression exposed as a piece of empty rhetoric.

A Last Word

The Great War ended in November 1918. The event was, for Sassoon, a damp squib. He "hurried to London" only to encounter "an outburst of mob patriotism" (*Diaries*, 11 November, 1918, p. 282), adding, "It was a wretched wet night, and very mild. It is a loathsome ending to the loathsome tragedy of the last four years." The war might be over but Sassoon's obsession with its excesses persisted. Two months later he wrote 'A Last Word,' an irregular ode of sixty-nine lines. Sassoon was unsure whether it was worth including in his next volume (*Picture Show*). Writing to Bartholemew he confessed, "I can't make up my mind about 'A Last Word.' Cockerill is keen for it to be cut out, Masefield thinks it may as well be retained. I dunno...." The poem was ultimately omitted (letter from Sassoon to Bartholemew, 20 February, 1919, quoted by Keynes, p. 49).

Not only are its formal constituents atypical. The game of cricket, so adored by Sassoon and frequently used by older poets as an analogue for battle heroics, here provides the setting for a diatribe against "scarlet majors." Waiting to bat, the poet meets up with an old cricket adversary and decides to let him know what he really thinks of him. For though the rival player has previously made him feel distinctly inferior and even got the better of him at cricket ("And when you bowled / You got me out"), he is, the speaker now realizes, a representative of everything he despises. Gradually his mounting animosity is revealed towards an older man who "hated Labour," who thought "imperially" and bought conservative newspapers.

In sections two and three the speaker warms to his subject. Had he refused to fight, the old man *would* have regarded him with contempt as "an unspeakable blighter." But the real "blighter" is this back-room major who has vegetated in "Blighty" for four years, and, like so many old imperials, has contributed to the catalogue of despair by court-marshaling recalcitrant recruits or worse, sending them to a muddy grave.

In section four the ironic note dominates. Here is a man, sardonically congratulated by the poet, who has apparently "stuck it fine!" But what, the reader inquires, has he *had* to stick? Four years on the home front have merely ossified his already reactionary views: for him life is a simplistic cricket match world of winners and losers, in which the defeated receive their just deserts.

Section five is hard-hitting, even though the speaker's most private thoughts remain unspoken ("I'm too well-bred to rub it in"). The younger man can now confidently take the moral high ground; he *has* done his bit and so have numberless other soldiers — "tough chaps" who *did* volunteer for active service. The rival player is revealed for what he really is — a bully, a coward and a hypocrite. The poet/cricketer hopes, in the parlance of the sport, that "they'll put you on to bowl": it will give the younger man a chance to prove his superiority in areas where previously the stay-at-home officer had an edge both moral and physical.

Vicarious Christ

On 16 June, 1918, Sassoon had been privy to a lecture by another "Blighty" figure, an English bishop described in the diary as "a well-nourished Anglican Gramophone." The encounter provoked a lengthy and humorous entry: "Today he gave us one of his well-worn records; Patriotism, Insular Imperialism, Hun-Hatred, all with a strong flavour of *Morning Post*, and the Bishop of London somewhere in the offing" (*Diaries*, 16 June, p. 272). Now, seven months on and in a final fusillade against establishment clerics, Sassoon raided his notebook for details he could use in his satirical piece. The ironic title is a reference to the bishop's perceived role as a latter-day prophet, but his nickname — Byegumb (By Gum!) — both reflects Sassoon's growing predilection for Dickensian surnames and emphasizes the prelate's "gung-ho" values, values with which the listening poet has no sympathy whatsoever. It is a vigorous piece of caricature written, appropriately, in rollicking anapests and, on the evidence of the diary, only slightly in excess of the facts, as the crusader bishop preaches a bellicose sermon on Christ as the Warrior Son of God, and on the moral imperatives facing soldiers who must identify with those early Christian martyrs "who were burnt alive and strangled." Only in the conclusion, where Sassoon uses internal rhymes to deflate his sermonizing bishop, does the poet allow his irritation to burst through:

> But when I was his victim, how I wished I could have kicked him,
> For he made me love Religion less and less.

Devotion to Duty

By the early months of 1919, Sassoon, despite being lionized by academics and fellow poets, was working hard at developing his socialist sympathies and consolidating his pacifist position. In *Siegfried's Journey* he drew a remarkably candid picture of himself at the time:

> Wearing corduroy trousers and a bright red tie, I went about exploiting my Labour Movement personality and my reputation as an anti-war poet. Now and again I reverted to riding-breeches and a loud check cap, a form of dress which caused me to be more my authentic self than I realised. For the fox-hunting man was irrepressible, and the superficially adopted Socialism — though generous in impulse and intention — required more than corduroy to conceal its inadequate repertoire [SJ, p. 135].

One of the poems of this period, "Devotion to Duty" is not quite as innocuous as it seems. Yet another retrospective look at the war, it describes an incident in which the king, watched by an attentive poet, reads out a dispatch in which an officer has been routinely commended for heroism:

> The spirit of the troops was by his fine
> Example most effectively sustained.

The overt moral is typically Sassoonesque. Being mentioned in dispatches is one thing, but what is the point if the heroic husband gets killed in the process. The monarch, presumably George the Third, must tell the soldier's widow personally; after all he is a king respected for his punctilious attitude towards royal duties. But there is a scurrilous and anti-royalist sting in the tail, so scurrilous it can only be implied. For the widow's name, Bathsheba, recalls an incident in the Book of Samuel where a woman of that name becomes one of the wives of David after the king has been responsible for the death of her husband in battle. George the Third likewise has a responsibility to bear concerning the conduct of the war and its murderous outcomes; worse, and the inference is clear, he may, like David, take advantage of Bathsheba's enforced widowhood. Where does the king's devotion to "duty" begin and where does it end?

Aftermath

"Aftermath," which Sassoon labeled "an effective recitation poem," would, he hoped, be his "last word on the subject, for I assumed that War 'as an instrument of national policy' was completely discredited" (SJ, p. 141). While the poem's sentiments are anything but new, it does demonstrate the poet's determination to continue his prosodic experiments. Its irregular stanzas and metrics, its italicized refrain and run-on lines all mark it as an attempt at innovative versification. But the continuing flirtation with anapests, while contributing to the poem's reflective tone does not, despite Sassoon's claims, make for easy reading. If the thrice-repeated question, "Have you forgotten yet?" is central to his haunted post-war consciousness, the potted summary of trench experience recalls dozens of earlier verse accounts. The problem is that "Aftermath" is no more than a reprise, a hackneyed summary of remembered effects lacking in that very particularity that informed the bulletins from the battlefield. Sandbags, rats, the "stench of corpses," a "dirty-white" dawn, the "hopeless rain" and the "ashen-grey masks" of dying comrades, all these flit through the poem, a catalogue of ghastly memories that Sassoon wants to imprint on the national consciousness. Rather than hectoring his readers, he would have been better off trying to involve them imaginatively. As a chronicler of trench conditions, Sassoon is understandably losing his inspiration.

Everyone Sang

If "Aftermath" attempted to reinvent the "dark months at Mametz," "Everyone Sang" heralded a new beginning. In *Siegfried's Journey*, Sassoon offered an interpretation of the poem:

> The "singing" that would "never be done" was the Social Revolution which I believed to be at hand ... its form was invisible to me. No doubt I anticipated that there would be some comparatively harmless rioting, but on the whole I merely thought of it as the sun-light of Liberty spreading across the landscape and Everyone being obliged to admit that the opinions of the *Daily Herald* were, at any rate, worthy of their serious consideration [SJ, p. 142].

Such an explanation accounts for the poem's optimism, its tone of romantic affirmation. It is, as befits the occasion, a lyric, but unlike the lyrical pieces Sassoon composed in the early months of the war, it is not a paean of praise to modern knightliness; instead it describes a promised land where, released from their confining shackles, "poisoned birds ... find ... freedom," as "Everyone" (thrice repeated) rejoices in the brave new post-war order. After all the vituperation engendered by the past, it was hardly surprising that Sassoon should crave an outlet for his burgeoning social optimism.

The poem, praised by Masefield as "the only adequate peace celebration he had seen" (SJ, p. 141), was widely anthologized in years to come; it became, as Sassoon called it after the example of Yeats, his "Innisfree." Yet Sassoon, though enthusiastic about the result, was perplexed by the atypical creative process that gave rise to the poem. After all, he recollected, it was spawned in a unique way, at speed and without any corresponding sense of emotional release:

> "Everyone Sang" was composed without emotion, and needed no alteration afterwards. Its rather free form was spontaneous, and unlike any other poem I have written. I wasn't aware of any technical contriving. Yet it was essentially an expression of release, and signified a thankfulness for liberation from the war years which came to the surface with the advent of spring [SJ, p. 141].

Thus, Sassoon concludes, "I saluted the post-war future and my own part in it."

Return of the Heroes

But the old attitudes were still there, simmering beneath the surface. When provoked by public events or statements, they were liable to re-emerge, as they do in "Return of the Heroes," a poem which targets both the generals and the women who admire them. So often derided by Sassoon for promulgating hero-worship, for preferring decorated appearance to unvarnished reality, women become spokespersons for the kind of patriotic platitudes he so abhorred. As the heroes return, the watcher gushes with unaccountable pleasure at the sight of self-important and be-ribbonned generals processing in triumph. The star-gazer is Sassoon's stereotypical woman, breathlessly exclamatory and still dangerously "gung-ho," as she enthuses: "they must feel sad to know they can't win anymore."

The objects of her approbation fare even worse at Sassoon's hands. Employing his penchant for Dickensian surnames, his first target is the appropriately named "Sir Henry Dudster" (all dud ribbons and salutes), the next is Leggit (which implies he "legged it" as a coward), the third a "stout one," "Sir Geoffrey Stoomer," who, judging by his name, enjoys his food and wine. The final acclamation, delivered by the admiring lady, is as ludicrously wide of the mark as Sassoon can make it:

> "Great victories!... Aren't they glorious men?... so full of humour!"

A Footnote on the War

Nine years after the 1917 Spring Campaign, Sassoon was asked to write a piece for the regimental history of The Royal Welch Fusiliers. Though he afterwards "relented and wrote a twelve-page account" (WP, p. 150), his immediate reaction was to compose a poem explaining why he wanted to travel "onward away":

> ... from that Battalion history
> With all its expurgated dumps of dead;
> And what remains to say I leave unsaid.

"A Footnote on the War" is that poem. What makes it more successful than "Aftermath," Sassoon's other extended retrospective look at the conflict, is its low-key approach. No longer angry, no longer recalling its now clichéd horrors, Sassoon concentrates, as befits the original brief, on the minutiae of battalion life. The everyday world of a civilian Sunday with the reminiscent sounds of a "Lenten blackbird singing in the square," and with the familiar "patter of pacing feet," combine to trigger the poet's memory. He recognizes, though, that the Front is worlds away in atmosphere as well as in time, a hell "doubly damned with frost and snow" and staffed by new recruits, "under-sized arrivals from belated / Chunks of the population wrongly graded."

In stanza three Sassoon introduces his doctor — the same Doctor Dunn, D.S.O., M.C. who had requested the prose contribution — a medical officer who had calmly performed his harrowing duties as though the war was nothing more than a minor inconvenience. Asked to "contribute" his own "reminiscence," the poet explains how he has "erected a barrier" to protect himself from the ghosts of "what I saw / In years when Murder wore the mask of law." Indeed his "repression of war experience" has been far more effectively achieved than in the 1917 poem of that name. Even the diary, he adds in a typical gesture of self-deprecation, doesn't help ("the scribbled entries moribund — remote"). He can remember the moment when he was shot in the neck, but nothing more. Sassoon permits himself a few lines of self-parody, replete with stock-in-trade feminine rhymes ("morning"/"yawning"; "stumbled" / "grumbled"; "rattled" / "embattled"), but confesses that these words now ring false, "although he didn't know it" when he was embroiled in frontline activities. Only in the final stanza does one haunting memory suddenly intrude and equally rapidly disappear: that of a fair-haired young Scot "propped in his pool of blood." However, the poet does not want, for obvious reasons, to dwell on things normally "beyond my retrospection"; all horror and loss, all those "dumps of dead" must be finally expurgated and left behind.

To One Who Was with Me in the War

Another retrospective look at the events of 1914, "To One Who Was with Me in the War" was written at much the same time as "A Footnote," "early in 1926 after an evening with Ralph Greaves." In a letter to Michael Thorpe, Sassoon elaborated on the point ("Ralph Wilmot in the Infantry Officer — a brother of old man Barton who lost an arm ten days after I was sniped ... I had written nothing about the war since "Aftermath"—seven years before"). If Sassoon's normally infallible memory is correct, then this poem just pre-dates "A Footnote on the War." What is beyond dispute is that two quite different stimuli—one, a request for a written contribution, the other a conversation—prompted "afterthoughts that send your brain / Back beyond Peace." In a matter of weeks, and after a gap of seven years, Sassoon was moved to write two more pieces about his war. He did so reluctantly, all too conscious that to dredge up all those "visual fragments" might prove painful as well as unrewarding. But they do return, even if "much that was monstrous" is forgotten or at least softened by the passage of time or the selective processes of memory. By 1926 not only had the passion and rage ebbed away, but the vivid images generated by immediate experience had lost their sharpness. As the speaker remarks, he can "share again" during the process of conversation "*all but* the actual wetness of the flare-lit rain" (emphasis added). Everything now has a slightly remote, ghostly feel. The men, whose names "we've long forgotten" are specters, in part because many of them are dead, but also because to play this "game of ghosts" is to conjure up insubstantial forms now blurred by memory. Even the "drenched platoon-commander," Sassoon himself, is now ten years older; he needs to turn his head to remind himself how he "looked" all those years ago.

Like "A Footnote," this poem explains Sassoon's reluctance to write yet more verses about the war. There are a few vivid images — "jagged with trees / That loom like giant Germans"—("Clogged our souls with clay" recalls Owen's "Strange Meeting") and the persistent motif of rain pervades the poem. That Sassoon does go back with his old comrade-in-arms to revisit the past and "stand in some redoubt of Time" is commendable, but there is nothing new to record for posterity.

On Passing the New Menin Gate

Few post-war sights provoked Sassoon's wrath as much as memorials to the dead. The 1918 satires, "Great Men," triggered off by the erection of a "shrine" in Hyde Park, and "Memorial Tablet," had shown how futile Sassoon believed such monumental gestures to be. The post-war activities of the War Graves Commission did not help to alleviate the poet's condition. Seeing the Menin Gate in Brussels in 1927, a massive monolith replete with 54,889 names, brought back all the old feelings of disgust at an establishment that could complacently absolve itself of all moral responsibility by erecting such a "pile of peace-complacent stone." There is irony in the disparity between war's victims, these "doomed, conscripted, unvictorious ones," and the huge memorial that celebrates their "achievement." How, the poet demands, can the "unheroic dead" be "paid" (the word is used twice for emphasis) by such a grandiose gesture? The gateway's very existence celebrates two lies: one, that "Their Name liveth for ever," and two, that the conflict, "the world's worst wound," offered opportunities for personal heroism. The conclusion is as bleak and damning as anything Sassoon had written during the war:

> Well might the Dead who struggled in the slime
> Rise and deride this sepulchre of crime.

That it is a "sepulchre" hints at collusion with the religious establishment; that the word is juxtaposed to "crime" implies that its presence is an act of monumental hypocrisy.

War Experience

The years 1933 and 1934 saw Sassoon publishing three short poems about the Great War, two in the *Spectator*, one in *Time and Tide*. Compared with the output of prose memories — *Memoirs of an Infantry Officer* was published in 1930 and the complete *Sherston's Progress* in 1936 — they are drops in an ocean of reminiscence. But mining the diaries for the chatty prose memoirs was one thing; to relive intense experiences through the medium of poetry quite another. Understandably the three poems Sassoon did compose are pretty low-key, though "Asking for It" does essay an ironic stance.

Of these occasional pieces the first is "War Experience." The only connection these eight lines have with the similarly titled "(Repression of) War Experience" is that the distant sound of guns, there dimly heard and here only remembered, sparks off a vivid recollection of the war. The image here is a solitary one: Sassoon knew, and his infrequent poetic incursions into the trenches remind us of the fact, that repression and forgetfulness had combined to ensure that

> not much remains, twelve winters later
> Of the hater of purgatorial pains.

Characteristically it is the sounds of gunfire that invade his consciousness and with it the haunting image of a solitary sentry "staring over Kiel Trench crater."

The poem is of passing technical interest since it employs — the only war piece to do so — a twelve-syllable line linked by enjambment. There is no punctuation, apart from a dash in mid-stanza and a caesural break in line six where the speaker's brief experience begins.

Ex-Service

Both "Ex-Service" and "Asking for It" also display a degree of technical virtuosity. "Ex-Service," with its syntactic inversions and "Some with" followed by "but most went glumly through it / Dumbly doomed to rue it," carries a trace of Ezra Pound's "Hugh Selwyn Mauberley." However, the theme is quintessential Sassoon: dream voices of the dead "denying dud laurels to the last" are anxious to give the lie to a war record that, like their dark dying, seeks to cloak the reality in a darkness that obfuscates the truth. For these ghosts are "swindled," unable, like the trooper in "Memorial Tablet," to set the record straight:

> Our deeds with lies were lauded
> Our bones with wrongs rewarded.

Asking for It

"Asking for It" is Sassoon's final stab at an establishment God. Like the rulers of "Ex-Service" who encouraged men to bear "arms for earth," he exhorts his worshippers to indulge in torture and killing. The form of the poem, that of a supplicatory prayer from the Anglican church service, lends a grim irony to the verses. "Lord God," instead of delivering us from sin and temptation, positively encourages it. The piece is an exercise in vituperation, a catalogue of the ways in which God's multifarious "mercy" issues in feats of torture, cruelty and "bungle." But the crowning irony is reserved for the last stanza, where God is asked to approve the use of poison gas. If he does this — and Sassoon was only too well aware that future tyrants might capitalize on its use — then an ultimate hypocrisy can be devised for the warmongers: there will be no need to shed any human blood. Gas, in the form of propagandist hot air or the equally deadly dichlorodiethylsulphide or cyanide, will do the business. The events of World War Two proved his prophecy to be all too accurate.

Appendix: Diary Poems

The following poems, not published in Sassoon's lifetime or in Sir Rupert Hart-Davis's edition of *The War Poems* (Faber and Faber, 1983), are included in their probable order of composition. These poems are discussed in the second part of this book.

The Quarter-Master

Bad stations and good liquor and long service
Have aged his looks beyond their forty-five;
For eight and twenty years he's been a soldier;
And nineteen months of war have made him thrive.
He's got a face to match his breast of medals,
All stained and veined with purple and deep red.
His heart is somewhat bigger than his body,
And there's a holy anger in his head.

See where he sits before the evening embers,
Warming his knotted fingers at the blaze,
The man whose life is in the old battalion,
And all its battles in his gleaming gaze,
That looks you through and through: his smile is kindly,
And humbugs are the only thing he hates:
He's risen from a private to be captain,
And still he cracks a joke with his old mates.

But when the rum is hot, his eyes will kindle,
And all that's nearest to his heart he'll speak,
Lifting his banner over the tired and humble,
Who toil and die with nothing good to seek.

His words go questing in the swarming cities,
For men whose faces get no glimpse of green;
And he would march them out to win fresh fortune,
And freedom from injustice that has been.

He's chanced his arm with fate and found his glory;
He's swung the lead with many a roaring lad:
Good-luck to him; good-luck to all his kindred!
It's meeting men like him that makes me glad.

March 17, 1916

Peace

Down glaring dusty roads, a sanctuary of trees,
Green for my gaze and cool, and hushed with pigeon's croon:
Chill pitcher'd water for my thirst; and sweet as these,
Anger grown tired of hate, and peace returning soon.
In my heart there's cruel war that must be waged
In darkness vile with moans and bleeding bodies maimed;
A gnawing hunger drives me, wild to be assuaged,
And bitter lust chuckles within me unashamed.

Come back to heal me when my feckless course is run,
Peace, that I sought in life; crown me among the dead;
Stoop to me like a lover when the fight is done;
Fold me in sleep; and let the stars be overhead.

April 2, 1916

The Giant-Killer

When first I came to fight the swarming Huns,
I thought how England used me for her need;
And I was eager then to face the guns,
Share the long watch, and suffer, and succeed.
I was the Giant-Killer in a story,
Armed to the teeth and out for blood and glory.

What Paladin is this who bleakly peers
Across the parapets while dawn comes grey,
Hungry for music, and the living years,
And songs that sleep until their destined day?

This is the Giant-Killer who is learning
That heroes walk the road of no returning.

April 14, 1916

Elegy: For Marcus Goodall

Was it for English morning, spilled and flowing,
Across grey hummock'd fields, dim cattle showing,
Was it for this I longed? The glittering brass
Of rays low on brown roofs and steaming grass,
A garden spiked with blue and splashed with white,
Yellow and red and all the eye's delight.
Was it for these I longed, while you were dead,
Your mirth destroyed and from your lolling head
The racing thoughts gone out like smoke on air,
Thinning and whirling and subsiding — where?

Sad victim, could you see your body thrown
Into a shallow pit along that wood
Thronged by the dead? O, there you lie not lone,
Under the splinter'd trees; for the brotherhood
Of discontented slain, with eyes that scowl,
And bristly cheeks and chins all bloody-smears,
Will hug their rank red wounds and limp and prowl,
Squatting around your grave with moans and tears.

But soon, I hope a monster shell will burst,
And all such filth be blotted and dispersed:
You'll no more need to cling to the dead clay,
Dancing through fields of heaven to meet the day,
Slow-rising, saintless, confident and kind,
Dear, red-faced father God who lit your mind.

July 28, 1916

For England

He ducked and cowered and almost yelped with fear,
Thought "Christ! I wish they wouldn't burst so near!"
Then stumbled on — afraid of turning back —
Till something smashed his neck; he choked and swore;
A glorious end; killed in the big attack.

His relatives who thought him such a bore,
Grew pale with grief and dressed themselves in black.

August 12, 1916

The Stunt

One night he crawled through wire and mud and found a score
Of Saxon peasants half-asleep, and wet and scared.
Three men he killed outright, and wounded several more.
But Gentle Jesus kept *him* safe; his life was spared.
At dawn we took the trench; and found it full of dead.
And for his deed the man received a D.S.O.
"How splendid. O how splendid!" his relations said,
But what the weeping Saxons said I do not know.

August 12, 1916

Via Crucis

"Mud and rain and wretchedness and blood."
Why should jolly soldier-boys complain?
God made these before the roofless Flood —
Mud and rain.

Mangling crumps and bullets through the brain,
Jesus never guessed them when He died.
Jesus had a purpose for His pain,
Ay, like abject beasts we shed our blood,
Often asking if we die in vain.
Gloom conceals us in a soaking sack —
Mud and rain.

August 12, 1916

England Has Many Heroes...

England has many heroes, they are known
To all who read of German armies beat.
One chap got drunk and took a trench alone,
And grinned to cheering mobs in every street.
Though England's proud of him — her stuffed V.C. —

No medal was attached to his D.T.
Think of the D.C.M's and D.S.O's
And breasts that swell with Military Crosses;
They are the pomps of War; and no one knows
Nor cares to count the bungling and the losses.
But I would rather shoot one General Dolt
Than fifty harmless Germans; and I've seen
Ten thousand soldiers, tabbed with blue and green,
Who, if they heard one shell, would crouch and bolt.
But when the War is done they'll shout and sing,
And fetch bright medals from their German King.

January 15, 1917

The Elgar Violin Concerto

I have seen Christ, when music wove
Exulting vision; storms of prayer
Deep-voiced within me marched and strove.
The sorrows of the world were there.

A God for beauty shamed and wronged?
A sign where faith and ruin meet,
In glooms of vanquished glory thronged
By spirits blinded with defeat?

His head forever bowed with pain,
In all my dreams he looms above
The violin that speaks in vain —
The crowned humility of love.

O music undeterred by death,
And darkness closing on your flame,
Christ whispers in your dying breath,
And haunts you with his tragic name.

January 23, 1917

Life-Belts (Southampton to Havre)

The Boat begins to throb; the Docks slide past;
And soldiers stop their chattering, mute and grave;
Doomed to the Push, they think "We're off at last!"

Then, like the wash and welter of a wave,
Comfortless War breaks into each blind brain,
Swamping the hopes they've hugged to carry abroad;
And half-recovering, they must grope again
For some girl-face, or guess what pay they'll hoard
To start a home with, while they're out in France.
For, after all, each lad has got his chance
Of seeing the end. Like life-belts in a wreck,
They clutch at gentle plans — pathetic schemes
For peace next year. Meanwhile I pace the deck
And curse the Fate that lours above their dreams.

February 15, 1917

Foot Inspection

The twilight barn was chinked with gleams; I saw
Soldiers with naked feet stretched on the straw,
Stiff-limbed from the long muddy march we'd done,
And ruddy-faced with April wind and sun.
With pity and stabbing tenderness I see
Those stupid, trustful eyes stare up at me.
Yet, while I stoop to Morgan's blistered toes
And ask about his boots, he never knows
How glad I'd be to die, if dying could set him free
From battles. Shyly grinning at my joke,
He pulls his grimy socks on; lights a smoke,
And thinks "Our officer's a decent bloke."

April 3, 1917

Wounded

Waking, I seem to drift upon a mere
Of swaying silence; windless gleams the way
Where I may drift from darkness into day.
Through fractious healing languors I can hear
Rumours of strife I need no longer share;
Slowly through fallen eyelids growing aware
Of colour, warmth of light, and songs unseen
From leaves along some shore, when breezes bear
Peace through a forest murmurous with green

I lift my hands only to touch the flowers,
Rose and narcissus, ranged beside my bed;
Morn comes with mercy of the clean fresh hours,
And lays cool hands on my untroubled head.
And the sombre evening dyes my glowing dreams
With tranquil glory clov'n by fiery streams.

April 24, 1917

Death in the Garden

I never thought to see him; but he came
When the first strangeness of the dawn was grey.
He stood before me, a remembered name,
A twilight face, poor lonely ghost astray.
Flowers glimmered in the garden where I stood
And yet no more than darkness was the green.
Then the wind stirred; and dawn came up the wood;
And he was gone away: or had I seen
That figure in my brain? for he was dead;
I knew that he was killed when I awoke.
At zero-hour they shot him through the head
Far off in France, before the morning broke.

May 28, 1917

A War Widow

"Life is so wonderful, so vast!— and yet
We waste it in this senseless war," she said,
Staring at me with goggling eye-balls set
Like large star-sapphires in her empty head.

I watched the pearls that dangled from her ears,
Wondering how much was left for *her* to buy
From Time but chattering, comfortable years,
And lust that dwindles to a jewelled sigh.

May 26, 1917

A Quiet Walk

He'd walked three miles along the sunken lane,
A warm breeze blowing through the hawthorn-drifts

Of silver in the hedgerows; sunlit clouds
Moving aloft in level, slow processions.

And he'd seen nobody for over an hour,
But grazing sheep and birds among the gorse.

He all-but passed the thing; half-checked his stride,
And looked — old, ugly horrors crowding back.

A man was humped face downward in the grass,
With clutching hands, full-skirted grey-green coat,
And something stiff wrong about the legs.
He gripped his loathing quick ... some hideous wound ...
And then the stench... A stubbly-bearded tramp
Coughed and rolled over and asked him for the time.

June 1, 1917

A Wooden Cross (To S.G.H.)

My friends are dying young; while I remain,
Doomed to outlive these tragedies of pain
And half-forget how once I said farewell
To those who fought and suffered till they fell —
To you, the dearest of them, and the last
Of all whose gladness linked me with the past.
And in this hour I wonder, seeing you go,
What further jest war keeps, having laid you low.

Men grey with years get wisdom from the strange
Procession of new faces, and the change
That keeps them eager. I am young, and yet
I've scores of banished eyes I can't forget;
The dead were my companions and my peers,
And I have lost them in a storm of tears.

I cannot call you back; I cannot say
One word to speed you on your hidden way.
Only I hoard the hours we spent together
Ranging brown Sussex woods in wintry weather.
Till, blotting out to-day, I half-believe
That I shall find you home again on leave,
As I last saw you, riding down the lane,
And lost in lowering dusk and drizzling rain,
Contented with the hunt we'd had, and then
Sad lest we'd never ride a hunt again.

You didn't mean to die; it wasn't fair
That you should go when we'd so much to share.
Good nags were all your need, and not a grave,
Or people testifying that you were brave.

The world's too full of heroes, mostly dead,
Mocked by rich wreaths and tributes nobly said,
And it's no gain to you, nor mends our loss,
To know you've earned a glorious wooden cross;
Nor, while the parson preaches from his perch,
To read your name gold-lettered in the church.

Come back, come back; you didn't want to die;
And all this war's a sham, a stinking lie;
And all the glory that our fathers laud so well
A crowd of corpses freed from pangs of hell.

August 14, 1917

A Moment of Waking

I awoke; evilly tired, and startled from sleep;
Came home to seeing and thinking; shuddered; and shook
An ugly dream from my shoulders: death, with a look
Of malice, retreated and vanished. I cowered, a horrible heap,
And knew that my body must die; that my spirit must wait
The utmost blinding of pain, and doom's perilous drop,
To learn at last the procedure and ruling of fate.
... I awoke; clutching at life; afraid lest my heart should stop.

January 8, 1918

Journey's End (To W.M.M.)

Saved by unnumbered miracles of chance,
You'll stand, with war's unholiness behind,
Its years, like gutted villages in France,
Done with; its shell-burst drifting out of mind.
Then will you look upon your time to be,
Like a man staring over a foreign town,
Who hears strange bells, and knows himself set free;
And quietly to the twinkling lights goes gladly down,
To find new faces in the streets, and win
Companionship from life's warm firelit inn.

January 8, 1918

In Palestine

On the thyme-scented hills
In the morning and freshness of day
I heard the voices of rills
Quietly going their way.

Warm from the west was the breeze;
There were wandering bees in the clover;
Grey were the olive-trees;
And a flight of finches went over.

On the rock-strewn hills I heard
The anger of guns that shook
Echoes along the glen.
In my heart was the song of a bird,
And the sorrowless tale of the brook,
And scorn for the deeds of men.

March 30, 1918

Shadows

In the gold of morning we march; our swaying shadows are long,
We are risen from sleep to the grey-green world and our limbs move free.
Day is delight and adventure, and all save speech is a song;
Our thoughts are travelling birds going southward across the sea.
We march in the swelter of noon; our straggling shadows are squat;
They creep at our feet like toads,
Our feet that are blistered and hot:
The light-winged hours are forgot;
We are bruised by the ache of our loads.

Sunset burns from behind; we would march no more; but we must:
And our shadows deride us like dervishes dancing along in the dust.

April 10, 1918

Colin

One by one they've passed across the scene;
One by one; the lads I've known and met;
Laughing, swearing, shivering in the wet.

On their graves the grass is green;
Lads whose words and eyes I can't forget.

Colin's dead to-day; he's gone away;
Cheery little Colin, keen to hunt;
Firm and cool and quiet in a stunt.
Is there any more to say?
Colin's name's been printed in *The Times*,
"Killed in action." *He* can't read my rhymes.

June 12, 1918

Can I Forget ?...

Can I forget the voice of one who cried
For me to save him, save him, as he died?...

Can I forget the face of one whose eyes
Could trust me in his utmost agonies? ...

I will remember you; and from your wrongs
Shall rise the power and poignance of my songs:
And this shall comfort me until the end,
That I have been your captain and your friend.

August 10, 1918

Select Bibliography

A. Works by Siegfried Sassoon

Collected Poems: 1908–1956. London: Faber and Faber, 1947.
The Complete Memoirs of George Sherston. London: World Books, 1940.
Counter-Attack and Other Poems. London: Heinemann, 1918.
The Daffodil Murderer. London: John Richmond, 1913.
Diaries 1915–1918, ed. Rupert Hart-Davis. London: Faber and Faber, 1983.
Diaries 1920–1922, ed. Rupert Hart-Davis. London: Faber and Faber, 1981.
Letters to a Critic, ed. Michael Thorpe. London: John Roberts Press, 1976.
Letters to Max Beerbohm, ed. Rupert Hart-Davis. London: Faber and Faber, 1986.
The Old Century and Seven More Years. London: Faber and Faber, 1938.
The Old Huntsman and Other Poems. London: Heinemann, 1917.
On Poetry. Bristol: University of Bristol, 1939.
Picture Show. London: Heinemannn, 1919.
Selected Poems. London: Faber and Faber, 1968.
Siegfried's Journey: 1916–1920. London: Faber and Faber, 1946, 1973.
A Suppressed Poem. London: The Unknown Press, 1929.
The War Poems. London: Heinemann, 1919.
The War Poems, ed. Rupert Hart-Davis. London: Faber and Faber, 1983.
The Weald of Youth. London: Faber and Faber, 1942.
Unpublished Letters to Robert Graves: 1917–1926 (Morris Library, Southern Illinois University, Carbondale)
Unpublished Letters to Roderick Meiklejohn: 1916–1950 (Harry Ransom Humanities Research Center, University of Texas, Austin)
Unpublished Letters to Lady Ottoline Morrell: 1916–1936 (Harry Ransom Humanities Research Center, University of Texas, Austin)
Unpublished Letters to Robert Graves, J. W. Pinker and Paul Lemperly; 1919–1930 (The Poetry/Rare Books Collection, State University of New York at Buffalo)
In addition to the works mentioned above, Sassoon also published a good deal of verse before the war, mainly in privately printed anthologies. These include *Orpheus in Diloeryum* (1908), *Sonnets and Verses* (1909), *Sonnets* (1909), *Twelve Sonnets* (1911), *Poems* (1911), *Amyntas: A Mystery* (1911), *Melodies* (1912), *Hyacinth* (1912), *Ode For Music* (1912).

B. Secondary Sources

Barbusse, Henri. *Under Fire (Le Feu)*, trans. Fitzwater Wray. London: Dent, 1917.
Barth, R.L. "Sassoon's 'Counter-Attack,'" in *The Explicator* (winter 1991).
Bergonzi, Bernard. *Heroes' Twilight: A Study of the Literature of the Great War*. London: Constable, 1965.
Blunden, Edmund. "Siegfried Sassoon's Poetry," in *Edmund Blunden: A Selection of His Poetry and Prose*. London: Hart-Davis, 1950.
Caesar, Adrian. *Taking It Like a Man: Suffering, Sexuality and the War Poets*. Manchester, England: Manchester University Press, 1993.
Campbell, Patrick. "Sassoon's Blighters," in *The Explicator*, 53, no. 3 (spring 1995).
_____. "Sassoon's 'They,'" in *The Explicator*, 52, no. 4 (summer 1994).
_____. "Sassoon's 'To Any Dead Officer,'" in *The Explicator*, 54, no. 2 (winter 1996).
_____. "A Suppressed Poem ('Dear Roberto')," in *Focus on Robert Graves*, 2, no. 2 (spring 1994).
Cohen, Joseph. "The Three Roles of Siegfried Sassoon," in *Tulane Studies in English*, 7 (1957).
Corrigan, Dame Felicitas. *Siegfried Sassoon: Poet's Pilgrimage*. London: Gollancz, 1973.
Devine, Kathleen. "Silkin: Sassoon and the Imagery of Loss," in *Focus on Robert Graves*, 2, no. 2 (spring 1994).
Farmer, David. *Siegfried Sassoon: A Memorial Exhibition Catalogue*. Harry Ransom Humanities Research Center, University of Texas at Austin, 1969.
Freud, Sigmund. *Introductory Lectures on Psychoanalysis 1916–1917*. London: Penguin, 1973.
Fussell, Paul. *The Great War and Modern Memory*. London: Oxford University Press, 1975.
Graves, Robert. *Complete Poems*, vol. 1, ed. B. Graves and D. Ward. Manchester: Carcanet, 1995.
_____. *Goodbye to All That*. London: Cape, 1929, 1957.
Hibberd, Dominic. *Poetry of the First World War: A Casebook*. London: Macmillan, 1981.
_____. "Some Notes on 'Sassoon's Counter-Attack and Other Poems,'" in *Notes and Queries*. London: Oxford University Press, August 1982.
Hildebible, John. "Neither Worthy Nor Capable: The War Memoires of Graves, Blunden and Sassoon," in *Modernism Revisited*, ed. R. Kiely. Cambridge: Harvard University Press, 1983.
Johnston, John. H. *English Poetry of the First World War*. Princeton: Princeton University Press, 1964.
Keynes, Geoffrey. *A Bibliography of Siegfried Sassoon*. London: Hart-Davis, 1962.
Lane, Arthur. *An Adequate Response: The War Poetry of Wilfred Owen and Siegfried Sassoon*. Detroit: Wayne State University Press, 1972.
Lefler, K. "Sassoon's 'Repression of War Experience,'" in *The Explicator* (spring 1987).
Mallon, Thomas. "The Great War and Sassoon's Memory," in *Modernism Reconsidered*, ed. R. Kiely. Cambridge: Harvard University Press, 1983.
Morrell, Lady Ottoline. *The Early Memoirs of Lady Ottoline Morrell*, ed. R. Gathorne-Hardy. London: Faber and Faber, 1963.
_____. *Ottoline at Garsington: Memoirs of Lady Ottoline Morrell: 1915–1918*. London: Faber and Faber, 1974.
Murry, John Middleton. "Mr. Sassoon's War Verses," in *The Nation* (13 July, 1918), reprinted in *The Evolution of an Intellectual* (London, 1920, 1927).
O'Prey, Paul, ed. *In Broken Images: Robert Graves: Selected Correspondence*. New York: Moyer Bell, 1988.
Owen, Wilfred. *Collected Letters*, ed. H. Owen and J. Bell. London: Oxford University Press, 1967.

———. *Collected Poems*, ed. C. Day Lewis. London: Chatto and Windus, 1963.
Parfitt, George. *English Poetry of the First World War*. London: Harvester, 1990.
Pinto, Vivian de S. *Crisis in English Poetry*. London: Hutchinson, 1939, 1951.
Quinn, Patrick. *The Great War and the Missing Muse*. Selingsgrove, Penn.: Susquehanna University Press, 1994.
Reilly, Catherine. *Scars Upon My Heart: Women's Poetry of the First World War*. London: Virago, 1981.
Rivers, William H.R. *Conflict and Dream*, ed. G. Smith. London: Kegan Paul, 1923.
———. *Instinct and the Unconscious*. Cambridge: Cambridge University Press, 1920.
Ross, Robert. *The Georgian Revolt*. London: Faber and Faber, 1967.
Shelton, Carole. "War Protest, Heroism and Shellshock: Siegfried Sassoon: A Case Study," in *Focus on Robert Graves*, 1, no. 13 (winter 1992).
Showalter, Elaine. "Rivers and Sassoon: The Inscription of Male Gender Anxieties," in *Behind the Lines: Gender and the Two World Wars*. New Haven: Yale University Press, 1987.
Silkin, Jon. *Out of Battle: The Poetry of the Great War*. London: Oxford University Press, 1972, Macmillan, 1998.
Stallworthy, Jon. *Wilfred Owen*. London: Chatto and Windus, Oxford University Press, 1974.
Stead, C. K. *The New Poetic*. London: Hutchinson, 1964.
Thorpe, Michael. *Siegfried Sassoon: A Critical Study*. Leiden, Netherlands: Universitaire Pers, 1966.
Wormleighton, Simon. "Something in Sassoon's Style: Notes on Owen's 'The Dead-Beat,'" in *Notes and Queries*. Oxford: Oxford University Press, 37 (March 1990).

Index

Diary poems which appear in full in the Appendix are included with the page number given in **boldface.**

Abraham 91
"Absolution" 15, 23, 63, 87, 88–9, 196
Ackerley, J.R. 156
"Aftermath" 200
Alexandria 135, 181
Amiens (hospital) 110, 111, 113, 118
Amyntas (1912) 16, 19, 20–1, 35, 87
anapestic meter 94, 124, 178, 187, 200
"The Ancient Mariner" (1798) 47, 105, 124, 180
"Arms and the Man" 26, 59, 78, 126–7
Arras (battle of) 144, 146, 158, 183
"Asking for It" 205
"At Carnoy" 107–8, 112
"At Daybreak" (1911) 37, 105
The Athenaeum 81, 83, 95
"Atrocities" 170
"The Attack" 46, 73, 164–5
Auden, W.H.: (*The Age of Anxiety*) 35; ("September 1, 1939") 96
"Autumn" 74, 166, 168, 172

"A Ballad" 26, 72, 124
"Banishment" 34, 38, 77, 166, 171–2
Barbusse, Henri (*Le Feu*) 57, 71, 73, 74, 80, 165, 172, 173
Bartholomew, A.T. 149, 197
"Base Details" 27, 49, 59, 78, 131–2, 138–9, 140, 144, 196
"Battalion Relief" 188
"Before the Battle" 39, 53, 54, 58, 87, 107

Bergonzi, Bernard (*Heroes' Twilight*) 5, 16, 76, 78–9, 84, 108, 117
birds, bird-song 54, 202
Bishop of London 198–9
Blake, William: "Holy Thursday" 124
"Blighters" 25, 27, 57–9, 134–5
"Blighty" 42–3, 77–8, 94, 122, 134–5, 163, 166, 169–70, 179, 182, 196
Blunden, Edmund 3, 58, 81, 83–4
Brassey, Lady 146, 147
"Break of Day" 54, 58, 73, 170–1
Brooke, Rupert 63–4, 88–9, 91, 98, 99
Browning, Robert: *Pippa Passes* 53
Byron, Lord 78

Caesar, Adrian 5, 23, 35, 36, 82–3, 89–90, 91, 137–8
Campbell, Major 36, 101–4,
Campbell, Thomas 124,
The Cambridge Magazine 118, 129, 161, 167, 168, 181, 195
"Can I Forget?" **217**
Carpenter, Edward 35
Chapelwood Manor 146
The Cherwell 120
"Christ and the Soldier" 26, 46, 55, 58–9, 113–15
Churchill, Winston 191
Cockerill, George 184
Cockerill, S.C. 19, 171, 197
"Colin" 186, **216–7**
Collected Poems 3, 145, 184, 187
"Concert-Party" 79, 181–2

223

"Conscripts" 27, 39, 82, 136–7
Corrigan, Dame Felicitas 24, 46, 47, 48, 69, 76, 83, 114
Cottrill, Joe (quarter-master) 12, 14–15, 97
Counter-Attack 29, 70, 71, 73, 138, 148, 172, 176, 178, 185, 187, 189–90
"The Counter-Attack" 51, 56, 73, 80, 158, 173–5
Craiglockhart ("Dottyville") 1, 28, 35, 42, 73, 80, 130, 147, 149, 158, 160ff

Dadd, Julian 14, 118, 130
The Daffodil Murder (1913) 19, 20–22, 24
The Daffodil Murderer 19, 20–2, 24
Daiches, David 16
Dante 142, 143
"Dead Musicians" 47, 53, 180
"The Death-Bed" 27, 64, 77, 84, 109, 115, 118, 120–1, 162
"Death in the Garden" 45, 145–6, **213**
"Decorated" 26, 126
De La Mare, Walter 64
Denmark Hill (hospital) 143–4, 148
"Devotion to Duty" 190, 199–200
Diaries (1915–1918) 11, 12, 14, 25, 27, 32, 33, 36, 37, 41, 42, 43, 44, 47, 49–53, 62, 67, 74, 89, 90, 92, 94, 96, 97, 98, 99, 100, 101, 102, 103, 104, 105, 106, 107, 109, 111, 112, 115, 118, 119, 128, 130, 131, 133, 135, 136, 138, 139, 140, 142, 145, 147, 150, 152, 156, 158–9, 160, 162, 165, 167, 168, 172, 174, 176, 178, 182, 183, 184, 189, 190, 191, 195, 197
"Died of Wounds" 25, 38, 55, 68, 77, 84, 111–12
"The Distant Song" 130–1
Dobell, Lt. Colin 37, 186
"Does It Matter?" 28, 55, 58, 71, 78, 162–3, 165
Donne, John 56, 121, 132
"Dottyville" *see* Craiglockhart
"The Dragon and the Undying" 24, 46, 64, 81, 95–6, 105, 115
"The Dream" 51, 58, 171
"Dreamers" 160
Dryden, John 56
"The Dug-Out" 39, 77, 79, 188–9

Duhamel, Georges (*La Vie des martyrs*) 30, 74, 183
Dunn, Doctor 202

"Editorial Impressions" 58–9, 161, 163, 167
"The Effect" 38, 59, 77, 158, 159, 161, 167
"Elegy: For Marcus Goodall" 37, 109–10, **209**
Elgar, Sir Edward 133, 180
"The Elgar Violin Concerto" 47, 133–4, 180, **211**
Eliot, T.S. 4, 143
"Enemies" 79, 83, 132–3
"Everyone Sang" 81, 177, 191, 200–1
The Explicator 5, 57
"Ex-Service" 204

Farmer, D. 170, 178
"The Fathers" 28, 32, 44, 55, 58, 164, 179, 196
"Fight to a Finish" 28, 58, 59, 78, 166–7
Flixécourt 24, 101, 104, 132
"Foot Inspection" 38, 39, 140–1 **212**
"A Footnote on the War" 36, 201–2
"For England" 26, 115–16, **209–10**
Formby (golf club) 131, 164
"For the Last Time" (unpublished letter poem) 51
"France" 24, 45, 53, 57, 104
Freud, Sigmund 151–8
Fussell, Paul 5, 35, 64, 65, 156

Gallipoli 91
Garsington 122
"The General" 59, 78, 144, 148
Georgian Poetry 18, 27, 64–5, 78, 80, 104, 115, 119, 127, 128, 160
Germans, attitude to 39, 43–44, 74, 110–11, 123, 132–3, 141, 164, 170, 179, 190, 196
"The Giant-Killer" 87, 99 **208–9**
Gibson 65
"Glory of Women" 44, 145, 158, 168–9, 179
"Golgotha" 24, 96
Goodall, Marcus 24, 25, 34, 104, 109–10, 113, 160, 186
Gosse, Edmund 18,19, 124, 137

Graves, Robert 17, 21, 25, 30, 40, 46, 82, 94, 95, 99, 101, 106, 110, 112, 127, 148, 149, 165, 171, 177, 190, 193, 194; "The Assault Logic" 143; "Dead Boche" 74; "Goliath and David" 37; *Goodbye to All That* 28, 33, 102, 117, 170; influence on Sassoon 66–70; It's a Queer Time" 113; "The Shadow of Death" 93
Greaves, Ralph 203

Half-Moon Street 127, 192
Hanmer, Bobby 31, 34, 36, 37
Harbord, Gordon 37, 160, 167, 178, 186
Hardy, Thomas 59, 61–2, 74, 128, 143, 145; *The Dynasts* 67; *Satires of Circumstance* 123
Harry Ransom Humanities Research Center 4
Hart-Davis, Rupert 53, 93, 110, 178
"Haunted" 64, 115–16
"The Hawthorn Tree" 79, 145
Henley, W.E.: "Song of the Sword" 102
"The Hero" 26, 32, 59, 109, 111, 117–18, 124, 147, 159
Hibberd, Dominic 71
The Hindenburg Line 141, 148, 159
homoeroticism 31–41, 65–6, 77, 82, 103–4, 156, 182, 184
Hood, Thomas 93; "The Bridge of Sighs" 16
Housman, A.E. 21, 35, 38, 65–6, 91, 106, 179, 181, 186
"How to Die" 28, 162, 163–4
Hyacinth (1912) 19
The Hydra 161

"I Stood with the Dead" 30, 38, 55, 77, 82, 184–5, 186, 192
Imperial War Museum 4
"In an Underground Dressing-Station" 77, 146–7
"In Barracks" 65, 177–8
"In Palestine" **216**
"In the Church of St. Ouen" 139–40
"In the Pink" 24, 64, 94–5, 103, 115
"The Investiture" 46, 167–8
"Invocation" 33, 38, 39, 57, 83, 180

Jews 17–18, 47–8, 68, 193
Johnson, Lionel 66

Johnston, J.H. 5, 15, 63, 73, 80, 138, 173, 174
"Journey's End" 140, 178, **215**
Jowett, Lieutenant 34, 39, 189
"Joy-Bells" 46, 81, 185
Junkers 167

Keats, John 54, 93, 155, 172, 179, 180; "Ode on Melancholy" 74; "Ode to a Nightingale" 171; "When I Have Fears That I May Cease to Be" 74
Keynes, Sir Geoffrey 149, 197
Kipling, Rudyard 63
"The Kiss" 25, 35, 36, 38, 64, 78, 101–4, 115, 179, 184

"Lamentations" 77, 158–9
Lancaster Gate (military hospital) 189–95
"The Last Meeting" 25, 36, 37, 38, 39, 45, 68, 104–5, 149, 155, 180
"A Last Word" 40, 190, 197–8
Lennell 190, 191
"A Letter Home" 25, 37, 54, 64, 65, 105–7, 115
"Letter to Robert Graves" ("Dear Roberto") 18, 30, 47, 66, 81, 142, 190, 191–5
Letters to a Critic 2, 3, 68
"Life-Belts" 135–6, **211–12**
Limerick (Ireland) 176, 178–81
Linthwaite, Jim 183
Litherland 136, 138

Mametz 174
"The March-Past" 27, 47, 131–2, 138, 144
Marsh, Edward 68, 69
Masefield, John 62, 65, 197, 201; *The Everlasting Mercy* 21
Massingham, H.W. 168
Meiklejohn, Roderick 4, 14, 31, 40, 44, 50, 62, 73, 148, 161, 183, 190, 191, 192, 193
Melodies (1912) 19, 20
The Memoirs of George Sherston 2, 11, 17, 23, 38, 90, 91, 92, 111, 119, 124, 126–7, 131, 165, 177, 182, 185, 204
"Memorial Tablet" 30, 58, 59, 196–7
"Memory" 56, 178–9
metaphor 81

Molyneux, Private 50
"A Moment of Waking" 178, **215**
Montague 92–3
Morgan, W.M. 140, 178
Morlancourt 100
"Morning Glory" 32
The Morning Post 198
Morrell, Lady Ottoline 4, 31, 34, 42, 43, 44, 49, 51, 62, 74, 76, 77, 79, 94, 122, 136, 142, 148, 160, 165, 176, 189, 190, 191, 193
Murry, J.M. 77, 81
music 47, 53–55, 79, 133–4, 180
"A Mystic as Soldier" 128, 129

The Nation 77, 81, 184
New Menin Gate 197, 203
Newbolt, Sir Henry: "Vitai Lampada" 97
Nichols, Robert 90
"A Night Attack" 26, 34, 43, 110–11, 112
"Night on the Convoy" 79, 182–3

Ode to Music (1912) 19
The Old Huntsman 14, 16, 70, 112, 113, 115, 119, 123, 124, 129, 145
"On Passing the New Menin Gate" 203–4
On Poetry 53, 56, 61
"The One-Legged Man" 26, 59, 111, 116–17, 138
"The Optimist" 44, 58, 141
Orme, Lieutenant 150
Orpheus in Diloeryum (1908) 19
Owen, Wilfred 1, 12, 28, 38, 76, 84, 89, 121, 143, 195; "A Terre" 163; "Anthem for Doomed Youth" 57, 95; "Disabled" 163; "Dulce et Decorum Est" 33, 98, 128, 175; "Futility" 110; influence on Sassoon 70–73; "Mental Cases" 163; "Miners" 81; "Parable of the Old Man and the Young" 91; "The Show" 81, 83; "Strange Meeting" 27, 83, 132, 203

Palestine 176
Parfitt, George 78
"Peace" 63, 87, 98, **208**
Picture-Show 13, 170
Pinto, Vivian De Sola 78, 79, 191
Plath, Sylvia 17
Poems (1911) 19

"The Poet as Hero" 21, 36, 64, 128, 129, 184
Pope, Jessie 33
Pound, Ezra 4, 205
"Prelude: The Troops" 56, 73, 158, 172–3
"The Prince of Wounds" 23, 45, 46, 91–2, 95
protest (statement, 6 July, 1917) 28, 32, 42, 44, 94, 148–9, 152

"The Quarter-Master" 56, 87, 97, **207**
"A Quiet Walk" 51, *146*, **213–14**
Quinn, Patrick 5, 16, 34, 98, 172

Ravel, Maurice 133
Rawlinson, General 132
"The Rear-Guard" 27, 50, 141–3, 148
"Reconciliation" 77, 196
"The Redeemer" 23, 36, 45, 46, 54, 63, 82, 89–90, 95
Reed, Henry: "Lessons of the War" 136
"Remorse" 179–80
"Repression of War Experience" 40, 45, 54, 74, 81, 82, 133, 149, 151–8, 162, 193, 204
"Return" 140, 141
"Return of the Heroes" 58, 201
"Reward" 29, 38, 53, 83, 183–4
Richardson, "Tracker" 96
Rivers, Dr. W.H.R. 28, 38, 110, 149, 151–8, 167, 172, 192, 193, 194
"The Road" 57, 109, 119–20
Rouen 138, 164
Roman Catholicism 3, 45, 48, 83
Rosenberg, Isaac 12, 84
Ross, Robbie 16, 40, 59, 127, 138, 147, 161, 163, 168
Russell, Bertrand 42, 148

St. Ouen 139–40
Sassoon, Hamo 91, 96, 170
Sassoon, Sir Philip 1
Sassoon, Siegfried: achievement as war poet 78–86; contrasts in poetry 57–9; diaries, importance of as source for poems 49–60; family background 17–18; homoeroticism 31–41; literary influences 61–75 (passim); repression of war feelings 151–8; vernacular, use of 55–6; visual method of composi-

tion 56–7; women, attitudes towards 31–4, 44, 168–9; working methods 49–61
satires 58–9, 78, 84, 113, 117, 149, 150, 166–7, 172
Satirical Poems (1926) 3
The Saturday Review 91
"Secret Music" 53, 128, 129, 180
Sequences (1956) 3
"Shadows" **216**
Shelley, Percy Bysshe 74, 168
"Sick Leave" 34, 39, 166
Siegfried's Journey (1945) 16, 23, 50, 59, 61, 70, 71, 73, 78, 84, 87, 88, 93, 100, 101, 111, 116, 118, 120, 122, 124, 126, 150, 178, 199, 200, 201
Silkin, Jon 5, 58, 81, 89, 107, 102, 144, 150, 167, 169
The Somme 11–12, 107, 109–11, 122, 175
"Song Books of the War" 83, 186–7
sonnets 53, 95, 122–3, 171, 178
Sonnets (1909) 19
Sonnets & Verses 19
Sorley, Charles 12, 67–8, 84, 106
The Spectator 136 204
Stallworthy, Jon 5, 72
"Stand-To: Good Friday Morning" 23, 46, 47, 55, 100–1, 103, 131
Stansfield, "Birdie" 12
"Stretcher-Case" 26, 65, 118–19
Stubbs, Corporal 126
"The Stunt" 26, 43, 115–116, **210**
"A Subaltern" 24, 37, 68, 96, 122, 130, 150
"Suicide in the Trenches" 66, 77, 181
"Supreme Sacrifice" 58, 147
"Survivors" 29, 72, 162, 165–6

Tennyson, Alfred Lord 36
"A Testament" 23, 45, 57, 92
"Their Frailty" 28, 33, 145, 158, 169–70
"They" 26–7, 46, 57, 58, 64, 78, 115, 124–5, 185
Thomas, David ("Tommy") 24, 34, 36, 96, 98 105, 106, 128, 132, 149, 186
Thomas, Edward 12
Thorpe, Michael: *Letters to a Critic* 2, 3, 5; *Siegfried Sassoon*, 5, 25, 63, 73, 77, 79, 87, 91, 95, 102, 130, 132, 133, 145, 166, 170, 189, 202–3
"Thrushes" 39, 46, 54, 74, 131, 168
Tiltwood, "Dick" 38
Time and Tide 204
The Times 94
"To Any Dead Officer" 28, 58, 68, 81, 84, 96, 149–51, 152
"To His Dead Body" 110, 112–13, 149, 167
"To My Brother" 23, 45, 63, 90
"To One Who Was with Me in the War" 202–3
"To the Warmongers" 58, 143–4, 148
"To Victory" 15, 19, 23, 36, 45, 49, 64, 67, 93–4
"Together" 50, 178
"The Tombstone-Maker" 26, 58, 122
"Trade Boycott" 44, 58, 195–6
"Trench Duty" 185
"The Triumph" 39, 54, 187–8, 193
"Twelve Months After" 51, 175, 177
"Two Hundred Years After" 79, 83, 127–8, 173

Vaughan, Henry 4
"Via Crucis" 26, 116, **210**
"Vicarious Christ" 46, 58, 185, 198

"War Experience" 204
The War Poems 13, 94, 96, 111, 113, 114, 118, 119, 131, 142, 178, 185, 201
"A War Widow" 32, 145, 146 **213**
Weirleigh 45, 92, 93, 122
The Westminster 24, 94
"When I'm Among a Blaze of Lights" 27, 49, 133
"A Whispered Tale" 14, 130
Wilde, Oscar 17
Wilson, Jean Moorcroft 5, 16
"Wirers" 73, 162
"A Wooden Cross" 160, **214**
"Wounded" 144, **212**
"A Working Party" 24, 63, 82, 97–8, 100, 128
Wordsworth, William 103, 145

Yeats, William Butler 143, 201